DEADLY SURPRISE

In the early-morning hours of December 30, 1978, Bob Spangler asked his wife, Nancy, to come down into the basement with him. He said he had a surprise for her. Perhaps she thought he had a late-arriving Christmas present for her. Perhaps she thought Bob was going to give her some gift of apology for the argument of a few nights past. Whatever the reason, Nancy Spangler followed him into the basement, sat down in a chair and closed her eyes as instructed.

Bob pulled a .38-caliber revolver out of hiding and aimed it at her forehead. The barrel was about three to four inches away from her skull and pointed down at about a forty-degree angle. As Nancy Spangler waited in anticipation for her surprise, Bob slowly pulled the hammer back on the revolver.

BOOK YOUR PLACE ON OUR WEBSITE AND MAKE THE READING CONNECTION!

We've created a customized website just for our very special readers, where you can get the inside scoop on everything that's going on with Zebra, Pinnacle and Kensington books.

When you come online, you'll have the exciting opportunity to:

- View covers of upcoming books
- Read sample chapters
- Learn about our future publishing schedule (listed by publication month *and author*)
- Find out when your favorite authors will be visiting a city near you
- Search for and order backlist books from our online catalog
- Check out author bios and background information
- Send e-mail to your favorite authors
- Meet the Kensington staff online
- Join us in weekly chats with authors, readers and other guests
- Get writing guidelines
- AND MUCH MORE!

**Visit our website at
http://www.kensingtonbooks.com**

MARRIED to MURDER

ROBERT SCOTT

PINNACLE BOOKS
Kensington Publishing Corp.
http://www.kensingtonbooks.com

Some names have been changed to protect the privacy of individuals connected to this story.

PINNACLE BOOKS are published by

Kensington Publishing Corp.
850 Third Avenue
New York, NY 10022

All Kensington Titles, Imprints, and Distributed Lines are available at special quantity discounts for bulk purchases for sales promotions, premiums, fund-raising, and educational or institutional use. Special book excerpts or customized printings can also be created to fit specific needs. For details, write or phone the office of the Kensington special sales manager: Kensington Publishing Corp., 850 Third Avenue, New York, NY 10022, attn: Special Sales Department, Phone: 1-800-221-2647.

Pinnacle and the P logo Reg. U.S. Pat. & TM Off.

First printing: March 2004
10 9 8 7 6 5 4 3 2 1

Printed in the United States of America

ACKNOWLEDGMENTS

I could not have written this book without the help of many individuals. These include Paul Berkowitz, Bruce Cornish, Randy Hampton, Debra Mayeux and Mark Schelper. I'd especially like to thank Jim and Janece Ohlman, Bev Perry, Chris Larsen, Paul Goodman, Lenny Johns and Camille Bibles. Lastly, I would be remiss if I didn't thank my terrific literary agent, Damaris Rowland, and my wonderful editor at Pinnacle, Michaela Hamilton.

It requires a singular focus in committing the actual crime, quite cold-bloodedly.

— Bob Spangler

Bob Spangler used the Grand Canyon, a place that is one of America's cathedrals, as a murder weapon.
— Camille Bibles, assistant United States attorney

Prologue

Grand Canyon, April 11, 1993

Donna Sundling Spangler had nightmares about hiking in the Grand Canyon. Her legs were not strong and she suffered from vertigo. But her husband, Bob Spangler, loved the area so much that she steeled her nerves for yet one more backpack trip into the Canyon on Easter week, 1993.

"You don't have to go!" her friend Sandy Brooks told her on the telephone before Donna left her home in Durango, Colorado.

"I know," Donna replied, "but Bob loves it so much. And he really wants me to go with him."

"How are things between you and Bob?" Brooks asked.

Donna sighed and said, "We'll have to talk when I get back."

Four days later, as Donna stood panting on the dangerous trail above the Redwall on Horseshoe Mesa in the Grand Canyon, she felt dizzy and leaned on a ski pole she used for balance while hiking. The view down the side of the cliff was magnificent and terrifying in its immensity.

Out of the corner of her eye, Donna casually noticed Bob walking toward her. Perhaps he was coming to straighten her backpack or give her a hug for being such a good sport and accompanying him on this difficult hike. Instead, she noticed a strange, almost quizzical, look on his face. He held out his arms to touch her; then, with all his strength, he pushed her backward over the cliff.

It happened so suddenly and unexpectedly that Donna didn't even have time to scream. In one horrifying instant her worst nightmare had come true. She was hurtling through space into the depths of the Grand Canyon.

Chapter 1

A Woman Named Sharon

Durango, Colorado, 1994

It was a street that dreams are made of—American dreams. Oak Drive in Durango, Colorado, is where people went when their ships had come in; the reward for a lifetime of hard work. Oak Drive wound through smart upscale homes with elegant designs and large plate glass widows that fronted the La Plata Mountains. Aspens and rock gardens abounded in well-landscaped yards, and Land Rovers and Mercedes-Benzes filled the driveways. The inhabitants of Oak Drive came from everywhere to capture a piece of the "Rocky Mountain High," leaving behind the endless flatlands of Kansas, the rat race of New York City and the mean streets of Los Angeles. Oak Drive at six thousand feet was about as close to paradise as you could get.

In 1994 Sharon Cooper Spangler was one of the inhabitants of Oak Drive. She was fifty-two years old and her own journey to Durango had been varied and colorful. She had grown up in the suburbs of St. Louis, Missouri, and had been an English teacher, yoga instructor, dog trainer and public-relations assistant for the American Water Works Association (AWWA) in the Denver area. Even more important, Sharon was the author of a well-respected book, *On Foot in the Grand Canyon*. It was more than just a guidebook of the canyon, it was a window into Sharon's soul.

She said of one particular hike with a friend: "We found a spot where I had rested, intoxicated by the forms, colors, and light. We rested in silence. In the silence you could hear the blood coursing in your skull, and you knew that it was being driven by the same primal energy that was driving everything around you, including the rock."

No less a person than Harvey Butchart, the dean of Grand Canyon trekking who had hiked more than anyone alive in the canyon, had nothing but praise for her writing. He said in the foreword to Sharon's book: "She has exhaustively researched and carefully written the most complete and reliable guidebook to hiking the trails of the South Rim. It's also an engaging personal adventure story, a good read for hiker and armchair adventurer alike. All of this is woven into a lively narrative that avoids the clichés and inadequacies of an attempt to rhapsodize over the indescribable grandeur of the scenery."

But despite all the acclaim and her beautiful surroundings in Durango, as the fall of 1994 approached, Sharon Cooper Spangler sank deeper and deeper into a mood of despair and foreboding. She had always been prone to bouts of depression and often used medication to ease her troubled mind, but there was something else adding to her sense of frustration and gloom that year. She was now living with the man whom she had once loved, then married and finally divorced. The man was Robert Merlin Spangler.

Once, Sharon would have done anything for Bob. She had called him "her soul mate, her beloved," but now she was only a guest in his house, a roommate paying rent for the right to exist under his roof. It was a testament of just how far she had fallen since their divorce in 1988 that Sharon had to come crawling back to him in the summer of 1994, seeking refuge from the strains of her life.

Life for Sharon after the divorce, which was supposed to have been liberating for her, was a disaster. She had tried teaching yoga and dog obedience training in Littleton, a suburb of Denver. Both had failed. One relationship after another, each seeming so promising, had all ended badly. One that finally held some promise sputtered along with an individual named Michael, who had his own set of emotional problems, and he needed medication for maintenance. Sharon tried writing another book. It never got off the ground. She thought of relocating to Arizona to be closer to the Grand Canyon, but that fizzled out as well. With the hopes that a new location might be beneficial for her state of mind, she moved to the beautiful small town of Pagosa Springs in southern Colorado. A gemlike location should have been a balm to her spirit, but more than ever, Sharon felt alone and separate from the individuals in this town.

Jim and Janece Ohlman, a couple of her best friends and hiking partners, knew Sharon very well over these difficult years. Jim related, "I don't know why Sharon moved to Pagosa Springs, other than to get away from old memories that lingered in Littleton and perhaps to give her and her dogs more room to move around in. Janece and I visited her in the last apartment she was in prior to leaving Littleton, and she was in the process of repainting it for sale then. Sharon really talked up the move to Pagosa Springs, but once there, things just never seemed to suit her. She wanted to teach yoga and dog obedience training while there, but I'm not sure she ever got either of those two ventures going."

Janece added, "Sharon had a lifelong battle with depression. It was always looming in her background. She would maintain it for a while. And then it would slip out of control."

Sharon's actions became more and more chaotic during 1994. Janece related that Sharon would call her up day or night to talk about her troubles. Good friend that she was, Janece always listened. She knew what pain Sharon was suffering.

Janece recalled, "Sharon would buy some expensive item, only to sell it for a loss a few weeks later. She would accumulate things to make her feel better then get rid of them as if trying to purge herself of some bad memory."

And then there was the matter of her boyfriend, Michael. Jim recalled, "Michael was Sharon's boyfriend after the divorce, before Sharon left Littleton. She spoke often of him, and at one time said that because he had more problems than she, there probably wasn't any future in their relationship. According to her, he later found the right set of medications for whatever ailed him, and they became an item. After Sharon moved to Pagosa Springs, she and Michael still found time to see each other."

But this relationship was always rocky at best. If Michael had found the right medications, as

Sharon had said, apparently she had not. She bounced from one extreme to another. Manic activity was followed by mind-numbing lethargy and hopelessness. To make matters worse, her mother was now gravely ill in St. Louis, Missouri. Sharon made long road trips there during a time she could barely take care of herself. By May 1994 it had all become too much and she ran for shelter under the roof of her former husband, Bob Spangler.

In June 1994 Sharon began writing her last will and testament, with references to how chaotic and miserable her life had become. She wrote that she was now living in Bob's house as merely a rent-paying housemate. She said that their relationship was somewhat strained but not intolerable. She noted that she'd been on numerous trips back to St. Louis because of her mom's heart condition. She said that her trips there "had been a nightmare for me. I was only in St. Louis two and a half days (on the latest trip) and thank God I'm back home in Durango now." She stated that all her furniture, linens, hardware and large household items were still in her Pagosa Springs home, while all her clothes and personal items were in Bob's home in Durango. She seemed to be living in two worlds and not inhabiting either one of them well.

Sharon spoke of perhaps selling her own home in Pagosa Springs and thought that she might put the earnings into money market mutual funds. She went into some detail about her financial concerns. But before long, her thoughts wandered back to more important things on her mind—the direction her life had gone.

Sharon wrote, "It's been hell to be torn and traveling so much among St. Louis (Mom's health and loneliness), Denver (Dr. Bell and my health), and this still somewhat alien type of life in Pagosa and Durango. It's culture shock of small town USA."

In another document she related, "This (Durango) isn't a normative small town. The entire region's towns are growing amazingly fast, are tourist draws, multi-ethnic and socio-demographically just downright weird. However, I seem to be getting used to this strange world and am accepting that for now and however long, I need to be in a small town and not live alone." But the man she had chosen "not to live alone" with carried a lot of emotional baggage for Sharon. He was a man she had both loved and despised and ultimately feared. But by 1994 her sense of despair was stronger than fear. In fact, when it came to Bob Spangler, all her emotions ran the gamut and they were irretrievably tied in an immense knot.

Adding to her sense of despair was the fact that her longtime companion, a dog named Shadow, died that summer. Sharon was disconsolate for days, crying uncontrollably at this new loss.

Finally, in a separate document, Sharon got down to the nitty-gritty of her burial instructions. "Even given the high level of stress and trauma of the past weeks and months, and agreed to by Bob, I do NOT WANT to be cached in St. Louis! I am to be cremated. My ashes are to be buried with Shadow, nestled as closely with her as possible, where she is buried adjacent to Bob's patio on Oak Drive in Durango."

Then as a footnote she added, "Bob will likely be the one to perform this task, including with my cremains a photo or two with me and Shadow and with all three of the Spangler girls (dogs), Mollie,

Shadow and Sunshine. And likely including one with Bob in the photo."

Sharon soon related in a letter to a cousin just what her relationship with Bob Spangler had become: "I'm grateful to have this safe harbor as we call it. To live in it for however long. To have the proferred opportunity to gain time to heal from the hurts and heart-crushing loss of Shadow, who rests under the sod just outside my window. And though I still cry for her and miss her so much, Sunshine and Mollie do help fill the void. And Bob is just wonderfully here for me."

Just what hurts and disappointments she had suffered, Sharon soon related to her cousin. She said she had been involved recently with a man named Michael, whom she loved, but could no longer live with. She said, "Michael is my psychic twin. My beloved dear one, who has shared and struggled with me during my illness. We wanted to make a life together, as lovers, as friends, perhaps as man and wife someday."

But her illness was paramount now and Michael had struggled with his own demons. He could barely take care of himself, much less her. As Sharon's life spiraled down, she could no longer think of a normal life with Michael. She couldn't think of a normal life at all.

Racked with manic-depressive fits, Sharon Cooper's life was becoming a living hell on the quiet street of Oak Drive. She didn't feel like she fit in anywhere—not in Pagosa Springs, not in Durango and certainly not on Oak Drive. Sharon was once a very active walker, but now some neighbors were not even aware that she lived in Bob Spangler's home. She was like a zombie, hiding in the shadows of the house, mourning her dead dog, Shadow, who lay in a grave right outside her window, and trying to cope with powerful bouts of anxiety and deep depression. Within a short time her "safe harbor" had become a self-imposed prison.

Adding to Sharon's sense of gloom was the knowledge that the "warden" of her prison, Bob Spangler, had some dark secrets in his past. Rumors had always swirled around him—vague, nebulous speculations about what had happened to his first family and third wife. Even though he rarely talked about it, Sharon knew that her ex-husband's first wife, Nancy, his daughter, Susan, his son, David, and third wife, Donna, had all died violent and mysterious deaths. Nancy had supposedly shot the children, then herself, back in Littleton, Colorado, in 1978. And Donna had fallen to her death at Sharon's favorite spot in the world, the Grand Canyon. No matter how she looked at it, people close to Bob Spangler seemed to die sudden and tragic deaths.

Death was like the third presence in their house now. The ghosts of Bob's former wives and children hovered constantly in the background, and Shadow's own ghost haunted Sharon with unrelenting pain.

Janece Ohlman noticed the worsening of Sharon's depression during August and September 1994. Though Janece lived many miles away in Arizona, Sharon kept up a constant stream of late-night calls to ease her pain. These were rambling soliloquies bordering on madness. Janece wondered if Sharon had stopped taking her medication. She tried to help talk Sharon through these dark spells, but there was only so much she could do.

By the end of September 1994, neither the shelter of Bob's roof nor the late-night phone calls were enough for Sharon Cooper's tormented soul. She sought a more permanent solution to all her agonies. On October 1, while Bob Spangler was away officiating a soccer game, Sharon sat down and began to write her final good-byes. In a letter to Bob she wrote, "You've said you wanted one of your former wives' lives to turn out okay. Your nurturing love gave me so much. And this release is, for me, a turning out okay. Please, my dear friend, acknowledge that this is the only way I could finally be okay and be well. To join God, and Shadow and Dad. Love, Sharon."

Having second thoughts about Michael, she wrote a separate note that he was to receive $35,000 and all her personal effects. And to her friends Jim and Janece Ohlman were to go all royalties she received from her book, *On Foot in the Grand Canyon*.

Then in a last-minute rush she dashed off a hurried note that said, "10-1-94. I would like it if Rich (her cousin) and Michael would be present to help you, Bob, and me, when my ashes and tokens are buried with Shadow. My dear Bob, thanks for all you've tried to do for me. Give my love to Mollie and Sunshine."

She signed the note with a simple letter *S*.

Sharon then took out a bottle of prescription drugs and swallowed them all at once, along with large swigs of alcohol. Before she lay down on the bed in her room, she tacked a note to the door for Bob to find. It read: "I've done it this time."

At around 3:30 P.M., according to Bob Spangler, he returned from officiating a soccer game to find Sharon's door closed. He didn't think much about it at the time and went on about his business for almost an hour, before passing the door once again and spying the note. "Damn it!" he swore when he read its contents, then burst into the room to find Sharon conscious but dazed and slipping into toxic shock. Scooping her off the bed, he managed to slide her into his car and rushed her to Durango's Mercy Medical Center, about seven miles away from his home in West Durango.

According to one source, Sharon was still conscious enough when they arrived to tell a physician named Dr. John Boyd that she had taken an overdose of drugs. She was administered a charcoal treatment in the intensive care unit to try and clear her system. The process went on for hour after hour. And strangely enough, during part of this time Bob Spangler was left alone with his ex-wife in ICU. His presence there would only add more rumors to his already mysterious past. What transpired between Bob and Sharon in the time they were alone? What medical knowledge did he have about her condition and ways to either improve it or make it worse? And was she more important to him dead or alive? After all, everything that had transpired in his home earlier that day would later be recounted only by him. There were no other eyewitnesses.

Whatever happened to Sharon Cooper while no one was watching in the ICU, except Bob, one fact became clear—the poisons in Sharon's body were more powerful than the antidotes. After twelve hours of struggle Sharon Cooper died from her self-inflicted overdose.

Bob Spangler cursed once more and muttered, "I always knew she would do something stupid."

But Bob's anger wasn't directed at her loss. It was

directed at the fact that she had brought attention to him. He now had one more dead ex-wife to add to an already long list of dead spouses and children. His third wife, Donna, had suspiciously slipped and fallen off a cliff at the Grand Canyon, where he and Sharon used to hike. And his first wife, Nancy, had supposedly killed the children and herself back in 1978. But Bob knew the terrible truth. He had killed them all. He'd pushed Donna off a cliff at Horseshoe Mesa in the Grand Canyon. And he'd murdered his entire first family just so he could be with the young Sharon Cooper. And now she was dead as well.

As Sharon's heart stopped beating, Bob Spangler knew one more thing: law enforcement officers would once again come pawing around his door, looking for clues that all these deaths were somehow more than tragic acts that had befallen his wives and children.

Chapter 2

The Deadly Surprise

Littleton, Colorado, 1978

Bob Spangler had once been in love with pretty, petite, dark-eyed Nancy Stahlman Spangler, but that had been years before in the 1950s when they'd gone together in high school. Now after twenty-three years of marriage, with two teenage children, he felt restless and trapped in a boring, middle-class existence. His seventeen-year-old son, David, wore long hair and played in a loud rock and roll band that often practiced in the basement of the Spanglers' comfortable home on South Franklin Way in Littleton. And fifteen-year-old daughter, Susan, had numerous boyfriends, none of which Bob cared for very much.

Even though Nancy still doted on him, life seemed stale and ennervating to Bob despite his interesting job as a public-relations director at the nearby American Water Works Association. He was good at what he did and had a gift for gab and raising money for the association. He was either a friendly mentor or a hard-driving boss, depending on whom you talked to there. But no one denied that he was bright and articulate. The only thing missing from his world was something or someone exciting to renew his zest for life.

That someone appeared one day in the mid-1970s in the form of Sharon Cooper. She became his assistant at the American Water Works Association, and she felt like a breath of fresh air to Bob after all the years of married life. Sharon was talkative and flirtatious, where Nancy was conventional and quiet. Sharon was filled with flamboyant ideas and of New Age sensibility, where Nancy was basically old-fashioned. And Sharon was an outdoor person, much like Bob who loved to hike and ride his motorcycle, where Nancy was a stay-at-home mom.

Before long, it came to the attention of coworkers that Bob Spangler was spending an awful lot of time with Sharon Cooper. And it was obvious he was more than just breaking her in on a new job. It was the way he talked to her, the way they stood together and seemed more intimate than was necessary. Before long, almost everyone in his department knew that Bob Spangler was having an affair with the pretty and young Sharon Cooper. In time he couldn't even keep this fact from his wife, Nancy. Nor did he want to.

Heated arguments erupted in the Spangler household between Bob and Nancy. In January 1978 he moved out of the house and into a home with Sharon Cooper. He liked her style and extravagant nature, but living with Sharon was no bed of roses either. She had a temper and, unlike Nancy, would not back down in arguments. One coworker said, "They would fight like cats and dogs. She would even throw things at him when she was angry. She had a nasty temper. So did he on occasion."

All the backpacking trips in the nearby Colorado Rockies with Sharon may have been fun for Bob, but there were arguments and quarrels that went along with them. Perhaps missing a quiet spell of domesticity and wanting one last chance at reconciliation, Bob moved back in with Nancy and the kids in November 1978. Nancy did try to make a go of it. She wrote to her cousin Martha Winter that she and Bob were planning to take a motorcycle trip together in Colorado. Also, in some attempt to turn Nancy into Sharon, Bob had convinced her to take a backpacking trip with him into the nearby Rockies, even though she wasn't very strong physically and suffered from arthritis in her right hand. Nancy was willing to go, however. She'd try about anything to get her family back together.

Because of his attempts at reconciliation, Nancy was upbeat and optimistic about their future together. She said she had been working at a temp agency and particularly enjoyed marketing and public relations. She said she planned to seek full-time employment in the new year.

Nancy wrote her cousin that David was getting pretty good at his guitar playing with his band and they all practiced in the basement. And she related that Susan practically had a live-in boyfriend, Timothy Trevithick. As for the Christmas holiday that had just occurred, Nancy wrote, "Had a fine time this year for Christmas. I have bought him (Bob) a backpack so we can try hiking again."

Christmas with Bob had been so good, in fact, that Nancy was sure she'd heard the last of Sharon Cooper. Bob Spangler, however, had drawn a whole

different conclusion about family life on South
Franklin Way in Littleton. The reconciliation may
have been working out for Nancy, but it was not
working for him. He was tired of the chaos that his
teenage children brought to the house. Both David
and Susan had little respect for a father who had
deserted them for nearly a year. He knew they
smoked marijuana with their friends. He suspected
they took harder drugs than that. And above all
else, when he compared the quiet, somewhat shy,
Nancy to the flamboyant Sharon Cooper—even
with all her problems—it was Sharon that he
wanted.

There was just one sticking point. Bob knew that
Sharon did not want kids, especially some hand-me-
down teenage kids from another marriage. She had
stated more than once, "I'm not a children-type
person." And besides, divorce could be so contentious and expensive. He would have to think of
another way to get out of his marriage. Something
more permanent.

As the days after Christmas wound down, Bob
Spangler devised an alternative to divorce. It was so
breathtaking in scope it even left him a little
stunned by the clarity of its image. He would eliminate his entire family and start over fresh with
Sharon. As he said later, "It was like a curtain
dropped."

One thing for certain was that once he decided
to act, he would proceed with careful planning and
no undo haste. It was the way he tackled all big projects in his life. As far as he was concerned, this was
just one more difficult project. The first order of
business was to create a diversion at the murder
scene. Something to draw attention away from him-

self and onto someone else. And what better way to do it than create an argument with his wife in front of Susan's and David's friends—something to let them see just how wound up and emotional Nancy was. A woman capable of doing anything.

At around 8:15 P.M. on December 28, 1978, two of Susan's friends, Kelly Kitchen and Ilbhlhin Mahoney, arrived at the Spangler home. David answered the door and led them upstairs to Susan's room, where Susan and her boyfriend, Timothy, were listening to the stereo. They all planned a New Year's Eve party, which in part would also be a birthday party for Tim. Susan asked her mother if they could have the party at the Spangler residence and Nancy agreed.

It was a perfect excuse for Bob Spangler to create an argument with his wife, one where he could accuse her of being too lenient where the kids were concerned. At around 10:00 P.M., when Kitchen and Mahoney were getting ready to leave, they became aware of Bob having a violent argument with David and Nancy down in the kitchen. Bob was yelling and swearing at them both, especially at David. Nancy looked on the verge of tears. She seemed incredibly distraught from the scene that was taking place. Mahoney had seen arguments in the Spangler family before, but nothing like this one. She thought that Bob might even strike his son. In embarrassment, Susan hustled the two girls out the door and said good-bye to them, then she slunk back into the house.

Mission accomplished, Bob Spangler broke off the argument and went to bed.

The next day, December 29, 1978, between 9:30 A.M. and 10:00 A.M., Tim Trevithick went over to the

Spangler residence again to see Susan. He'd caught several hints from Susan the night before that things were not going well between her parents and she was pretty sure they'd get a divorce. In a way she didn't care. She was tired of her father's presence in the home anyway.

At around 3:00 P.M. Tim noticed that Bob Spangler came home early from work. He even heard Bob apologize to David for the previous night's argument, saying, "I'm sorry. It was just your old man blowing up." He did not have any similar apology for Nancy.

Tim went home for dinner between 5:30 P.M. and 6:00 P.M. but returned to the Spangler residence about 7:30 P.M. and went upstairs to Susan's room. According to Tim later, he and Susan dropped some LSD and listened to music.

During their acid trip Tim became aware that Bob Spangler had received a phone call from Iowa saying that his mother had fallen down the stairs and was in bad shape. The news seemed to upset Bob very badly.

Tim stayed with Susan until nearly 1:30 A.M. on December 30 before going home. When he left, everything seemed to be all right in the Spangler home. But it wasn't. Bob Spangler was already putting plans into motion for eliminating his entire family.

Bob kept a .38 caliber revolver in a shoe box in the master bedroom closet. He had bought it, or so he told Nancy, for protection on his motorcycle trips. (Another alternate theory is that he never told her about it at all.) Even though he was a tall man, 6'1", he placed a footstool in front of the closet as if a shorter person were reaching for the shoe box. Then he took the pistol to the basement and hid it.

In the early-morning hours of December 30, 1978, Bob Spangler went down to the basement and placed a typewritten letter into a Corona typewriter that Nancy often used. The letter was supposed to have been written by her, but, in fact, he had concocted it. The letter stated: "What do I say now that I decided to do this? I found the gun by accident some time ago and couldn't help thinking about this. I don't know why I didn't say anything to you. I feel shattered. We have always argued about who'd have the kids. I will. I know you will get along. You always have."

At the bottom of the note was a handwritten letter *N*. Bob had already tricked Nancy into signing her first initial there. She thought she was signing a Christmas letter that he had typed. Placing the "suicide note" in the typewriter, the only thing Bob needed now was the victim.

He casually went upstairs and asked Nancy to come down into the basement with him. He said he had a surprise for her.

Perhaps she thought he had a late-arriving Christmas present for her. Perhaps she thought Bob was going to give her some gift of apology for the argument of a few nights past. Whatever the reason, Nancy sat down in a chair next to a table that held the typewriter and closed her eyes as instructed.

Bob pulled the .38-caliber revolver out of hiding and aimed it at his wife's forehead. The barrel was about three to four inches away from her skull and pointed at about a forty-degree angle in a downward slant. As Nancy waited in anticipation for her surprise, Bob Spangler gave it to her. He pulled the trigger and fired. The bullet ripped through Nancy's skull and brain and she slumped over in the chair. Even if she didn't die immediately, she was now beyond all hope. The wound was ultimately fatal.

Bob's bloody morning was only beginning. For one instant he thought of leaving the house, but then he decided that Sharon Cooper would never want his children. And the one thing he wanted most in life at that moment was Sharon Cooper. The children had to go as well.

Both Susan and David were heavy sleepers, especially on a Saturday morning as this was. Apparently, neither one of them heard the gunshot in the basement. Bob made his way up to Susan's room and found her asleep. She was wearing a cream-colored nightgown and a pair of blue briefs; she was lying on her stomach as she slept.

Bob sneaked up, as close as he dared, to the bed and aimed the pistol at the center of her back, in the area he thought her heart would be. He fired once and the shot couldn't have been more well aimed than if he had been an expert marksman. The bullet pierced her heart and Susan died with hardly a sound.

David, however, was another story. He was large and strong, and unlike his sister, David could be a problem if only wounded. As Bob Spangler moved closer, perhaps David awoke and shifted in bed. Or perhaps Bob suddenly lost his nerve. After all, David was his favorite, and despite their numerous arguments, he was proud of the boy. For whatever reason, his aim was not good this time and the bullet ripped off-center near the midline of the boy's sternum.

Awake now and in shock, David must have looked up in disbelief at his father with the smoking gun in his hand. Bob made ready to fire again but quickly changed his mind. To fire again would be out of alignment with his plan—one bullet for each victim.

As David's blood began to pour over the sheets, Bob grabbed a pillow from beneath his son's head and smashed it down over the boy's face. There must have been a terrible struggle despite David's wound. He twisted and turned and fell halfway off the bed. There was blood everywhere.

David was just as big as his father, and strong, but with a bullet wound in his body, he was no match for the now-frantic Bob Spangler. Bob smothered his son for all he was worth. Slowly but surely, the boy's strength began to ebb. Then his struggles ceased all together. He was dead too, just like his mother and sister.

Within a short period of time, Bob Spangler returned to the basement and dropped the pistol on the floor a few feet away from Nancy's body. He looked around the room, feeling as if he were an actor in a play. And then he simply walked out the door and away from the scene of terrible slaughter on quiet South Franklin Way.

Chapter 3

Gun Shot Residue

At approximately 10:30 A.M. on December 30, 1978, Timothy Trevithick phoned the Spangler residence to contact Susan. Receiving no answer, he decided to go there and wake her up. Tim knew she and David were late sleepers on the weekends and it wasn't too unusual for no one to answer the phone.

Upon arriving at the Spangler home, he went to the front of the house, but the door was locked. Moving around toward the garage, Tim noticed that the maroon station wagon was gone and the side door into the house was locked. Returning to the front door, he rang the bell, but no one answered. He picked up some pebbles from the neighbor's yard and threw them at Susan's window, to no avail. Frustrated, he grabbed the Spanglers' morning newspaper and threw it at her window. It bounced off the glass, making a loud noise. Still, there was no response.

Determined to get into the house, Tim went to a basement window, pushed the window open and crawled inside. It was dark in the basement and he passed right by the body of Nancy Spangler, slumped over in a chair, without even knowing it. He climbed the basement staircase into the main portion of the house and went up the stairs to the second floor.

Susan's bedroom door was closed, but Tim went inside and saw her in the bed. She looked so peaceful, he thought she was sleeping. As a joke he threw his hat and gloves at her to wake her up. Susan, however, did not move a muscle as the hat and gloves landed on her bed.

Concerned now, Tim strode forward and saw that she was lying facedown, her head was buried in the pillow and she did not appear to be breathing. Incredibly enough, there was no blood present, even though a bullet had pierced her heart. Tim rolled Susan over and felt for a pulse on her neck. He even may have lifted her nightgown up over her chest to check there, but later he did not remember doing this. There was no blood on her chest. Finding no pulse, Tim panicked and ran to David's bedroom. Flinging open the door, he was greeted by the sight that there nearly made him faint. There was blood everywhere and David's body lay sprawled halfway off the bed and onto the floor.

In a daze Tim ran to the master bedroom and phoned paramedics. Then he waited, shivering with shock. The first paramedics to arrive on the scene were Gary Roberts and Emmett Adams from the Littleton Fire Department. They met Tim in the Spangler home and followed him up to Susan's and David's rooms. But it soon became apparent to the two paramedics that nothing could be done for either teenager. Neither one recorded any vital signs.

A few minutes later, Arapahoe County sheriff's sergeant Gene Martin and Deputies Greg Williams and Bruce Hayward arrived on the scene. Deputy Williams stayed with Tim while Sergeant Martin wrote in his report, "There is a body of a white male, approximately sixteen years of age, located in the northwest bedroom. This individual is lying face down with his head to the east and feet to the west. His upper torso is touching the floor with his feet on the bed at a higher level. There are numerous blood pools spotting the bottom sheet of the bed. The top bed clothing is rumpled at the foot of the bed. A larger pool of blood is directly under the part of the torso that is neither touching the floor nor the bed.

"A patterned pillow is under his head and his face is buried in it. The pillow is also blood stained. The male is clad in a pair of red nylon briefs. His body shows numerous abrasions, most prevalent about the knees and lower legs, with two linear abrasions about the upper middle shoulders. The bedroom itself is extremely cluttered."

Sergeant Martin noted later, "Upon moving the deceased, it was found that he had suffered a single gunshot puncture wound, located midline of the superior aspect of the sternum."

As for Susan Spangler, Sergeant Martin noted: "She is lying face up with her head to the east and her feet to the west. Her bed clothing is pulled up exposing her chest. She is clad in a cream colored nightgown and a pair of blue briefs."

A short time later, he wrote, "There were no signs of puncture upon first viewing. It was later discovered that she had a single puncture gun shot wound in midline, slightly to the left of her back, with no extrusion of blood."

Walking to the master bedroom, Sergeant Martin discovered Bob Spangler's little stage prop. It was the step stool in front of the closet, as if someone of a small stature had used it to reach the open box of .38-caliber ammunition that was on a high shelf.

At around 12:05 P.M., Lieutenant Les Murray and Investigator Marv Tucker of the Arapahoe County Sheriff's Office arrived at the Spangler home, followed by Deputy Coroner Mark Hamilton. According to Tucker, Hamilton went downstairs and nearly jumped out of his skin when he turned on the light and saw the body of Nancy Spangler slumped over in a chair. As Tucker said later, "He had no idea a body was there. That's the first we knew about Nancy Spangler."

Tucker noted in his report: "The victim was slumped over to her right side with her right arm hanging straight down and blood dripping from her nose. Her left arm is in her lap. There is what appears to be a gun shot wound to her head area. In front of the chair is a round table with a small Corona typewriter on it. On top of the typewriter is a typewritten note." Then he wrote down what was contained in the note.

This, of course, was the fake "suicide note" that Bob Spangler had typed expressly for the investigator to find and attribute to Nancy.

Tucker went on to record, "A Smith and Wesson, Model 12.3, two inch barreled six shot revolver, serial number 3067041, was found approximately five and a half feet from Nancy Spangler's body. That weapon contained three fired rounds and three live rounds. There was a man's sock covering half of the grip."

After the shock of discovering Nancy's body, Deputy Coroner Hamilton moved through the house as well, from victim to victim, and he jotted down: "Victim #1, identified as one David A Spangler, age 17. Pronounced dead at 11:48 AM. On the deceased body were numerous abrasions that were most prevalent about the knees and lower legs, although two linear abrasions were noted about the upper middle shoulders. The room was extremely cluttered with bizarre paraphernalia. This male had a single puncture apparently from a bullet. This was located at the midline at the superior aspect of the sternum. A sample was taken from [his] lips and given to CBI (Colorado Bureau of Investigation) to analyze.

"Victim #2, identified as one Susan E Spangler, age 15. Pronounced dead at 11:51 AM. Deceased appeared to be sleeping. It was later known that the boyfriend of the deceased had turned this particular person over upon discovery of no movement upon numerous attempts to waken her. Upon moving the deceased at a later time it was discovered that the deceased had a single puncture apparently from a bullet at the midline slightly left of the back with no exudation of blood. No other signs of foul play were observed on this body."

Moving to the basement, Hamilton wrote: "Victim #3, identified as one Nancy Spangler, age 45. Pronounced dead at 12:24 PM. It is apparent to this office that the above top two victims were the result of an apparent homicide. The last victim appears to have been the victim of suicide. This is not a final interpretation of the above scenes. The final interpretation will result from investigations of the Sheriff's Office."

It wasn't until 4:45 P.M. that Bob Spangler returned to his home to find yellow police tape marking the yard and a street filled with law enforcement vehicles and television news vans. He put on his game face, ready for anything the investigators would throw at him. He knew this would have to be the performance of his life.

Bob was met at the door by Sergeant Martin, who talked to him briefly and told him to wait in his vehicle. Then Bob was transported down to the Arapahoe County Sheriff's Office for questioning. There he was taken into a room for an interview with Investigator Tucker and Lieutenant Murray. Bob had taken all day to concoct a story and he began to relate it to them. It was filled with an assortment of truths, half-truths and lies.

To their questions, he answered, "My wife and I had an argument on December twenty-ninth and I told her I was planning on leaving her. We went to bed that night in our bedroom. In the morning she and I awakened and went downstairs. The argument continued. At about 8:30 A.M. she told me to leave the house. I put on my jacket and left the house through the back sliding-glass doors, crossed the backyard and over a fence to the back of King Soopers store. I walked down South University to the Southglenn Mall and walked around for a while.

"I was gone about an hour and a half. I returned to the house, crossed the fence through the backyard and went immediately into the garage. I didn't go inside the house. I got in my car and drove around."

Spangler told them that he had driven around

Denver listening to the Broncos football game on the car radio. Then he went to see an animated movie, *The Lord of the Rings,* at a theater in the University Hills Shopping Center. After the movie he'd driven home to find all the police in his house.

Bob agreed to take a trace metal detection (TMD) gunshot residue (GSR) test. And an incredible coincidence occurred, the testing lab technician was Jack Swanburg, who happened to be a friend of Bob's. They had worked together in conjunction with the Honeywell Corporation before Swanburg moved on to become a lab technician for Arapahoe County. In fact, Bob coached Swanburg's son in a soccer league.

As Swanburg administered the tests, he was looking for traces of gunshot residue on Bob's hands and clothing. Gunshot residues are composed of soot, lead, barium and antimony from the discharging cartridge primer compound. The soot portion contains mainly graphite dust. The trace elements of lead, barium and antimony mainly come from the discharging primer's explosive compound. When a gun is fired, there is a small puff of soot over the chamber area. This puff of GSR is usually deposited over the shooter's hand that holds the weapon. The palm, however, is generally free of this residue because it grips the butt of the pistol, while the web and back of the hand are coated with the residue. Someone who picks up a gun after it has been fired can get gunshot residue on the palm of his hand. In Bob Spangler's case he did seem to have trace elements of GSR on the web and backside of his hand, but he also had GSR on both palms as well.

Following the completion of the gunshot residue

test, administered by Swanburg, Bob was transported to Bullock's Mortuary, where he identified the bodies of Nancy, Susan and David. After this was done, he was taken back to the Arapahoe County Sheriff's Office. At this juncture Jack Swanburg spoke up and told the investigators that he was a friend of Bob's. He also said that Bob didn't have any relatives in the area, and Swanburg asked if it would be all right if Bob stayed at his home that night. Even though this was highly irregular, there were no objections from the investigators.

The next day, December 31, 1978, Jack Swanburg told Investigator Tucker that Spangler was willing to take a polygraph test. Swanburg took Bob Spangler to Ralph Severance's office within the Arapahoe County Sheriff's Office; once there, Spangler seemed eager to take the test, but he was also acting very agitated and hyperventilating. Severance determined that Bob was in no shape to take the test and told him to go home.

Spangler replied, "I'll take the test at a later time if it's okay with my attorney."

By now he had retained the services of attorney John Burns.

At nine-thirty that same morning Investigator Tucker and Investigator Karen Beauchamp went to Bullock's Mortuary to meet Dr. John Wood, the chief coroner. As Dr. Wood began the autopsy on Nancy Spangler, he explained to the investigators that the broken capillaries on her right wrist could have been caused by the recoil from firing the pistol. The dark spots that collected there were known as Tardieu spots. He said that a person her size could have suffered bruising if she was not used to firing a pistol.

As to the bullet wound in her forehead, he noted, "a bullet entrance area is seen in the right frontal bone. There is evidence of metallic tracking through the right hemisphere with an exit site in the right occipital bone almost at the midline."

Meanwhile, the crime scene processing at the Spangler home was being completed by lab technicians Al Sprigg and Dick Hopkins. Document examiner Andrew Bradley examined the "suicide note" and the Corona 70 portable electric typewriter. He compared these with several typewritten and handwritten examples coming from Nancy Spangler. Some of them were from cashed checks.

After careful examination Bradley recorded the following conclusions, and they seemed to confirm what others had already surmised:

- The suicide note was typed on the Corona 70 typewriter.
- The capital *N* written in ink was written by the same person as the canceled checks initialed N Spangler.

One thing he didn't add in his notations at the time was that it was Bob Spangler who gave him the canceled checks that were used for comparison.

On January 3, 1979, Dr. Wood completed his examinations on the bodies of Nancy, Susan and David and issued death certificates. He ruled the manner of death for Susan and David to be homicide. For Nancy he listed the death as a suicide, but the case was still open as far as the Arapahoe County Sheriff's Office was concerned.

Not long after Dr. Wood's final assessment, the victims' remains were cremated. This request seemed to have come from Bob Spangler. Whether they wanted to be cremated or not was unknown, but one thing was for certain now—their bodies could not be disinterred later for further examinations.

Some of the items from the Spangler home were sent to the Colorado Bureau of Investigation Laboratory. On January 17, 1979, Agent Ted Ritter reported on several of the items he had received:

1. One Ziploc plastic bag containing a .38 special Smith & Wesson model 12 revolver
2. Five plastic tubes containing nitric acid hand swabs from Nancy Spangler
3. Five plastic tubes containing nitric hand swabs from Robert Spangler
4. One plastic cup containing one fired lead bullet, taken from the skull of Nancy Spangler
5. One paper bag containing a gold-colored turtleneck, pants, bra, plaid shirt and panties
6. One plastic cup containing one fired bullet from the body of David Spangler
7. One plastic cup containing one fired bullet from the body of Susan Spangler

Among Ritter's test results he noted that the Smith & Wesson pistol was operable and capable of producing serious injury or death. He also discovered that bullets numbered 4, 6 and 7 were all fired from the same gun.

But the nitric acid hand swabs (#2 and #3 of the list) analyzed by Dr. Richard Lehmann at CBI really set off alarm bells. Dr. Lehmann wrote in his report, "The amounts of antimony found in exhibit

#2 taken from Nancy Spangler were not sufficient to indicate the presence of gun shot residue. No powder pattern was developed on exhibit #5 A (Nancy) which would be indicative of a very close muzzle contact distance. The amount of barium and antimony found on the right palm of R. (Robert) Spangler, exhibit #3, were sufficient to indicate gun shot residue. The results are consistent with the possibility that the subject handled a weapon with the right hand."

The Corona electric typewriter was also at the CBI lab and Agent Steven Sedlacek noted that there were distinct wipe marks on the typewriter as if someone had tried to wipe away fingerprints.

With these new facts, the investigative team at the Arapahoe County Sheriff's Office asked Bob Spangler to come back for further questioning. He arrived at their office on February 1, 1979, with his lawyer, John Burns. He was met by Investigator Beauchamp. Advised of his rights, he said he understood them. He also said that he wanted to make a statement. And this one varied in quite a number of areas from his first statements on December 30, 1978.

First of all, Bob contradicted his earlier statement about an argument between himself and Nancy on the morning of December 30. He said, in fact, that not many words had been exchanged between them that morning. Bob explained, "I went downstairs, made breakfast and was starting to eat when Nancy ordered me to leave the house. I became somewhat huffy, grabbed my coat and left by the back door. I went over the back fence."

Bob gave more details about his absence from the house during the critical hour between nine and ten in the morning. He said, "I walked down toward King Soopers Shopping Center. Then down the sidewalk on University Boulevard to Easter Avenue and proceeded down the street, south of Southglenn, to Franklin Street and back up to the Kings Ridge Subdivision entrance. I came to the front of the house and opened the garage and drove my car out of the garage. As I approached the entrance to the subdivision, I decided I needed to go back and discuss things further with my wife.

"I went back to the house by the way of Vine Street and pulled into the driveway. I went into the garage through the family room. I called Nancy, but got no answer. I didn't see her in the living room, kitchen or family room. She'd been in the kitchen when I left earlier.

"I noticed the basement door was ajar and the basement lights were on. I proceeded down the basement stairs and walked around the corner. I saw Nancy sitting in the chair with her head slumped over to the side and blood dripping from her head.

"I walked over to the table and stood across from her. Then I noticed the gun on the floor, partially covered with a sock, that covered most of the grip. I reached down and picked up the gun with my right hand.

"I know I had the gun in both of my hands. I stepped back a couple of steps and dropped the gun on the floor. I left by going back up the stairs and through the garage door. I think I locked the garage as I left.

"All I could feel was that I had to get away from there. I couldn't believe what had happened."

Investigator Beauchamp asked him about the suicide note in the typewriter.

Bob said, "I saw the typewriter. But I did not see a note on top of it. My only thoughts were to get out of the house."

Bob continued, telling of his journey through the rest of the day on December 30. "I drove all over Denver, all day long. I listened to the Denver Broncos football game on the radio. And I ate lunch at Burger King. While I was near University Hills, I decided to go see a movie at the University Hills Cinema. While I was there, I began to worry about seeing my wife (dead) and not calling anyone. I didn't see the end of the movie but went back home."

Investigator Beauchamp asked him about the step stool found in front of the master bedroom closet.

He answered, "I last remember seeing it under the sink in the washroom near the kitchen, where it was kept."

"Where were the bullets for the pistol kept?" Investigator Beauchamp asked.

"Upstairs in the bedroom with the gun," Spangler answered.

Investigator Beauchamp asked why there was a gun in the house.

Bob answered, "The reason I bought it in the first place was due to the discussion I had with Nancy approximately a year before while we were separated. I'd become interested in motorcycles. Nancy felt it was important that I have some type of protection with me. I bought the gun and never showed it to her. I kept it on a high shelf in the back corner of my closet. I kept it in a shaving kit, and to my knowledge she did not know about it."

Beauchamp asked Spangler if Nancy ever used the letter *N* to sign her name.

He said, "I received a birthday card from her once, which was signed with just the initial *N*."

Bob then volunteered that he was embarrassed about lying to sheriff's investigators on December 30 when he'd first come into their office right after the deaths. He said he was frightened because he'd left his residence after seeing Nancy dead without reporting it to anyone. Then he added he would take a polygraph test to prove that he was telling the truth now.

Bob Spangler did take a polygraph test on February 28, 1979. It was conducted by a private firm that specialized in such procedures. A polygraph test consists of several different phases. There is a pretest interview, where the interviewer tells the person to be tested about the range of questions that will be administered. This part generally takes anywhere from forty-five minutes to an hour. Then the tester shows the subject the actual instruments of the polygraph machine and explains their functions.

The polygraph machine in Bob's case consisted of a pneumograph, which recorded respiration, the galvanograph, which recorded galvanic skin response and changes in skin resistance, and the cardiosphygmograph, which recorded relative blood pressure and pulse rate.

Four attachments were placed on Bob Spangler's body, including two rubber pneumograph tubes across the upper chest and abdomen and two metal fingerplates across the ring and index finger and a blood pressure cuff around the upper arm. During the collection of data the examiner asked him the same set of questions three times. Each time Spangler's responses were recorded on a chart that ran out of the machine like a large piece of ticker tape.

Even though it is expected that anyone taking a polygraph test will be nervous, the machine and examiner takes this into account. Nervousness is presented in a regular set of patterns. Lying is something else again. When a question is asked, the respondent automatically determines whether to tell the truth or lie. When a person decides to lie, the heart rate flucuates, either faster or slower; blood pressure will change; skin resistance will become different.

But Bob Spangler brought a new element to his test. When he began, he immediately started to control his breathing. He hyperventilated on all the questions, even the easy ones such as the date and what city he lived in. It skewed the test so badly that the examiner could not tell whether he was telling the truth or lying about any of the questions, including whether he had killed his family.

On March 1, 1979, he was retested. Again he hyperventilated throughout all the tests. As the police report stated later, "His actions appeared voluntary but the examiner could not determine if it was a purposeful attempt to hide deception."

On March 2, 1979, Bob Spangler retold his story to investigators about the hours after he left his home on the morning of December 30, 1978. And once again his story changed as far as certain details went. In part he stated, "On Friday night, December 29, 1978, I told my wife our life together wasn't working out as I'd hoped it might and that I felt a divorce would be necessary. There was no big fight. Mostly tears, shocked silence and evident anger.

"On Saturday, December thirtieth, we got up together about eight A.M. or slightly before, dressed and came downstairs without speaking. As I began to look for breakfast things, Nancy very clearly indicated she'd just as soon I got out of the house right then. She was very grim about it, very determined. I reacted with a fairly typical 'if that's the way you want it, fine' attitude. We didn't fight. I went to the hall closet, got my coat and went out the back door, across the backyard and over the back fence, which faces a new shopping center."

He then added a few more details about his walking around in the neighborhood. The details were meant to add veracity to his story. They were also meant to give him an alibi. He recounted, "It was too darn cold to stay out walking all day. We (his lawyer and himself) measured the distance later and found the round-trip was something over two miles, so the time consumed was somewhere between thirty and forty minutes." (The minutes in which Nancy had supposedly killed the children and then herself.)

"As I approached the house, I recall a neighbor whose dog was out by the Franklin Way curb in our area. I'm not sure he saw me at the time. I also recall seeing another neighbor, who lives two or three doors farther down, drive away from his house in a gray car. I picked up the morning paper from the driveway and tossed it onto the front porch. Then I went to the garage, got into our '73 Chevy wagon and drove off."

Bob told of returning home, changing bits of information once again. "I realized I'd gotten into a huff rather unfairly and that we actually had quite a lot to talk over. We were going to have to talk sooner or later and that it might as well be now."

As far as seeing Nancy slumped in the chair, Bob said, "There was an immense amount of blood. I cannot say what I thought. I know I just started repeating over and over, 'Oh, my God. Jesus. Oh, my God.' And staring at her. I know I crouched and reached to pick up the gun. I have no idea why. It still had the black sock I kept it wrapped in, down around the butt. I think I only glanced at it and then right back at her. I have no idea how many bullets were in it or anything else. I backed up a step or two and let the gun down. It was perhaps five feet or so from Nancy. And I just had a surge of feeling that I had to get out of there. I didn't even think of calling anyone. I didn't even think of my children at the time. As for them, earlier in the day, they were asleep in their rooms. Very typical of a Saturday morning. It could be like pulling teeth to get them out of bed."

He recalled wandering around Denver and watching *The Lord of the Rings* at the movie theater. And then he related, "Around five P.M. I did go back and found the sheriff's deputies."

Even after these latest admissions, the Arapahoe County sheriff's investigators took everything Bob Spangler said with a grain of salt. Investigators asked for and got the gloves that Bob had been wearing on December 30. These gloves were tested at the Colorado Bureau of Investigation. After the test Dr. Lehmann wrote, "The amounts of barium and antimony found on the palms of the right and left gloves was sufficient to indicate gun shot residue."

Then he added, "No conclusion can be drawn from these results since there is no statistical base for barium and antimony in leather gloves."

Several detectives within the Arapahoe County Sheriff's Office doubted that Bob Spangler was an innocent man. Just too many of his statements and actions didn't seem to jibe. He would tell one story and then change key details later, but time and circumstances were working in Bob Spangler's favor. There was no new evidence coming forward and the polygraph tests were inconclusive; so were the gunshot residue tests. However, more than anything else, there was that "suicide note." No one doubted that the letter *N* signed to it came from Nancy Spangler. The handwriting examples had proven that it was her handwriting. Why would she sign it if she hadn't written it?

A short article came out in the *Denver Post* around that time. It read: "Robert Spangler, husband of the dead woman, was questioned and released by authorities. He isn't considered a suspect in the deaths."

If the authorities officially didn't consider him a suspect (though many of them still did doubt that he was innocent), the doubt factor was even more prevalent amongst Nancy Stahlman Spangler's relatives. The news that reached the Stahlmans in Iowa, where Nancy had grown up, was devastating to say the least. Jo Stahlman, Nancy's stepmother, related years later to the *Denver Post* that a deputy sheriff phoned from Littleton, Colorado, to say that Nancy and both of her children were gone. Clarence Stahlman, Nancy's father, told the reporter that the deputy had related the facts with almost no sympathy. The deputy merely stated that Nancy had shot her children and then herself.

David Fitch, Nancy's stepbrother told the *Rocky Mountain News* years later, "I can smell the place I was at, standing in the basement when the phone rang." Then he added about his suspicions: "If she (Nancy) had all her clothes on and you soaked her with water, she probably weighed 105 pounds. How could she have overpowered her seventeen-year-old son?"

Clarence Stahlman had doubts as well. He told Jo, "She (Nancy) was always afraid to handle guns."

As time went by, Clarence Stahlman began to believe more and more firmly that his son-in-law, Bob, had killed all three members of his family and somehow blamed it on Nancy. But no one in authority would listen to him.

Strangely enough, there was one more death that could be linked to Bob Spangler's massacre on Franklin Way. Something he never imagined. Soon after his elderly mother, Ione, heard the terrible news, she had a massive stroke. Ten days after Nancy, Susan and David died, Ione Spangler passed away in Iowa. Some people said she died of a broken heart.

The cremated ashes of Nancy, Susan and David were shipped back to Ames, Iowa, the town that Nancy had grown up in and where she had first met Bob Spangler. Their ashes were interred in the Spangler plot on a small rise in the main municipal cemetery, but there was something missing on their grave markers. Only their first names and middle initials were imprinted on the markers, and no mention was made that their last names were Spangler, as if part of them ceased to exist.

Meanwhile, back in Littleton, Colorado, Bob

Spangler had Sharon Cooper all to himself now. Within days after the murders, Sharon moved in with him to the "death" house on Franklin Way. If Sharon was disturbed about being in such a tainted residence, she didn't let her feelings be known to coworkers. After all, she had Bob all to herself now.

A next-door neighbor who knew all the Spanglers well thought this situation was odd. The bodies of Bob's wife and children were barely cold and here was this new woman moving in with the widower. The female neighbor had always liked Nancy and found it hard to believe that she had killed her children. She knew that Nancy had been upset by Bob's affair with another woman, but Nancy had doted on her children so much, it was almost inconceivable that she had murdered them.

And this woman's eyebrows were really raised a few days later when Bob and Sharon dragged much of Nancy's belongings out into the driveway and had a yard sale. It was as if he were trying to erase all memories of his newly departed wife.

"What's going on here?" the woman rhetorically asked.

What was going on was that for the time being Bob Spangler had gotten away with murder three times over.

Chapter 4

Young Bob

Robert Merlin Spangler, known as Bob through much of his life, was born in Des Moines, Iowa, on January 10, 1933. The fact of the matter is, no records have been kept as to who his real parents were. He was adopted at a very young age by Merlin Grant Spangler and Ione Spangler of Ames, Iowa, and this was one of the most important factors of his life. It was a dual-edged sword. He could have hardly been adopted by a more prominent or caring Iowa family of that period, but the mere fact that he was adopted would always haunt him and make him wonder about his real parents.

Bob's young life would be shaped and molded by his adopted town as well. Ames, Iowa, is situated right in the middle of this Midwestern state, surrounded by farmland as far as the eye can see. But Ames itself is somehow separate and apart from the agricultural vastness that surrounds it. It is a university town, through and through, with Iowa State University as its center. More than just a physical entity, Iowa State dominates the city in all aspects, both culturally and economically. In one way or another, almost everyone in town has some links to the university. And this carried right over into Bob Spangler's life as his adoptive father, Merlin, was a well-respected professor at Iowa State in the field of soil engineering. For many years Bob would live in the shadow of his adoptive father, and it is impossible to understand Bob without understanding Merlin Grant Spangler as well. For Bob was in awe of him and perhaps a little envious as well. Merlin had traveled far from very humble beginnings in the Hawkeye State.

Merlin Spangler was born in 1894 in Des Moines, Iowa, and embodied the hardworking ethic of mid-America at the turn of the twentieth century. He studied hard as well and earned his degree at Iowa State University in civil engineering in 1919, following 1½ years in the United States Army during World War I. In his army life he was a lieutenant of field artillery.

During the war years he married his Iowa sweetheart, Ione Amsberry. From 1919 to 1924 he served as a bridge designer with the Iowa State Highway Commission, but higher learning was always his passion. Merlin took the time to earn his Master of Science degree in 1928. Not content with just teaching others, he took on the job as a researcher of soil pressure on underground conduits as well.

This dual role became the focus of his life. Merlin loved to teach and he loved research. He once joked to a colleague, "After fifteen years of working next to students without the formal opportunity to teach, I began to feel like a young person under a full moon without a date."

He approached Dean Marston, head of the civil engineering department at Iowa State, and asked if he could become a professor. Marston agreed and Merlin became a researcher/mentor/teacher.

Of his teaching abilities a colleague wrote later, "Professor Spangler's many years of teaching on the Iowa State faculty, his expertness, and his humble and pleasant manner, have carried a position of respect, admiration and endearment for many students and alumni. His textbook also has won him many friends and is widely regarded as the best organized and most simply written for the beginning student."

World War II interrupted Merlin's life once again in 1941. Always a patriot willing to do his duty, Merlin became an officer in the navy of all places, having been a lieutenant in the army during World War I. But the navy immediately saw his expertise in engineering and wanted him in their new wartime construction units, a Seabee Construction Battalion. Merlin did such a good job during his stint in the navy that he ended the war at the grade of Lt. Commander.

After the war Merlin went on with his teaching/research career at Iowa State. And he was eminently successful at this. So much so, in fact, that he joined the rare group of individuals who have a scientific theory named after themselves. In this case it was the Marston/Spangler Theory.

In brief, the Marston/Spangler Theory concerns the aspects of soil pressure on underground conduits. In a mathematical manner it theorized at what pressure certain conduits would fail. By use of the theory an engineer could take certain measures to ensure the successful implementation of a conduit. The Marston/ Spangler Theory became implemented worldwide as the accepted design for underground conduits.

Young Bob Spangler obviously had a lot to live up to in the Spangler household in Ames with such an eminent father. It's hard to know at this juncture whether he felt intimidated by his adoptive father or whether something else was at play. Wayne, his adopted brother, who was not a blood relation, never seemed to have the same kind of trouble in his early years that Bob had. And it brings up the question of nature versus nurture. There may have been something in Bob's genes or psychological makeup that made him different no matter what family he grew up with. To paraphrase Paul Newman in the movie *Hud,* when talking to his respected and honest father played by Melvyn Douglas, "You're so damned good, I just had to turn out bad."

And indeed there was a bad start for Bob Spangler in Ames, Iowa. One schoolmate remembered years later that Bob got into a lot of fights in grade school. In one instance, this schoolmate said, Bob got into a fight with another boy and beat the hell out of him: "He had to be pulled off because he was going to keep beating him. He thoroughly enjoyed hurting people." This same person was asked years later by the FBI if young Bob Spangler liked to torture animals or set fires. The man said he could not remember. All he could remember was Bob's anger when he was in the middle of a fight. He wouldn't give up.

An even more serious and disturbing event occurred in 1944. A schoolboy, whom Bob despised, mysteriously drowned at a sewer treatment plant near Ames. Bob was considered enough of a suspect to be taken down to the police department for questioning. All documents relating to this incident have since disappeared, but it was widely known by those around him that he had a violent streak when angered. And the fact that he was now a murder suspect did not surprise some.

But young Bob was more than just a violence-prone bully. He was also bright, inquisitive, athletic and full of confidence about one thing—Bob Spangler. By high school he managed to channel his aggressions into sports and clubs. He joined the band, journalism club, film operators club, tennis team, track team and basketball team. Bob was a member of the Varsity Club, a select group of boys at Ames High. As the high school yearbook of that era stated: "The Varsity Club consists of those boys who have won that elusive black and orange A in athletics."

Though Bob was good at all sports, he excelled in football. And the Ames High School football team of 1950 in his senior year was one for the record books. Bob was a fullback on the team, and their name, the Little Cyclones, was appropriate in every respect. The 1950 Little Cyclones tore through their competition like their wild namesake.

In their first game against Mason City they won 38 to 0, and Bob scored a touchdown. It wasn't so easy in the next game against Newton, until Bob helped, winning the game by scoring the only touchdown in a 7 to 6 victory. Ames was all over Marshalltown, 33 to 13, and Bob scored another touchdown in game number four to help beat Oskaloosa, 20 to 14.

It was game number five where Bob really shone. He scored three touchdowns against Waterloo for a final score of 20 to 14. There was no contest in game number six, 47 to 6 over Grinnell, but game number seven proved to be the hardest contest of the year. The first touchdown came on a pass to Spangler with fifteen seconds left in the first half. The score was tied 7 to 7 until the waning minutes of the game when Ames won 14 to 7.

In the last game Ames won handily, 25 to 0, over Boone to cap off an undefeated season. The yearbook gloated, "Captain Bob Spangler and all of the team brought a successful season to a close."

What a season it was. Coach Kenny Wells was named Iowa's Football Coach of the Year. And for Bob Spangler, that winning season was one of the major highlights of his life. He would remember it years later when other aspects of his life seemed tarnished and dull. And rooting him on from the sidelines all season long was his pretty, petite, dark-eyed girlfriend, Nancy Stahlman.

Nancy was born to Clarence and Manzella Groth Stahlman on September 11, 1933, in Ames, Iowa. Clarence, like Bob's adoptive father, Merlin, was an Iowa boy. And the two men's early careers had a remarkable resemblance to each other. Clarence attended Iowa State University and during World War II became a petty officer in a Navy Seabee Battalion. But after the war the two men's careers diverged. Clarence worked for the Standard Oil Company and eventually owned his own gasoline station on the corner of Kellogg and Lincoln Streets in Ames.

When Nancy was young, her father divorced her mother and remarried a woman named Jo Fitch. Nancy then had a stepbrother, David, and stepsister, Cathy. Apparently she got along well with both, because they had nothing but praise for her in later years. In fact, Nancy got along with just about everybody. She grew up in a household that wasn't as exotic or quite as well-to-do as the Spangler one in Ames. But it was a middle-class, comfortable home life none the less. For someone so quiet, she joined an immense amount of school clubs and organizations, putting even Bob Spangler's numerous school activities in the shade. Nancy was in the Girls Athletic Association, pep club, glee club, photo club, film operators club, Cubs Club, yearbook staff and school newspaper staff, and served as homeroom secretary.

In her newspaper staff duties she was an assignment editor and on the yearbook committee a member of the copy editor staff. In that capacity she had to contact and write about all the various school organizations. She obviously knew her way around this area, since she was in so many organizations.

Nancy somehow found time to sing in the glee club and even win a doubles badminton tournament, but her favorite activities were those that brought her into contact with Bob Spangler in the film operators club and, especially, Cubs Club. This was an organization open to all students interested in journalism. And despite Bob's overwhelming interest in athletic activities, he also became enamored with journalism. He did have a knack for a certain kind of writing and a way with words. In fact, after high school he planned to make some sort of journalism his major at college. He was good at newspaper tasks, radio announcing and even had an interest in the new field of television.

The Cubs Club had Nancy and Bob rubbing shoulders as they wrote articles for the school newspaper, edited pieces and put all the principles of journalism into practice. Bob became a features editor on the paper, a position that allowed him to highlight his own achievements on the football field. Bob was always one of his own best promoters.

It must have been heady times for young Nancy Stahlman at Ames High. She was well liked in all her clubs and her boyfriend was the football hero on campus. They had dated ever since junior high school and there were no plans to stop dating after he entered college. Bob was intelligent, talkative, funny and full of energy. His occasional flashes of anger could be written off as the moodiness of all teenage boys. Nancy Stahlman was too much in love with young Bob Spangler to see the flaws in his character.

But Nancy's cousin Martha Winter would say years later, "Way back in high school, [Bob's] head started growing. Bob Spangler was in love with one person, himself."

Bob was on top of the world in 1951 when he graduated from Ames High School, but something strange happened when he went to college, attending the campus that was literally down the street at Iowa State University, Ames. He ceased being a big fish in a small pond and joined all the other small fish in a very large one. Whether he tried out for the college football team is not recorded, but he was not on it or any other college athletic team. This must have been a real comedown for someone who had excelled in all high school sports. And whereas his name and image had been constantly portrayed in the high school newspaper and yearbook, his photo and name almost ceased to exist in Iowa State yearbooks. From 1952 to 1955 his photo only appeared once in all the yearbooks. It was in the 1954 yearbook, where he stood in a group of fellow members of Sigma Delta Chi, the men's journalism fraternity.

The photo told a lot. He was no longer the smiling, cocky Bob Spangler looking directly at the camera. He glanced to the side with a half smile, a look of partial bewilderment on his face as if he didn't really belong there. What happened to him in those college years was a mystery. No one was singing his praises anymore and even his grades remained a mystery. It must have felt strange to him to be going to the same university where his father was still a well-respected professor. Many people around campus knew eminent professor Merlin Spangler. Not many people knew Bob.

One of the people who did was Nancy Stahlman, who also attended Iowa State after high school. She was still very much in love with Bob and seemed to have had a more pleasant college experience than he did. She worked on the journalism staff and was a member of the university's yearbook staff, *The Bomb* as it was called. She lived in Birch Hall, an all-girls dormitory on campus, and there was a sorority-type atmosphere typical of the 1950s. Each floor of Birch Hall entertained the other two floors in a series of open houses once a year. As the yearbook stated, "The girls paraded from room to room, getting acquainted and munching on candy favors. Each corridor followed a theme, such as Melody Lane or Hawaiian Nights, and rooms were decorated accordingly."

It seems like a time of lost innocence, looking back at it now. The school newspaper spoke of a dance at Birch Hall called Rendezvous of the Roses, where "a satiny rose centered on black velvet furnished a back drop for Ron Vogelsang and his Orchestra, which set the tempo for dancing."

Whether Bob Spangler danced with Nancy at the Rendezvous of the Roses is not known. What is known is that he graduated from Iowa State University in 1955 with a degree in technical journalism and disappeared from its ivied halls. He didn't even bother to have his photograph taken for the yearbook. Today it's difficult to know what happened to Bob there. Why did someone who was always into self-promotion become almost a ghost at Iowa State University? The only thing that was certain was that he still wanted Nancy Stahlman. In 1955 they were married at a Presbyterian church, but it must have been a whirlwind honeymoon. By September 1955 Bob Spangler was off to the army, joining as a second lieutenant.

During basic training Bob qualified with a rifle and carbine on the firing range at Fort Monmouth, New Jersey. In fact, he was so proficient with a carbine that he earned sharpshooter status with that weapon. Bob knew his way around guns and was not afraid to use them.

Putting his college degree to use in the army, Bob entered the Signal Corps in the Motion Picture and Television Division. He received nine weeks of Signal Corps training in the army's use of communications. What is interesting was that the army confirmed what did not show up elsewhere, especially during Bob's college days. The army records stated that he had worked as a civilian at Ames television station WOI as a news gatherer, editor and occasional on-air reporter. He was deemed to be proficient with film editing and a Bell & Howell movie camera.

Maybe it took a new environment for Bob to blossom once again. Once outside of the constraints of Ames, Iowa, he seemed to become much more confident. He and his new wife, Nancy, could have hardly asked for a more glamorous army posting after basic training. He became a motion picture camera officer in January 1956 at an army base not far outside of New York City. He was well qualified for this and the Big Apple must have seemed enthralling indeed for the young couple from Iowa.

Bob's tenure in the army seemed to have gone by without a hitch. There are no negative reports on his record. In 1957 he was discharged at Fort Hamilton, New York, and a whole new world of civilian life opened up for Bob and Nancy Spangler. He worked for a while in television in New York City, but Bob always had "itchy" feet. When a better job, in his opinion, opened up in Minneapolis, Minnesota, he took it. Son David was born there on November 27, 1961, but before long, Bob was dragging the family back to the East Coast in the New York area for another stint in broadcasting. Daughter Susan was born on August 14, 1963, and an FBI report much later stated that Bob worked for a while on *Sesame Street* in its infancy.

One thing noted by Martha Winter, Nancy's cousin, was wherever Bob wanted to go, that's where the family ended up. She said that Nancy's aspirations and career always took a backseat to Bob's. Winter later told a *Rocky Mountain News* reporter, "She eagerly put career aspirations on hold, replacing them with a passion for gourmet cooking, motherhood and her husband. Even back then as a kid, I thought Bob was somewhat controlling of her. He wanted her at his beck and call. She literally worshiped the ground the man walked on."

Winter later added, "She seemed like a mom who wanted to have the perfect family. She was always just sparkling. You'd never know there were problems."

Bob worked for a while with the firm of Carl Byoir in the New York area. In his job there he was a public-relations administrator and also an account executive handling an account with the Honeywell Corporation. With this particular account for Honeywell he had to make many trips to Denver, Colorado. It also brought him into contact with Jack Swanburg, who worked for Honeywell before becoming a technician at the Arapahoe County Sheriff's Office. Bob fell in love with Denver and before long was dragging the family along to a new residence in the area.

When the Spangler family moved to Littleton, Colorado, a neighbor picked up the refrain about Nancy where Martha Winter left off. The neighbor lady said, "She was a real nice woman. Kind of quiet sometimes, but she really doted on the kids. Husband too, as far as I could see. Though he was at work a lot and I didn't see much of him. I mostly saw her and the kids. They were what I'd call a typical family for the area. She was always friendly to me. She didn't put on airs. She basically seemed like a stay-at-home mom."

Bob's move to the Littleton area was caused by his new job in public relations with the American Water Works Association, based in nearby Denver. The AWWA is an international nonprofit organization dedicated to the improvement of drinking-water standards around the globe. Founded in 1881, it is the largest organization of its kind in the world dealing with water quality managers, treatment plant operators, scientists, environmentalists, manufacturers, professors and regulators. The four thousand utilities in North America that were associated with the AWWA brought drinking water to 180 million customers. Worldwide it was affiliated with fifty thousand members.

This organization was right up Bob Spangler's alley—he did have a way with words, both spoken and written. And he felt right at home with liaisons and trips to the Washington, DC, area with lawmakers and policy makers. He had the gift of gab and knew how to play the game. One of his duties was raising money for the AWWA and he was good at it. Bob always had a way of attuning himself to people's likes and dislikes, and presenting himself to them in a manner he thought would be most in line with their personalities. If they were boisterous and outgoing, he became the same. If they were quiet and introspective, Bob could be bookish and academic. It was hard to say if he believed in everything he presented. The trick was he could do it effortlessly. To him the whole world was indeed a stage and the most important actor on it was himself.

These many sides of Bob Spangler weren't just evident to his clients; his coworkers at AWWA saw him in different lights as well, being whatever image he projected to them. And their recollections of him years later mirrored the images he wanted them to see. Coworker Cathy Noler thought that Bob was very confident. She said, "He was good at his job. Very polished, but egotistical. He knew how to manipulate people."

Another coworker at AAWA, who wished to remain anonymous, said, "Bob was a quiet and polite gentleman. He never seemed to get angry and always remained on an even keel. Even when things got crazy."

Elaine Youngren saw Bob in a slightly different light than the other two did. She said, "Bob was a charismatic speaker. He was mostly a gentleman, but he could get very angry on occasion. When he flared up, watch out. He could also become very withdrawn for short periods of time. He had a Jekyll and Hyde personality."

Youngren knew Nancy Spangler as well. She said of Nancy: "She was quiet and old-fashioned. She adored Bob and especially the kids. The Spangler children were typical teenagers of that time and place and the same age as my own kids. So I knew the whole family pretty well. From the outside they didn't look any different than any other family living in the Denver area."

It should have been an idyllic life for Bob Spangler on South Franklin Way in 1976. He had a doting wife, two healthy children and a nice suburban home, but Bob was always restless and wanted more. And then one day in 1976 he got it. It came to him in the form of a young and vivacious temporary secretary named Sharon Arnst Cooper.

Bob's coworkers remembered Sharon Cooper very well and the effect she had on Bob. Their perceptions of Sharon were just as varied as their opinions were about Spangler.

Cathy Noler thought that Sharon was flirtatious and, in a very short time, after Bob Spangler. "She was very talkative and high-strung," Noler said. "A bit much at times. The two began an affair and pretty soon just about everybody knew about it."

The anonymous coworker had a somewhat different take on Sharon Cooper. She said, "Sharon was more outgoing than Bob. She flitted about the office and was bubbly. But she was also neurotic. She had a lot of New Age ideas. She openly talked about her breast augmentation to everyone in the office. It was kind of weird and so was she. Bob was director of public relations at the time and Sharon was his administrative assistant."

As for Bob and Sharon's affair, this coworker thought it wasn't out in the open as much as Noler remembered. The coworker stated, "They sneaked around. It wasn't overt. I don't think a lot of people knew about it. Sharon was always touchy-feely, so it was hard to tell."

Elaine Youngren's take on the affair between Bob and Sharon was different from the other two women's observations. She said, "A lot of people didn't like Sharon. But she was pleasant to me and I liked her. Sharon had real mood swings. She was an attractive woman, but had low self-esteem. Because of this, it made her try harder. Just like Nancy, she adored Bob."

Youngren agreed with Noler that most of the department knew about Bob and Sharon's affair. Before long even Nancy knew about it. It can only be guessed at what scenes went on in the Spangler household that year. There must have been arguments and accusations. Whatever happened, Bob moved out of the house and into Sharon Cooper's place on Pearl Street in Denver in the spring of 1977, according to one source. But a more reliable source has them moving in together in January 1978, and Bob's later comments on the matter seem to substantiate this date.

Glimpses of that tumultuous year come from several people acquainted with Bob Spangler. One was a friend of Susan Spangler's named Kelly Kitchen. She said, "I knew David and Sue for about three years prior to that time. They were super people and their mom was really cool. I didn't really know their dad. I never heard much about him. David and Susan didn't talk about him much (when he was gone)." In effect, they didn't want to talk about the father who had deserted them.

Another source was Bob Spangler himself. He said years later, "During the year I was away, I wasn't in touch with my children on a regular basis. I saw them on occasion but only had activities with them once or twice the whole time. Nancy had lost control of the kids then. They were taking advantage of her. I know through some neighbor kids they were demanding and foulmouthed with Nancy. I guess both she and I kept our emotions to ourselves and never discussed our feelings about the kids. I know that both kids smoked marijuana. I used to let them do it at home because I was afraid of them doing it on the street."

The overall impression of Bob that year is that he didn't like his family very much, especially his kids. Even though he admitted that David was a good musician, he didn't like his smoking marijuana or his friends. He didn't like Susan's friends any better. In fact, he hardly knew his children at all anymore. They were like strangers to him. It was much more fun to go backpacking and hiking with Sharon up in the nearby mountains. She was vivacious and funny and made him feel alive. She also brought out his athletic abilities once again, something he was always proud of. One thing he knew for certain was that Sharon didn't want any kids around the house. Especially teenage ones.

But life with Sharon was not all sunshine and blue skies either. They had their ups and downs and Sharon had much more of a temper than Nancy. One of Bob and Sharon's coworkers at the American Water Works Association was a man named Dennis Hill. A number of years later, he told a reporter for the *Grand Junction Sentinel,* "She (Sharon) sometimes threw things at him during their fights in the office." Sharon was always prone to wild mood swings, and when her ire was up, she had no problem with giving Bob a piece of her mind.

Things were an absolute mess for Bob in the autumn of 1978. It seemed that he couldn't live with Sharon and he couldn't live without her. Perhaps yearning for some peace and quiet, he moved back in with his family on South Franklin Way in October 1978. And he may have even tried to make their relationship work.

Right after Christmas 1978 Nancy sent her father and stepmother a chatty Christmas letter. She said, "Bob and I are happy together after a nine-month separation." She spoke of their motorcycle trips around the area and plans for hiking in the mountains. She also said that she'd just obtained a higher degree in education at one of the nearby universities and was looking forward to becoming a full-time public-relations person in the near future. It was an upbeat, optimistic letter, the very antithesis of someone who was considering killing her children and then herself. Somehow, though, this letter never surfaced in police investigations until years later. If it had, it might have shed a whole new light on Nancy Spangler and her frame of mind in the days before December 30, 1978.

In Sharon Cooper's short absence from Bob, Dennis Hill confided some very interesting things to her. He later told the *Grand Junction Sentinel,* "I told Sharon [that] Bob is a guy who can become anybody he wants to be. Whatever role he needed to take on, he took on. He was the consummate public relations guy that way. He was 100 per cent facade."

On the morning of December 30, 1978, Bob Spangler took on the role of cold-blooded killer. He shot Nancy, Susan and David with unemotional detachment. It was no more than any other unpleasant task he had to perform. Meeting with an unhappy client, making cold calls, killing his family—they all had equal weight and had to be taken care of his own way.

Later that day, he would play the role of survivor of a terrible tragedy. He would play this role for years, embellishing and refining it. He would embrace it and take some pleasure of being the poor unfortunate man who had lost his family because of his wife's insanity. In the end he would half convince himself that the events he lied about had actually taken place. Myth and reality became blurred in his mind until he could barely tell one from the other.

With the elimination of his family, his new role for 1979 was one he looked forward to—a fresh start with the woman he had murdered for, Sharon Cooper.

Chapter 5

Lure of the Canyon

Bob Spangler was an athletic man of forty-six when Sharon moved in with him in the home where he had murdered his family on South Franklin Way. Instead of dwelling on what he had done, he sloughed off their memories as if they were an old snake skin that had to be shed. Bob had other things on his mind, like taking long hikes in the mountains with Sharon, and becoming a referee for a nearby soccer league. In fact, despite his age, he could run up and down the field with the best of them. It was as if he were regaining some of his past glory as a football star on the Ames High School team. If life with Nancy and the kids reminded him of his limitations and advancing age, his new life with Sharon spoke of renewed energy and new possibilities.

As far as athleticism went, Sharon was more than his match. She taught hatha yoga and was very balanced and nimble. A good walker, she kept fit and exercised constantly. Sharon also had a yen for dog training, instilling in them a discipline that matched Bob's own need for order and control.

Sharon adopted three dogs from the Denver Dumb Friends League. She called them Shadow, Sunshine and Mollie. One person who knew Sharon remarked that she had never seen dogs so well trained. If Sharon took her dogs into a strange house and told them to sit, they would stay without moving a muscle until she released them. Sharon may not have been a "children person" as Bob had stated, but she was certainly a "dog person." In effect, the three dogs became her children. And in some respects they became Bob's children as well. These were "children" that he could control and they didn't talk back. Nor did they take drugs, have boyfriends or play loud music all hours of the day and night.

Bob even brought the dogs down to his office at the American Water Works Association on occasion. He liked to show them off in front of his coworkers. Cathy Noler noticed a growing egotistical streak in Bob after the death of Nancy. She wondered how much it had to do with Sharon and how much it had to do with the levelheaded restraint that Nancy had imposed upon Bob, but was now gone. One memory of this new image stuck out in her mind. She said, "He once had his dogs pose with his secretary for a photo. He said, 'I want a picture of my girls.' I guess his dogs and his secretary were 'his girls.' He was becoming a real male chauvinist."

If the dogs were a diversion for Bob, they were an absolute necessity for Sharon. They helped fill a void in her life caused by severe mental problems. Sharon needed medication to control her wild mood swings, which often bordered on panic and depression. Much of it may have been a chemical

imbalance; some of it may have been her own inability to cope with the stresses of everyday life. She
could not control everything in her environment,
especially at work. She could control her dogs.

Janece Ohlman had insights into Sharon's complex nature. She noted that Sharon was obviously
bright and brimming over with enthusiasm about
outdoor activities. But Janece stated, "She was very
high-strung. Very emotional." Janece also knew that
the dogs were good for her. They allowed Sharon
to take care of "someone" besides herself. They
gave her an emotional anchor.

Janece also knew one other fact about Sharon—
the most important balm of her life, besides her
dogs, was hiking in the Grand Canyon. It was the
one place Sharon could go to escape the demons
that tormented her soul. There was something
about the majesty and remoteness of the Canyon
that soothed Sharon's jangled nerves and quieted
the inner voices that assailed her.

In some ways it was strange that Sharon should
pick such a place to find comfort. She had grown
up in St. Louis, Missouri, and as a child she had
been terrified of bugs and stifled by the heat and
humidity of the area. Because of the hot, humid
summers, she didn't go outside often. The heat so
exhausted her that she became an indoor person.
But in 1968 she moved to New York City and discovered the joys of walking around Manhattan.
When she moved to Denver, Colorado, in 1970,
Sharon transferred her walking into taking long
hikes in the nearby Rocky Mountains. In the arid
West she found that she had much more strength
and energy, and her hiking abilities came into full
bloom. Not only her body was eased by the joys of

hiking, but her mind was as well. As she wrote later, "Thanks to the delightfully low humidity in the West, hiking became a major pastime."

Sharon took a long river-raft trip on the Colorado River through the Grand Canyon in 1978, when she and Bob weren't living together, and absolutely fell in love with the place. She would write later of enjoying sixteen days on the beautiful wooden and metal dory boats of Grand Canyon Dories. Sharon wrote that when ashore "I (did) a lot of day hiking up side canyons to see fossils and Indian ruins and frolic at fantastic little oases and waterfalls and swimming holes, and I wanted to come back."

But first she and Bob got married on July 14, 1979. They took a long motorcycle trip to the West Coast for their honeymoon and Sharon talked him into stopping by the Grand Canyon on the way home to Colorado. It was only seven months after the murders of Nancy, Susan and David, but as far as Bob was concerned, it might have been seven years. He had the woman he wanted by his side and a whole new area to explore. The past was not something he dwelled on very often.

They chose the Hermit Trail, which led down to the Colorado River from the South Rim for their first hike. He was in his element now, pitting his strength and athleticism against the Canyon. Even Sharon commented somewhat grudgingly and with a bit of jealousy about Bob's innate athletic abilities. After all, she considered herself the Canyon veteran and him a novice. But as she kept slipping and sliding on the rough Hermit Trail, which led down steeply toward the Colorado River, Bob kept giving her advice about how best to hike the trail.

He told her, "Try sighting your next few steps in advance."

Grudgingly she admitted he was right.

This trail had once been a main thoroughfare to the Canyon, but that had been years ago. It was rough and ill marked now, and it was slippery with loose rocks and crumbling sandstone. Despite the danger and the heat, Bob Spangler enjoyed himself immensely. Even when one of Bob's knees became sore and made walking hard, in Sharon's words, "he became transformed by the power of the Colorado River as we neared Hermit Rapids. Bob's face showed his pain, but his spirits lifted in the presence of such dazzling power."

When they fell asleep that night in the inner canyon, Sharon noted how quickly Bob fell asleep. There never seemed to be anything bothering his conscience—not the police investigations that had recently ended or the bloodstained rooms of his home. He slept like a baby on the sandy soil within the canyon, with no thoughts of a murdered wife and children to disturb his thoughts. Sharon was envious of his ability to fall asleep almost anywhere and under any conditions.

For her own part, Sharon lay awake a long time that night, drinking in the beauty and mystery of the place. She wrote later: "The moon worked a witchery on the walls around us, setting them in platinum-gray relief against the black sky. Frogs sang boisterously into the night."

Bob may have slept soundly through the night and was immune to the "witchery" of the canyon then, but he was hiking the next day somewhat ahead of Sharon alone and was entranced by his surroundings. When she caught up, he told her exactly how he felt about the Grand Canyon. He said, "I suddenly became aware of myself alone, in relation to the Canyon. It was one of those 'last man on earth' sensations, right out of *The Twilight Zone,* where the camera pulls up and away, leaving the character standing in the immensity of his aloneness. Those incredible distances, colors and textures had been here for so long, I thought, only seen by mankind in the past brief few thousand years, and by me for the first time now, a split instant in the Canyon's existence. I didn't feel insignificant, just fortunate to be experiencing it."

This was an interesting turn of phrase—"I didn't feel insignificant." Almost everyone else who has written about the Grand Canyon stressed just the opposite. How they felt small in its immensity; how insignificant they were in its vast grandeur. But not Bob Spangler. For him the world began and ended with himself. Whatever he saw, touched, smelled and heard could not be defined outside of himself. No matter how immense or beautiful or mysterious, the objects were always defined by his own self-importance.

In fact, Bob always had to feel he was in control of a situation, even when it came to something as immense as the Grand Canyon. One means he used to accomplish this was to compartmentalize and categorize everything by numbers. While looking at the rocks around them, he once told Sharon that they had been there for 6 million years. But just that notation was not enough for Bob. He went on to say that those years added up to roughly 2 billion 200 million days. By comparison, he said, he and Sharon had only been on the planet roughly 16,500 days.

At least Sharon wasn't as mathematical in her response. She told him, "That doesn't throw me. The brevity of human existence on the planet doesn't bother me, because I don't think of us as being special or outside the process. I feel very connected to it. That's one thing the Canyon reinforces in me. The numbers are so immense, and anyway, time and numbers are just constructs of the human mind. All that seems to matter is to really be here while we're here and let the Canyon work its mysteries on us."

In fact, she would soon grow even more poetic and detailed about what the Grand Canyon meant to her. She wrote: "The Canyon was becoming part of my interior landscape. When I wasn't in it, it dwelled inside me. The glow that rose from its depths, its vast and intricately defined space, and its engulfing silence at first seemed to hold secrets not just of the earth's history but of my own consciousness and mortality. Yet the Canyon didn't hold any clues to my condition, I just projected my own need for meaning into it. I would have to continue to look inside myself for answers."

As it had done for Sharon, the spell of the Grand Canyon soon affected Bob. Sharon put down in words just how he felt about it in her book, *On Foot in the Grand Canyon.* Bob's words mirrored early explorer Clarence Dutton's own comments: "Those who have long and carefully studied the Grand Canyon of the Colorado do not hesitate for a moment to pronounce it to be the most sublime of all earthly spectacles."

In 1980 Bob and Sharon were back, this time on a river trip down the Colorado River. And they enjoyed an exhilarating ride through Hermit Rapids, the same place that Bob had gazed on with awe at its power. But at heart both Sharon and Bob were hikers rather than river people, and as the years progressed, they took numerous hikes down into the wild inner canyon. Sharon even took a ten-day women's course at Colorado's Outward Bound school, to develop her rock-climbing skills and overall balance. Yet even with this accomplished, the trails within the Canyon could be tough and punishing. Sharon wrote of more than once having "thighs that were quivering with strain."

As Bob and Sharon became more adept at canyon hiking, which for the most part was harder than hiking in the Rockies because of the heat element and lack of water in the Canyon, they began to take longer and more difficult treks. Sharon commented on her newfound ability to incorporate her hatha yoga training into her hiking. She would breathe at specific rates, especially on scary, slippery spots along the trail, in order to maintain her balance and composure.

A coworker at the American Water Works Association commented to Bob, "Gee, you're lucky your wife goes with you on those backpack trips in the Grand Canyon."

But Bob corrected him. "You've got it all wrong," he said. "Sharon makes all the plans. I go to keep her company."

In their journeys Bob and Sharon became acquainted with veteran Grand Canyon hikers Jim and Janece Ohlman of Arizona. Jim was a geologist and Grand Canyon trail guide and Janece had a background in botany. Sharon was in awe of Jim, noting that by 1989 he had logged more than eight thousand miles in hikes through the Grand

Canyon. He had a photographic recall of map contours and an intimate knowledge of canyon geology and natural history. He could point out Indian ruins, fossils and geologic formations that she and Bob had missed on trails they had already taken.

According to Jim Ohlman, "Jan and I met Bob and Sharon at the old Grand Canyon Railway Depot in the fall of 1984. This depot at the time was being used by Canyoneers, Inc., of Flagstaff, as headquarters for their Grand Canyon Trail Guides operation. Jan and I were initially hired on as guides and then later as comanagers. Bob and Sharon came in off the street and inquired about transportation service out to the South Bass Trailhead."

Jim Ohlman related that in November 1984 he and Sharon hiked down to the Esplanade on a day hike. Later he hiked down the Tanner Trail with Sharon, and on another occasion he and Janece hiked the New Hance–Grandview Loop with Bob, Sharon and some friends.

Janece Ohlman, a biology graduate, was remarkable in her own way, blessed with a keen eye and a wide range of knowledge about the flora of the Canyon. In April 1985 Sharon and Janece took a backpacking expedition together on the South Bass Trail into the depths of the Grand Canyon. Of that trek Sharon wrote, "Morning dawned sunny and crisp. Lying inside the tent, I reflected on yesterday's hike and the special qualities Janece had brought to it. She was a sturdily built, dependable woman, keenly intelligent, with a warm gentle nature. And she had a quality of stillness."

For her part Janece described Sharon as outgoing, intelligent and always asking probing questions about geology and plants in the Canyon. "She dwelled on facts and stored everything away for future use. She was kind and generous. She could also be difficult. It was odd how she would hike and backpack under the most primitive conditions and not complain. But as soon as she was back on the rim, she wanted a luxurious motel and good food. There were always two sides to her. One thing was for certain, though. She was very loyal to friends and would cling to them no matter how much time had gone by or how far away they lived."

Bob and Sharon not only liked hiking alone, they enjoyed doing it with friends as well. And on one hike in particular, it was interesting to note Bob's reaction to being in the Havasupai Indian Village, within the Canyon, near Havasu Falls. Generally, he had no admiration for a person or people who had not triumphed in life. And in some regards it can be said that the Havasupai certainly hadn't triumphed over the white settlers in the nineteenth century. Their weapons and numbers were no match for the intruders, and they were pushed back into the wild and isolated depths of the Grand Canyon near Havasu Falls. But Bob surprisingly sympathized with their plight, telling Sharon that he was sorry that his society had disrupted the Havasupai's stable and traditional ways. He even expressed that he felt a "haunting sadness about it." This was the same man who wasn't haunted at all by the fact that he had murdered his wife and two children.

During her treks in the Canyon, Sharon met a woman who would remember her and Bob very well in years to come. She was the chief Backcountry Ranger, Bev Perry. Bev and Sharon had a long discussion one day about the Canyon and Sharon's plans to write a book about it. Bev's overall impression of Sharon was that she was intelligent, had a keen eye for detail and was very enthusiastic about the Grand Canyon. She also noted, as others had before her, that Sharon was somewhat of an "oddball." Her actions and speech weren't quite normal. She could become very wound up when excited about certain subjects.

For the most part, Bob Spangler was a good hiking companion for Sharon. He was athletic and enthusiastic about new hikes and didn't complain about the rigors of the trail. If she had looked closely, however, she might have glimpsed a flip side to his normal cheerful demeanor. As Bev Perry would comment later, "Suddenly the mask would drop and you saw a whole different side to Bob Spangler. It was a dark and dangerous side."

Perhaps Sharon got a glimpse of this side on a hike down the South Bass Trail in June 1983. Things were not going well on the hike. She and Bob became lost and had to do a lot of backtracking. They wandered around through the heat and dust and Sharon said, "Bob was dehydrated, but he wouldn't or couldn't recognize it. He was sullen and uncommunicative. It took some delicate persuading to get him to drink, but he finally grudgingly admitted that maybe he had been a little dehydrated after all."

Nor could Bob even admit to Sharon when he was lost. One time somewhere along the Tonto Trail, he missed a junction and they began to wander over the terrain. Not wanting to turn back, Bob took a shortcut and ended up walking into a prickly pear cactus, getting a shinful of spines for his trouble. He was even foolish in taking hikes that were just too long for a normal day's trek within the Canyon. Once he covered eighteen miles of difficult and strenuous country in a single day. This might have been all right in the Rockies, but not in the Grand Canyon, where dehydration is a real and often deadly danger. As Sharon noted later about Bob's hike that day, "It was a hike worthy of Harvey Butchart, and one which is not to be attempted except by the most athletic endurance-proven Grand Canyon hikers." Undoubtedly, Bob was pleased with her comparison of him to Harvey Butchart, a man many people called "the Dean of Grand Canyon hiking." Bob always wanted to be known as the best in what he did.

If Bob didn't want to talk about his skirting with the dangers of dehydration, Sharon certainly did. She could never withhold information about her emotions or physical problems. She once expressed, "When I was dehydrated, there were times on the trail when I wanted to lean out, spread my arms and fly. But my fifteen years of yoga practice saved me. It was like there were two of me, one that was disoriented and wanted to fly, and the other, deeper inside that remembered to breathe to regain my center."

If Sharon could occasionally be a danger to herself, Bob could be a danger to himself and others. He never liked to admit that he was wrong about anything, or that he was somehow less than physically fit. He always liked to feel that he was in control, and any hint that he wasn't would fuel his anger. It also made him foolish and dangerous.

John Azar, who knew both Bob Spangler and Jim Ohlman, related such an instance at Angel Gate.

Azar related, "Angel Gate is one of the most difficult and technical ascents in the Grand Canyon, and one needs to be a serious and qualified climber to attempt the last pitch. Jim was already on top when as he belayed Bob up, he noticed that Bob's anchor knot was a slipknot. Jim asked Bob to hold up and retie the knot. Bob laughed and told Jim to continue the belay. He reached the top safely, but Jim was pretty concerned about Bob's flippant attitude."

This attitude was also an indication of Bob's compunction for flirting with danger. He was daring to the degree that it did not fall under the category of bravery; rather, it was a disregard for life, both his own and those around him.

There was also an incident on a backpack trip on the Hermit Trail that gave another glimpse into Bob Spangler's "other self." A nineteen-year-old man had fallen forty feet off a cliff on the wall of Hermit Canyon. Both of his ankles were broken and he was in a great deal of pain. Bob was more concerned about playing the hero in a rescue than he was about the young man's physical state. Bob fetched a mirror from Sharon and trekked up to an unmanned ranger cabin on the Tonto Plateau, where he signaled until sunset. His flashes were seen on the rim and help did come. Bob later told about his part in this incident to several people. He was always excited about his role in the procedure rather than the severity of the boy's fall. "Bob as hero" was just one more of his life's ambitions.

Unfortunately for Sharon, on the day after this episode, she suffered a nervous breakdown in the Canyon, which would presage things to come. The incident with the boy must have triggered her memories of a friend she admired who had died at the age of forty-one from a rare heart ailment. Suddenly she began crying as she hiked along the trail and couldn't stop. Before long she was absolutely wailing. She told Bob to leave her and go on ahead. He did as instructed, and as she hiked alone, Sharon sobbed for the next two miles. It was only after she met up with Bob again that she related, "I had cried myself out."

Perhaps more than any other backpack trip that Sharon and Bob took in the Grand Canyon, their trek down to Horseshoe Mesa would have far-reaching effects unlike anything Sharon could have imagined. As they hiked the New Hance–Tonto–Grandview Loop, Sharon wrote, "If one word could sum up the descent of the New Hance Trail, I would choose 'Yiii!' Bob's choice would be 'Argh.' The trail takes hikers on a treacherously steep, rocky, screey (sic), slippy-slidy careen to the floor of Red Canyon. Even Bob was less than his usual serene self on the New Hance Trail."

By the second day they were on Horseshoe Mesa itself near a place called Miner's Spring. Sharon described the magnificent views of the Krishna and Rama Shrines and the Vishnu Temple of the inner canyon. She also described the dangerous trail conditions near an old mine shaft.

"Above the mine the trail became more and more difficult—narrower, rougher, steeper and exposed. Once or twice our metal pack frames bumped and scraped against the cliff wall, jostling our balance under the shifting loads. We would not want to come down this trail with or without packs on. The very top was the most treacherous. We skirted under a low overhang and had to make one unpleasant scramble. As we climbed the Redwall, I tried to ignore my fright."

Unknown to Sharon, Bob Spangler tucked away the image of that dangerous section of trail into his memory for future use. It was a perfect spot for a murder. Someone could be pushed from there and who could say that it wasn't an accident? A tiny shove could send them reeling into space. The fall was sure to be fatal. Small details like that were tucked away in Bob Spangler's memory, just in case they should be useful someday. At heart he was a planner and he planned for all contingencies.

A more immediate concern arose in 1986 for Bob Spangler. He was tired of working for a living and his elderly father, Merlin, was now ninety-two years old. As long as the old man lived, Bob could not touch the sizable estate that Merlin had accumulated. By now, the accolades and awards had piled up to an impressive height for the elder Spangler. In 1960 he'd received the Distinguished Service Award from the Iowa Engineering Society. In 1983 he gained their Honorary Life Membership Award. In 1984 Iowa State University named a geo-technical laboratory building after him. And there was always, of course, the Marston/Spangler Theory named in part after him.

By 1986 Merlin Spangler may have been of an advanced age, but he still did not show any signs of faltering. That is until Bob showed up that spring for a visit. Within a short time of Bob's arrival, Merlin Spangler had a nasty fall. Two weeks later he was dead.

It never has been proven if there was any correlation between Bob Spangler's visit and his adoptive father's death. One thing was certain—after the old man died, Bob Spangler received a hefty amount of money from the estate and was able to retire. It was only much later that law enforcement authorities would notice his trip to Iowa that year and the fact that people close to Bob Spangler seemed to die at unexpected times. Underlined on a memo were the words "Merlin Spangler died under suspicious circumstances when Robert Spangler had been visiting in Ames, Iowa."

Chapter 6

Incident at King Soopers

Sharon Spangler once may have considered Bob her soul mate and chief hiking partner, but by 1987 things began to change dramatically. She could barely control her emotional problems and was seeing a psychiatrist, not only for therapy but medication as well. She had to contend with all her inner turmoil, and there were all those rumors that constantly swirled around Bob and his former family. Whispered comments flittered through the neighborhood about how fast Sharon had moved into the house after the death of Bob's first family. Some neighbors, who had liked the quietly friendly Nancy Spangler, found Sharon to be strange. Sharon had no hesitancy about expressing her New Age beliefs. These were at odds with the traditional values in the fairly conservative enclave of Littleton. As one neighbor succinctly put it, "She was a nut."

Much of Sharon's outward extravagance and drama were not consciously her fault. She did suffer from manic-depressive symptoms, which only added to her sense of foreboding and uneasiness in the "death house" on South Franklin Way. Her trips to the Grand Canyon with Bob were often a reprieve from her anxiety, but they ended all too soon. Then it was right back to the neighborhood that would not embrace her and living with a man who became more quarrelsome as time went on.

Perhaps Bob was growing tired of Sharon's manic spells of hyperactivity, followed by the inertia of depression; or perhaps he was feeling the same ennui he had felt with Nancy. Sharon Cooper Spangler was not turning out to be the dream woman for whom he had murdered. Bit by bit their lives drifted apart, and not even the cement of Grand Canyon trips could keep them together.

On December 4, 1987, something dramatic happened in the Spangler home. The details are murky at best. Glimpses of what happened there that afternoon only come from Sharon's troubled mind and police reports that followed. It all began when Sharon phoned her mental-health therapist, Dr. Bell. Her call was frantic and incoherent. She said she was afraid of Bob, and may have even indicated suicidal tendencies. Whatever occurred, Dr. Bell was concerned enough to phone the Arapahoe County Sheriff's Office and have them send a deputy over to investigate the Spangler household on South Franklin Way. He told them, "Mrs. Spangler has been despondent and may need to be placed into the hospital."

Just as Officer Malsam reached the area, he received a car radio message that Sharon Spangler was seen at the nearby King Soopers market and was acting erratically. She was hysterical and apparently hiding from her husband there. She claimed he had threatened her.

Officer Malsam was met by Officer Hahl at King Soopers. They went inside and contacted a store manager named Vandenbrink, who told them Sharon Spangler had run into the store claiming that her husband had taken her car keys so that she couldn't leave town. He also indicated she was afraid of him and that he might harm her. She was very upset and badgered Vandenbrink to lend her his car keys so she could escape. When he refused, she ran into the storeroom at the back of the store and was hiding out there. She was so wild and crazy she asked him for a Baggie to place over her head so that no one would recognize her.

When Officers Malsam and Hahl entered the storeroom, they found Sharon with a Baggie wrapped around her neck. She screamed at them to leave her alone. Both officers told her to calm down. Instead, she attempted to rush by them, but they grabbed her. Sharon tried repeatedly to kick Officer Hahl in the groin. She was forced to the floor as Officer Hahl restrained her legs and Officer Malsam handcuffed her. She twisted and struggled and cursed them as she was led away.

Even in the squad car she was combative. As soon as the Littleton Rescue ambulance arrived, she was placed into it for evaluation of any injuries and possible medication. Just before she was driven to Davis Pavilion for an overnight stay, she told the officers one chilling thing: "My husband is trying to get me."

Just what she meant by that statement never became clear. Did "get" mean financially or emotionally? Or was it something even more permanent, like murder? She apparently didn't speak on the matter to others later on. And if she spoke to Dr. Bell about it, it stayed locked within his records, protected by doctor/client privilege.

By late December 1987 it was clear that the situation between Bob Spangler and Sharon was beyond repair. He told his friend and hiking buddy Jim Ohlman, "Looks like Sharon and I will be taking the divorce trail in 1988. It promises (so far) to be as amicable and nonacrimonious as these things can be, because we've both agreed: (A.) that we're really not all that well fitted for each other, and (B.) that we both prefer not to turn over all our funds to lawyers in an extended court battle. Plus with no kids or other conflicting factors, it should move relatively easily."

Bob told Jim that Sharon would remain in the house with him for the time being. He said it was uncomfortable but not awful. "We don't hate each other," he said. "We just have different values." He noted that they saw things through different eyes.

Then Bob added, "Among the things we will continue to share is a deep and lasting appreciation of the Canyon, and of the people, like you and Jan, who've helped us become close to it."

By April 1988 Bob was telling Jim, "Sharon and I finally have our first formal legal meetings set between us and attorney representatives set for May ninth. [I] hope good comes from it. We're both anxious to get on with our lives. And it would be nice if Sharon could get on the trail with Jan. But that remains to be seen. When lawyers are involved, I take nothing for granted."

On a happier front, Bob thanked Jim for the "super" hike they had recently been on together in the Grand Canyon. He described it as the single most difficult hike he had ever been on, but he said it was exhilarating. "A wonderfully satisfying trek," Bob pronounced. Then he joked and asked, "When will I learn not to make casual comments like 'Why can't we just cut across right there? It doesn't look so bad.'"

As for the divorce lawyers, about whom Bob worried, his worst fears began to come true. It became evident soon enough that Sharon wanted more financially than he was willing to give. There would be a battle. In the last days of April 1988 Bob released his lawyer, Daniel Glaess, and retained the services of Albert Bonin.

Jim Ohlman thought later that Sharon always had an acquisitive streak. She liked accumulating things for their own sake. And with the advent of a divorce she soon was out to get as much as she could from Bob. It wasn't particularly mean-spirited or vindictive. "It was just the way Sharon was wired," he said.

On June 24, 1988, Bob and Sharon met with their respective lawyers and hammered out a settlement. The documents they eventually drew up stated:

1. The parties are co-petitioners of the action of dissolution of marriage.
2. The marriage is irretrievably broken.
3. The parties have experienced unhappy differences and agree that it is for their best interests that they live separate from each other in the future.
4. The parties desire to settle all rights, claims and demands to each other's property, and to settle all claims which have arisen between the parties.

What all this meant was soon spelled out in detail. It was demanded that "neither molest the other, nor compel the other to cohabitate with him or her. Each shall have the right to conduct his or her social life and business affairs as he or she sees fit."

Bob was to pay Sharon $500 a month, up until February 1990. From that time until July 1997 he was to pay her $400 a month. He had to agree to designate Sharon as a beneficiary in his will for an amount adequate to cover the maintenance obligation.

Sharon was to receive their 1986 Mazda. Bob would retain their 1985 Chrysler station wagon. Sharon was to give up all claims to the house on South Franklin Way, but she was to receive $150,000 in compensation from stocks and bonds that Bob owned. If Sharon remarried, she was to return $20,000 to Bob. Bob was to pay all of her attorneys' fees.

One of the most contentious parts of the agreement concerned their dogs, Sunshine, Shadow and Mollie. The document stated, "The parties are currently the owners of three dogs. Each party shall be able to visit and enjoy the company of the dogs on a reasonable basis by agreement of the parties. In the event of either party's death or disability, the other party will provide a home for the dog or dogs not in his or her possession."

Sharon soon moved out of Bob's home on South Franklin Way and into a place on Knolls Way. She took only Shadow with her, since the accommodations were small. Just as Bob had worried, he felt that he had been taken to the cleaners by Sharon and her lawyers. In a letter to Jim Ohlman he explained, "Bringing you up to date, Sharon and I are officially and legally separate and single again. The settlement between us was, I guess, what compromises are made of, that is, not enough from her point of view, and far too much from mine. In any case, it's over."

Bob went on, telling of his attempts to sell the house on South Franklin Way so he could get something smaller. He said he still wanted to live in the Denver area, but it was a buyer's market and he was having trouble selling the place for a decent price.

Then Bob related that he was keeping in shape with a long series of soccer tournaments in 95-degree heat and filling in as a referee in an adult basketball league. He said that both of these sports gave his legs a good workout. He wrote, "If this place sells soon and if I can find and close another place quickly and if I can get reestablished in a new location with a minimum of trouble, I suppose I'll be looking to do some sort of Canyon experience."

Apparently, he did make it to the Grand Canyon soon thereafter, because he wrote Jim about a hike he had taken there. He also told of his new house on Utica Street in Denver. About the house he related that it was a real "fixer-upper" and that he'd have to replace the fireplace soon. "It looks fine now. But it will be a mess again."

Surprisingly, Bob stayed in touch with Sharon, despite their contentious divorce. He told Jim that she was off visiting relatives in St. Louis. He said he was watching her dog, Shadow, while she was gone, and he kidded, "Well, at least it's cheaper than keeping it at a kennel."

While on Utica Street, Bob for once opened up in his appreciation for another's abilities besides his own. Proud and vain about his own athleticism, Bob was nonetheless in awe of Jim Ohlman's hiking abilities in the Grand Canyon. He said, "Your maps continue to amaze me. I find myself wondering as the Butch Cassidy/Sundance character did when watching the relentless trackers coming along their back trail—'How does he do that? I couldn't do that. Could you do that?' If there is never another reason to do hikes with you, that will be sufficient." Coming from self-centered Bob, this was great praise indeed.

Sharon may now have been out of Bob Spangler's life, but his enthusiasm for hiking the Grand Canyon had not abated one bit. If anything, it became more pronounced and almost a fixation. He was always restless and looking for new challenges. The mundane, the ordinary, bored him. He liked to live on the edge of danger, and the Grand Canyon filled that need for adventure. He wrote Jim of a recent trip he had taken at the Canyon: "It was great scenery, challenging routes, a certain amount of real danger and tremendous sense of accomplishment. Of course it was demanding, especially that last godawful trudge up the South Kaibab [Trail] on those incredibly steep sections. But what an immense satisfaction afterward having done it all. And the memories of places seen that most people, even Canyon regulars, never dream of visiting."

For some reason, perhaps not even known to himself, Bob sought recognition and praise from the one man he admired so much—Jim Ohlman. He knew that Ohlman was one of the premier hikers of the rugged Grand Canyon. He realized that Ohlman's skills were greater than his own. He even admitted in one letter to Jim: "I've had a fine time describing our hike to friends as the single most difficult hike I've ever taken. I appreciate that you had to find out whether I could keep up with you. Seriously, I've never enjoyed myself more. Without your map reading skills, I'd never have found the way."

Bob—who was generally an entity unto himself, feeling superior to almost everyone—reached out for the one thing that may have been lacking in his life, the praise of an authority figure. (Here the authority stemmed from experience, not of paternal origin.) Bob Spangler may not have received it from his adoptive father, but he definitely wanted it from Jim Ohlman.

Bob sought Jim's praise for planning another hike in April of the coming year, a grand trek that would include the dangerous trail at Horseshoe Mesa above the Redwall. There was something exotic about that section of the trail. On its slippery, rocky edge he could feel the presence of danger and death. Bob Spangler liked toying with the concept of death, even his own, as long as he felt he had some control over it.

In February 1989 Bob talked to Jim about a possible hike with his (Bob's) nephew, who was taking a break from college. He also told of his brother, Wayne, who was planning a sailing trip with his wife clear to Australia. Wayne had asked him to come along, but he begged off. Bob said he had no desire for such a long sea voyage, and his brother had no desire to backpack in the Grand Canyon. "To each his own," Bob commented.

Interestingly enough, his next comments to Jim were about Sharon once again. Despite all their differences, they had stayed in touch. Their one common bond was the Grand Canyon, and it was a strong one. Bob said that Sharon was planning a backpack trip to Lava Falls with a woman friend and was thinking of moving to a city in Arizona, just to be closer to the Canyon. Then he related she recently had a nervous breakdown and possibly had been hospitalized. She was doing better now, he said.

Bob stated, "She's on quite a high with her recovery right now, and I hope it continues. But things have turned bad so many times before. I'm waiting to see what happens this time. Taking hikes, and moving and writing new books, has all been in the works a number of times, only to crash with a new bout of nerves and anxiety. Still, she seems to be moving very confidently through her recovery program now, so perhaps things really are changing for the better at long last."

During one of the sessions of recovery in Denver, Sharon met a man named Michael who was also recovering from emotional problems. They seemed to click and started dating. But before long, Sharon realized that Michael had even more emotional problems than she did. She was both drawn to him and repelled. It truly became a case of "can't live with him, can't live without him." One of his main problems was the inability to stay on medication, something she battled herself. It was the old conundrum that when they felt better, they stopped taking the medication. But feeling better and lack of medication only threw them back into a new cycle of depression. Despite Michael's problems, Sharon did not like living alone. She made plans to move in with him, only to change her mind, then changed it again. Both of their lives were constantly in turmoil.

Interestingly enough, at this same time, Bob Spangler was also struggling with his "aloneness."

In essence a man who could not live alone, he needed the presence of a woman around him. He began dating several women, but he also placed an ad in *Westword*, a Denver-area singles newspaper. As it turned out, the ad caught the eye of a woman named Donna Sundling, who lived in the nearby community of Evergreen.

She told a coworker about this time, "I'm ready to take a chance."

The chance she took was with Bob Spangler. She answered his ad and agreed to meet him at a local tavern. Just what implications her new bravery and search for adventure would have, she couldn't have guessed in her wildest dreams.

Chapter 7

Durango DJ

Donna Sundling met Bob Spangler at a bar in Denver called Proof of the Pudding. At the time Donna was living in a posh suburb in the mountains called Evergreen. She had been divorced since 1974, but by 1989 she seemed eager to be back in the dating game. Her first date with Bob went well and she looked forward to more.

She might have been surprised to learn that she was not the only candidate for Bob's affections at the time. There was also a woman from Alaska. In a letter to Jim Ohlman, dated March 16, 1989, Bob wrote that if interesting things developed, he would introduce the "developee" to "canyoneering." Neither woman had been to the Grand Canyon before but both claimed interest.

A short time later, he wrote Ohlman again and said: "I took your advice about carefully checking out the ladies."

Jim apparently knew about Spangler's habit of making rash decisions, especially when it came to dating, and then regretting them later. And Bob did have a bad track record when it came to women.

Bob went on in his letter: "I decided to change the two to a onesome. I liked one a lot (the woman from Alaska) but kept bumping into characteristics that I eventually realized were reminding me of life with Sharon." Spangler told Ohlman that he'd been through that "game plan" during the last several years and didn't want to experience it again. Which left one prospective woman, Donna Sundling.

He described her as 5'2", the same age as he was (fifty-six at the time) and unmarried for eighteen years. She was the mother of five grown children and an accountant at Martin-Marietta. She lived in a very nicely remodeled home in Evergreen. Bob said he planned to introduce her to the Grand Canyon in the fall.

Bruce Sundling, Donna's son, described her as "self-sacrificing, caring, gentle and protective." He also said, "She was full of life and energy. Mom loved the Evergreen area and all her friends there. She had a large network of friends."

One of Bruce's recollections typified the way Donna looked at life. He said, "I had just received my grades from my last semester at college. I was in the process of calling several family [members] and friends. Invariably, the grades would come up and I informed them, 'I got an A, three B's, a C and a D.' And the next question would be 'Oh yeah, what did you get the D in?'

"When I called my mom, we eventually got around to the grades, and her response was 'What did you get the A in?' That's the way she was. Always positive."

Strangely enough, according to one source, Barbara Dugan, a good friend of Donna Sundling's, just happened to have worked with Bob Spangler in Littleton. By the time he met Donna, Dugan was working with Donna at Martin-Marietta in the Denver area. She learned from Donna about her new friend, Bob Spangler. It's not clear if Dugan told Donna anything about Bob's past "tragedy" in Littleton. Bob eventually told Donna his version of what happened on South Franklin Way. It was the standard lie that Nancy had killed the children and then herself.

In order to pay for all the trips to the Grand Canyon, Bob Spangler started working again part-time for the American Water Works Association, raising money for them in the public-relations sphere. Bob told Jim Ohlman that he'd recently raised $800,000 and joked that the first million was always the hardest. Bob related that he would stay with the job for about a year and charge them by the hour. In the back of his mind must have been the thought that he was still paying Sharon support. Always tight with money, he must have been rankled that he had to give her anything.

With Donna around, though, Bob soon quit talking about Sharon and money matters and became more upbeat, speaking of Donna as a potential mate. He said to Jim Ohlman, "We'll be taking off for a nice little introduction to the Canyon jaunt down the Hermit Trail."

But the trip to the Grand Canyon with Donna didn't turn out as well as planned. Bob related later, "Donna banged up her knee about a week before, so [she] had a bit of a built-in handicap on the way down, especially her not being used to carrying a pack. However, with only a two-nighter in a nice place like Hermit, I could have carried everything myself without much difficulty."

He added, "I think we have a new convert to the Canyon."

Unfortunately for the both of them, Bob didn't realize that Donna was mainly putting up a good front for his behalf. The truth of the matter was that she was frightened of hiking in the Grand Canyon. Even though she was athletic, she was prone to dizzy spells and afraid of heights. But for the time being, she kept this knowledge from Bob because she knew how much he loved the place.

Bob's nephew from Wisconsin apparently came out around that time as well and had a good time hiking with his uncle in the Canyon. In fact, he liked it so much that he planned on another trip at a later date. Always proud of his hiking abilities, Bob couldn't help stating that he walked just as fast as the young man.

Yet there was always background noise in Bob's life, and in this case it was coming from Sharon once again. Bob told Jim Ohlman that Sharon's life was now one disaster after another. He said, "You may have heard that Sharon got down for the Escalante trip. The guy who was going with her broke down and had to be choppered out. He'd had a heart attack a while back and was a suspect repeater."

Bob said all this with a certain smugness, contrasting what good physical shape he was in himself, even though he was fifty-seven years old now.

The fact of the matter was, even though Bob had a very rocky relationship with Sharon and was angry with her in many ways, he still kept in touch with her. According to one of Donna's friends in the Evergreen area, Donna was upset because Bob still found excuses to be around Sharon so often. He would go over and repair things for her and baby-sit her dog.

Bob just couldn't seem to sever all his ties with the woman he had once murdered to have.

Sharon aside, the romance between Donna and Bob blossomed, and after a whirlwind courtship they were married on August 18, 1990, at her home in Evergreen, Colorado. About fifty people attended the reception. Carolyn Metzkis, one of Donna's friends in the Denver area, later told the *Denver Post,* "This man (Bob)—she was just thrilled with him. She just loved him. They were going to keep her house and sell his and travel around in a Winnebago."

But things did not work out that way. In some regards Donna was more like Nancy than Sharon. She more readily acceded to Bob's wishes and demands. The same friend who knew that Donna was upset by Bob's association with Sharon also said, "Bob was domineering but never mean to Donna. He seemed to control things that went on in the Spangler household. He had certain perceptions about how things had to be done."

Though Donna was well established in Evergreen and most of her friends were there, Bob had wanderlust as usual. Donna was so in love with him she was willing to go wherever he went—even if it meant pulling up stakes from the community she loved.

By September 1991 Bob had a great deal of news to tell his friends the Ohlmans. He wrote: "Let's see, since I wrote you last, I've been to Phantom Ranch for a birthday celebration, took a sailing vacation with my brother and his wife in the Virgin Islands, drove to Durango to see if any homes looked good enough to buy, decided one did, went back to Denver and sold our home." Bob also told Ohlman that he took time off to take a hike alone on the Phantom-Crystal Loop Trail, moved to Durango in

April, sold Donna's home in Evergreen and had been transplanting, lifting, hauling and building in the Durango home ever since they moved in.

One thing that he did not reveal to the Ohlmans was that he had tried to have Donna sign her portion of the new home completely over in his name alone. They eventually had both their names placed on the title. But soon after, Donna wrote up a will that stated if she died before Bob, he was to have her share of the house in Durango. This was a sizable amount of money.

Bob said he would soon be taking one of Donna's sons on a routine hike over to Horseshoe Mesa in the Grand Canyon. A place where Sharon had once said, "As we climbed the Redwall, I tried to ignore my fright."

Then Bob related some very unexpected news to the Ohlmans. He said that he'd decided to become a radio DJ in the Durango area. He tried out for the morning spot on the country-and-western station KRSJ, 104.9 FM, and got the job. His immediate boss, Dave Bray, said Bob got the job because he had a good delivery. "He had been in public relations," Bray said, "and had a good style. He came across as very professional." Bob began working mornings, Monday through Friday, on a regular basis.

What had started out as a lark on Bob's part turned into much more than either he or Durango expected. He went on the air about 5:30 A.M. every weekday and announced various items of news, sports, weather and shows recorded from the ABC network. He generally signed off at 8:00 A.M. What set him apart from all the other DJs was his style. Most country-and-western morning shows either had some guy acting like a good ol' boy, or a tough-guy act, or a team clowning around during the morning drive. But Bob's style was totally different. He came on in a well-modulated, cheerful style. No one had heard the likes of this on KRSJ before. It was as if the listeners had a personal friend talking to them in the morning, someone they'd like as their next-door neighbor.

Four Corners Broadcasting general manager Ward Holmes later told the *Denver Post,* "He was un-failingly polite and gracious. The only complaint I ever had about him was that he was too cheerful, too early in the morning."

And Linda Wallace, who was a news director/re-porter at the radio station, knew Bob Spangler as a good storyteller who could lend a sympathetic ear. As time went on, she became very attached to Bob, even though he was years older than she was. He seemed very tenderhearted in her estimation.

Others spoke of Bob's warm style, happy person-ality and positive attitude. It was as if Bob Spangler never had a bad day. To many it was comforting. To a few it was cloying. Mark Schelper, marketing di-rector at the time, was blunt in his assessment of Bob. He said, "Some people thought he was the nicest guy in the world. But other people thought he overdid it, saying things like 'Make it the best day possible'; 'Make it a wonderful day'; 'Go out-side and enjoy this beautiful day.' It could be real schmaltzy at times. Personally, I didn't like the style. And neither did some of my clients who advertised on the radio station. They thought it was too sappy. Some told me, 'Don't put my ads on when Spangler is on the air.' But others really liked it and wanted to be in his time slot."

Schelper added, "He was a mellow guy and a certain segment of the listeners liked that in the morning. Especially women. They'd come up to me and ask, 'Oh, what is Bob like?' He actually had this following among women in the area. They had this perception of him as some warm, cuddly teddy bear. In a word, he was charismatic. And he didn't seem like he was faking it. It just seemed to be a part of who he really was. I remember one line he used a lot, concerning women. Bob would say, 'Women are to be cherished.' One thing was for sure, people in the Durango area either loved or hated Bob Spangler. They couldn't keep from talking about him. I guess in one way it's that old line, 'I don't care if you love or hate me, as long as you don't stop talking about me.'"

Bob had a segment on his radio show called "Speakout," where callers could discuss hot issues of the day with him. This included such topics as gun control, domestic violence and social issues. Strangely enough, Bob was all for gun control. He said he didn't want to be anywhere near them. This was from the same man who qualified as a marksman with a carbine in the army and shot Nancy in the forehead with a .38-caliber pistol. On the issue of domestic violence, radio station vice president John Mackley recalled, "I remember some of the shows and Bob really pouring his heart out about how he had gone through it."

Bob intimated about the tragedy in his life, never revealing that he had been the instigator of that tragedy. Mackley went on to say that Bob told how women needed to be protected from abusive boyfriends and husbands. He obviously did not count himself amongst them.

People in Durango were also talking about Bob

Spangler because he was talking about them. He used anecdotes he picked up around town for part of his broadcast. One of Bob's neighbors across the street in his new neighborhood on Oak Drive saw Bob on the roof of his house soon after he arrived there. Bob was shoveling snow off the roof after a huge snowstorm. The neighbor laughed and said to Bob, "Welcome to Durango." Bob laughed as well at all the snow, and the next day he related his neighbor's comments on the radio show.

"He was an okay guy," the neighbor said later. "We'd have a beer or two once in a while. He was talkative and pretty friendly. I remember he had a lot of stuff in his house about the Grand Canyon. He was wild about the place. There seemed like two big things in his life, his radio show and the Grand Canyon."

The neighbor also had praise for Bob's new wife, Donna. He said, "She'd get right out there and shovel the snow too. She wasn't a shrinking violet. Or a klutz. She seemed pretty athletic. A nice lady."

In fact, Donna was very agile and into aerobics, but there was one thing the neighbor didn't know. Donna suffered from spells of vertigo and was afraid of heights. Able to move gracefully on the ground, she became terrified when even a few feet off the pavement.

If Donna was afraid of heights, she was not afraid of a good workout. In fact, she soon landed a part-time job in Durango as an instructor for seniors at the Durango Sports Club. Joan McCabe, her supervisor and friend, said, "Donna was friendly and outgoing. She had a lot of energy. The people in her classes just loved her. She would throw little parties for them. Hand out silly hats. That sort of thing. The people loved the parties and they loved her. She had a very pleasant, sweet personality."

During their time in Durango, Bob and Donna's social life expanded, especially as his "fame" as a local DJ spread. Pamela Mackley remembered one party at the elegant Spangler home where the two seemed like such a happy couple. She also remembered Bob's two incredibly trained dogs, Sunshine and Mollie. The dogs would be brought into a room, told to sit by Bob, and there they would stay without moving a muscle until he released them. Mark Schelper had also seen these dogs and said later, "Bob was a control freak. Everything had to be just so with him. You should have seen his desk. Everything in its place. Even his Subaru. Most Subarus around Durango are pretty junky, filled up with all sorts of stuff from everyday life. But not Bob's. It was immaculate. This sense of control ran right through his dogs, his car, his house and probably even his wife."

Bob had one dog story for Pamela Mackley that was very telling and interesting. He said he'd had Sunshine and Mollie trained by a friend who trained dogs for the Disney Studios out in Hollywood. But the fact of the matter was that Sunshine and Mollie had been trained by Sharon, years before. It was just one more lie by a man who always seemed to be toying with the truth.

Bob's lies in Durango didn't just concern his dogs. He told those around him different stories about how his first family had died. The main story was, of course, how Nancy had killed the children and then herself. But to one coworker he said that Susan had overdosed on drugs, David had been killed in a car accident and Nancy committed suicide after the children were gone. Bob told Pamela

Mackley that his son had killed his sister and mother, then himself. To others he said all had died in a car accident. There were even two versions of this story. One was that they died while he was driving and only he survived. The other was that they all died while he was at work.

The wonder of it all was that Bob, who had been so careful and precise in the murders, should have told such different stories. But perhaps at some level he knew these people wouldn't compare stories. Who, after all, would make up such terrible things? Certainly a man of Bob Spangler's stature wouldn't lie about such horrible tragedies that had happened in his life.

Bob had such a well-respected veneer that no one was likely to question his honesty as he told one lie after another. In fact, he lied his way right through life in Durango as he spoke on the radio and refereed at soccer games. He was so good at lying by this point that no one could tell. The common theme was picked up again by those on his street in West Durango: "He was a good neighbor." They referred to him as being funny, charming and a gentleman.

Donna loved Durango too, and the people she worked with, but because of her work and Bob's early-morning hours, it started to cause a strain on their marriage. Before long, the Spanglers were leading separate lives. Donna did not want it to be that way, but she found it hard to share his interests. He became increasingly annoyed with her. And Bob discovered the most annoying fact of all, Donna did not love hiking in the Grand Canyon the way he did. She was afraid of the slippery, steep trails at the Canyon and losing her sense of balance. In essence, she was afraid of the place he loved the most.

If there was a common bond left between Bob and Donna Spangler during this period, it was their appreciation of Durango. Spangler expressed his feelings to the Ohlmans in a letter: "Durango seems to be quite a low rent district as far as pay scales go. Not a place to make a decent living. But otherwise absolutely great. I cannot imagine having made a better decision in my life than the one to move here."

Besides his stint on the radio station as a DJ, Bob was also officiating local games of the soccer league. In this capacity he was widely regarded as one of the best refs in the business. He was a veteran at it now and knew all the nuances of the game. A stickler for rules and regulations, he took his job very seriously. He also took time to explain the rules to children. Having been almost a stranger to his own teenage children and often angry with them, by comparison he was kind and patient with other people's kids. As word spread about Bob's soccer skills in the area, teams wanted him to officiate their games.

Dave Bray noticed that Bob was always volunteering for some kind of sports activity. He even helped announce a couple of the local high school football games. Perhaps it reminded Bob of his own glory days on the football field in Ames, Iowa. Mark Schelper, who played soccer, noted that Bob was a very good soccer referee. "Here was a guy who was in his fifties and could run up and down the field with guys half his age. Soccer is an analytical game and so was Bob. They made a good match. All the teams wanted him to ref because he had a good eye and knew the game."

The one real complaint Bob had about his new life in Durango was that his schedule at the radio station kept him from taking off for the Grand Canyon whenever he wanted. He told Jim Ohlman, "It does cut into plans I might otherwise make for hiking."

He daydreamed about a long route in the Canyon to Utah Flats, Phantom, Shiva Saddle, Dragon Springs, Crystal, and South Kaibab. He always wanted to try new routes. New adventures. Pitting his skills against the Canyon. But there was another aspect to this. He also wanted to be seen as worthy in the eyes of his mentor, Jim Ohlman.

There were only a few clouds on the horizon of this "Rocky Mountain High" in Colorado. The strain in the marriage with Bob induced Donna to seek some counseling while in Durango. Not much of what she said there has survived, but a few glimpses of what she was thinking made their way into police reports later. These insights came via friends and family. Donna was depressed and said that there was a lot of loneliness in her marriage to Bob. She never felt that she had a good connection with him. She loved him, but he was set in his ways. She also worried about a Durango woman who used to come over to their house for barbecues. Bob would flirt with the woman more than what seemed appropriate. Donna wondered if they were having an affair. She already knew that Bob's affair with Sharon had split apart his first marriage. She worried what this woman might do to her own union with Bob.

To add to the friction, Donna wanted Bob to take up skiing. The idea may not have been to ski with her, but rather for Bob to ski with her children who enjoyed skiing in the surrounding area. He was not enthused about this sport and worried that if he banged up a knee or ankle skiing, it would ruin his hiking abilities and ability to officiate soccer games.

But more than anything else, it was Donna's lack of passion for the Grand Canyon that bothered him. As he noted later, the magic had gone out of their marriage. He would say there was nothing special about it and that marrying her was a mistake. When he had such thoughts as these, he was at his most dangerous.

Chapter 8

The Fatal Edge

By the fall of 1992, as Bob began to lose interest in Donna, she quit her accounting job at Fort Lewis College in the Durango area and went to Hawaii on her own for a six-weeks course in advanced aerobics training. After the course she received her certification and planned to work full-time at the Durango Sports Club. It was becoming more and more a part of her world, but not Bob's.

There was a Christmas party at the Spangler home during the holiday season in 1992. Pamela Mackley was there and remembered how good both Bob and Donna looked. To all outside appearances they seemed like a loving, happy couple. But at some point in the party, Donna took Pamela aside and mentioned how the Grand Canyon had become a hot issue between them. She admitted to Pamela, "I'm afraid of sheer drop-offs. I'm not balanced."

This seemed like an odd comment from someone who was so good at aerobics, but Donna had a whole host of medical problems. She had to take Meclizine for dizziness, Pepcid for stomach ulcers,

Pirbuterol Acetate for asthma and, because of all these problems, even Prozac for depression.

Bob was not happy with the way things were turning out either. Since he wasn't into skiing, the winter storms that year kept him inside and added to his sense of frustration. Thirty-seven inches of snow fell in one week in the Durango area and Donna told him to buy a snowblower because he was too old to be shoveling so much. This comment wounded his vanity. Despite his age he was still very vain about his physical fitness. And during the Christmas holiday that year, their house seemed to become a magnet for Donna's sons and relatives. Bob complained in a letter to a friend: "They (Donna's relatives) are here ostensibly to enjoy Christmas, but actually use us as a base camp for skiing."

Bob was also miffed that the radio station now used him as their "official designated hitter." He complained that "when anyone wants a vacation or day off or gets sick or whatever, I'm the one they call to fill in." Every day spent at the radio station was one less day he could be traveling in his beloved Grand Canyon.

There was one other fact bothering Bob Spangler that season. In January 1993 he turned sixty years old. He wistfully told Jim Ohlman that winter that he'd recently taken one of Donna's sons and a friend on a hike to the Grand Canyon. Both of them were in their thirties. He said he knew he was entering a new decade in his life and that his energy and strength were sure to abate. Though he never spoke of it openly, Bob Spangler was terrified of growing old.

Worst of all, it was now very plain that Donna was not going to be his "Grand Canyon partner" as

Sharon had been. For Bob, hiking in the Canyon was almost a religious experience. For Donna, it was a frightening nightmare that had to be endured.

By the spring of 1993 Bob Spangler was once again restless, bored with his wife and increasingly felt the constraints of his job. He both loved and hated it—loved it for the recognition he craved, hated it because of its time constraints. He had fallen into a deep rut, much as he had with Nancy and the kids back in 1978, except now there was no alluring young Sharon Cooper on the horizon to lift his spirits. He was sixty years old with diminishing possibilities. There were so many things he still wanted to do, and Donna seemed like a millstone around his neck, dragging him down. It didn't matter that she still worshiped the ground he walked on. According to him, she was very jealous and didn't even like him talking to the neighbor lady. Bob Spangler was the man she wanted, but more and more the main impediment was that she didn't want to do the things he wanted to do.

By April of 1993 the old malaise was back for Bob and with it vague and murderous plans drifted through his mind as they had in 1978. If Donna was an impediment to his dreams, he remembered that he had rid himself of larger problems before. He had been questioned about all the deaths by authorities and then let go. He had fooled them all. If he could fool them once, he could fool them again. Bob Spangler was never one to doubt his own abilities.

In April, Bob pleaded and cajoled Donna to come with him to the Grand Canyon for a backpack trip during Easter week. It would be their four-year anniversary since meeting in 1989. It was something he definitely wanted to do and he was very adamant about it.

Donna told her friend Joan McCabe about Bob's request. She said she didn't want to go. McCabe asked her how she and Bob were getting along. Donna answered, "We'll have to talk after the trip."

She also phoned her friend Sandy Brooks. Donna told her she was scared about the trip, but excited as well. Brooks told her that if she was scared, she didn't have to go. But Donna responded that it was important to Bob that she went along. Brooks asked Donna how things were between her and Bob. Donna said they would have to talk about it sometime.

Donna was so concerned about this upcoming trip to the Canyon that she phoned each and every one of her children before leaving. She didn't mention that she was afraid of Bob, but she did lay out her fears about the Grand Canyon. A couple of her children had the eerie feeling that she was saying good-bye. They were very unsettled by the tone of her voice.

Once at the Grand Canyon, on April 9, 1993, Bob and Donna hiked down the Grandview Trail from the South Rim to Horseshoe Mesa. This was an established trail used by numerous hikers in all seasons. At a certain point, though, Bob led her off onto the unmaintained and difficult Page Springs Trail to Hance Creek, where they camped for the night. The trail was rough going for Donna, and Bob was not pleased with her performance.

The next day, they made their way along the Page Springs Trail, which was not an easy task. Donna was not a strong hiker and this section must have been agony for her. Sharon Spangler had written years before about this section of trail: "It was steep, mind-numbingly steep."

Donna could not have been enjoying herself much on that day's hike, and Bob probably made a mental note about how unfavorably she compared to his other hiking companions. There seemed to be almost nothing they shared in common anymore. He didn't overtly dislike her, but where was the woman he had dreamed of in 1989? Where was the magic?

As they hiked along the trail, they met a group of four hikers, Mark Stephen, Kevin O'Leary, Rick Morgan and Rick's girlfriend, Elizabeth Duncan. This foursome did not always keep together as they hiked, and often they would individually bump into Bob and Donna Spangler along the trail. At one point Mark Stephen and Kevin O'Leary were standing together waiting for the others when Bob approached them and began chatting. He asked where they were going and where they planned to camp overnight. He seemed awfully nosy. Both of these men knew the name Spangler from Sharon's book and realized that this was the Bob she had been talking about within the book. They were surprised when Bob told them that he and Donna were planning to camp the night on Horseshoe Mesa near the old mine shaft. They knew this area was off-limits to camping and were sure that Bob knew this as well. They wondered why he would pick such a spot to camp. From this conversation Stephen felt that Bob was a "weird guy."

As the day progressed, the four hikers and the Spanglers would often intermix as they hiked along. At one point Donna and Mark Stephen were hiking by themselves. He recalled later that Donna

seemed like a nice lady and was acting normally
that day. She did have to hike with ski poles for balance, but she seemed to be doing okay. She didn't
seem frightened or dizzy.

Rick Morgan also thought Donna was a nice lady.
He remembered her later as "pleasant, outgoing
and not frightened." She didn't indicate to him
that anything was wrong between her and Bob or
that she needed help in any way. But he also found
it strange that Bob would pick the illegal spot near
the mine shaft to camp for the night. And he
thought that Bob asked a lot of questions about
where they were camping for the night.

Kevin O'Leary talked to Donna as well. He noted
she walked slowly with the ski poles and was very
wary about the edges of the trail—especially along
any cliff sides.

At some point along the trail the foursome split
off from Bob and Donna and went their own way
for the night. Bob and Donna struggled into camp
near the old mine tailings and camped illegally at
its entrance. Bob, indeed, knew that this place was
off-limits to campers. He also knew that no one
would be around to see whatever happened next.
That something *had* to happen became more apparent to him all the time. He couldn't go on living
life the way it was with Donna. In his mind she re-
stricted all that he wanted to be.

The spot Bob chose to camp in that night
couldn't have been much different than the way
Sharon had described the scene back in the 1980s.
Sharon had recorded the area near Miner's Spring
as "delicious and cool, hacked into a shady niche at
the base of the Redwall. The spring was overhung
with grasses and ferns. Redbud trees grew around

it and framed the view outward, creating a perfectly balanced composition. On the left, the Redwall cliff of Horseshoe Mesa, on the right, partially screened by redbuds, the steeply sloping terrace of the east wall. Center, in vibrant colors, Krishna, Vishnu and Rama Temples."

Whether Donna enjoyed the oasis where they camped illegally that night, only Bob knew for sure. And he had other things on his mind at the time.

The next morning, April 11, 1993, it was Easter Sunday and the fourth anniversary of Bob's meeting with Donna back in Denver. Bob woke up early, looked at Donna and decided what he must do. Just like Nancy and the kids, she had to go. If Bob had learned one lesson from his divorce with Sharon, it was this: divorce could be very expensive. But there were ways around divorce, if he was clever enough.

Bob and Donna broke camp around 8:30 A.M. and climbed two steep switchbacks above the mine shaft along the Redwall. As they paused to take a breath, Bob knew there was no place above this spot where a fall off the trail was certain to cause death.

"It's now or never," he said to himself.

On first glance, the spot he picked to kill her would not seem an ideal place for a murder. The cliff side was only about twenty-five to thirty feet high, but right below the cliff was a steep rocky chute that descended another hundred feet. Anyone falling off the cliff and into the chute would have little chance of survival. Bob had to act fast. As the morning wore on, chances grew that other hikers might travel along this stretch of trail. His choice of the previous night's campsite had been key. No one should be in the immediate area at present.

As Donna stood on the edge of the precipice,

breathing hard and looking at him, Bob Spangler silently moved forward and reached toward her. Perhaps she thought he was going to adjust her pack. Perhaps she thought he was going to hug her. Instead, Bob reached out and shoved her over the cliff.

God only knows what Donna Spangler thought in that terrible instant. The sheer unexpectedness of it must have been unfathomable. In one single moment her worst fears had been realized. She had always feared falling from some great height at the Grand Canyon and now she was hurtling backward through space.

She fell a full twenty-five feet before hitting the first rocks and her straw hat flew off. Then she tumbled another hundred feet down the rocky chute before coming to rest beneath a lone tree. Then everything became darkness.

During his fatal shove Bob Spangler hadn't counted on one thing. The trail at the spot where he pushed Donna over the side was rocky and slippery. His momentum nearly carried him over the precipice with her. He skidded and slipped and came within inches of tumbling over the side himself. An ironic justice was almost meted out upon him in his very act of murder.

Stunned and breathing hard from his near miss, Bob felt a rush of conflicting emotions: relief of having accomplished the deed without anyone seeing it, and shock that he had nearly perished himself. He later said that once again he felt as if he were watching himself from afar. It was as if he were an actor in a play or movie. This was a sensation he had once described to Sharon while in the Canyon, as if he were in a segment of *The Twilight*

Zone and the camera panned away farther and farther, leaving him alone in its immensity.

But soon enough he remembered the nonfatal wound he had inflicted upon son David back in 1978. He had to make sure that Donna was really dead. Bob found an alternate route down to where Donna's body lay. It was steep and treacherous, but negotiable. Once he got to her, he discovered she had numerous bruises and contusions all over her body and blood was oozing from various head wounds. Bob knelt down and checked her for any vital signs. If he had to, he would do as he had done to David—cover her mouth and nose until she stopped breathing. He didn't have to worry, though. Donna Spangler was dead.

Bob noticed that items had broken free from her backpack and were strewn down the steep slope. For some reason he washed her face, covered it with a red bandanna and placed a blue tarp over her body. Then he scrambled back up the slope, threw her backpack behind some rocks and began to concoct the story he would tell the park rangers once he reached the Back Country Office on the South Rim.

And then in one of those small twists of fate that constantly seemed to run through Bob Spangler's life, he ran into Mark Stephen, Kevin O'Leary, Rick Morgan and Elizabeth Duncan as they hiked back toward the South Rim. Each one of them would recall Bob's passing that day a little differently.

Mark Stephen recalled Bob running by Rick and Elizabeth, not saying a word, before stopping to tell him that Donna had fallen off a cliff and was dead. Rick Morgan also remembered Bob running by him and Liz, but that he did tell them that Donna was dead, without slowing down. He recalled that Bob looked distraught.

Kevin O'Leary had the most time to observe Bob Spangler that morning after Donna's fatal fall. Bob ran past him and then stopped, standing by the edge of the trail and catching his breath and crying. Kevin told Bob that he would walk to the top of the trail with him and they took off together. On the way to the rim Bob did not discuss Donna's "accident" very much, but he did mention to Kevin that he didn't know why he had run up the trail since Donna was already dead. It seemed like an odd comment to Kevin.

Bob's remark at the top of the trail was even more odd. As they parted company, each exchanged addresses. What Bob said next became somewhat garbled, depending upon whom you asked, but with only a few minor word changes it came out: "I'm taking a hike in the Canyon next November. Would you like to be my hiking partner?" It was as if he couldn't help himself. Just fifty minutes after he had murdered his third wife, he was already looking around for a replacement to hike in the Grand Canyon.

At 11:24 A.M., April 11, 1993, Ranger Dolly McHenry at the Back Country Office looked up and saw a man with a gray beard patiently waiting in line for his turn. When the man, dressed in hiking gear, reached the booth, he said in a calm, measured voice, "Yes, please, can you help me? My wife has fallen off the Redwall on Horseshoe Mesa. She fell to her death."

McHenry was stunned by the man's calm demeanor and thought perhaps he was in a state of shock. He seemed to show no emotion about his wife's death.

The strange man went on to say that he and his wife had stopped to take a photo at a point on the trail above the old mine. He said that as she posed for a picture, she fell. He said that he had scrambled down to her body and found that she was dead. He washed her face and covered her body with a tarp and had hiked and run back to the Back Country Office.

The Park Service made Bob Spangler fill out a report on the incident. He wrote: "We struck camp early, had breakfast and got on the trail about 8:30 AM. No more than a half hour later, we reached a promontory at a switchback and paused for one last photo down the drainage. I positioned Donna and turned to mount the camera on a rock for an automatic picture of us together. I heard a small sound from Donna and turned and she was gone. I looked over the edge and saw her some two hundred feet below, up against a small tree. I dropped my pack and ran back down the trail to a point where I could traverse to where she was. There was no pulse, her legs were badly broken; I pulled her into a better position; I got some water from her pack, which had broken free, and washed her face with her bandana. Then covered her with our blue ground cloth. I carried her pack back to where I'd dropped mine for some reason, then tossed it up behind some bushes and walked out."

At 11:45 A.M. Coconino County sheriff's deputy Brett Rye was informed of Donna Spangler's death. He arrived at the Back Country Office on the South Rim at noon and spoke to Ranger Ken Phillips about the incident. Twenty minutes later, Rye and Ranger

Jeff Kracht began interviewing Bob Spangler about Donna's fall. Bob told them that Donna wasn't much of a hiker and that she was feeling shaky and a little dizzy that morning. Then he began to repeat to them what he had already written in his report. He said at approximately 9:00 A.M. he and Donna had stopped at a view point to take some photos. He said she had stepped on a large rock while he turned away from her to set his camera on a rock so that he could take a picture of the both of them with the automatic timer. Then he recalled, "When I bent down to place the camera, I heard a breath or gasp from Donna. When I turned to look at her, she was gone. I stepped up on the rock, and when I looked down, I could see Donna had fallen over the side at least one hundred feet."

At 12:27 P.M. Deputy Rye informed Coconino County sheriff's sergeant Raul Osegueda about the fatal accident. Three minutes later, the coroner Dr. Forrest Ritland gave Rye permission to remove Donna's body from the site. But by now the winds were howling around the Grand Canyon and Ranger Phillips told Rye that it would be too dangerous to fly a helicopter into the inner canyon to extract the body. Rangers Carly Lober and Nick Herring would have to hike down there instead and secure the "accident" scene.

It took Lober and Herring over four hours to hike down to Donna Spangler's body. Once there they located her body under a tarp against a tree beneath a steep cliff off the Page Springs Trail. Lifting the tarp, they saw that Donna's face was covered with a red bandanna, just as Bob Spangler had reported. Various items belonging to her were scattered in descending order, suggesting the point from which she had fallen. The distance from the point was later measured and turned out to be 160 feet.

A story that could not later be verified by park officials had a curious twist. A man who claimed to be a friend of one of the rangers who checked on Donna Spangler that day said that his friend bent down for a closer look at her hands. The ranger didn't quite believe Bob Spangler's story about this being an accident. He checked underneath her fingernails to see if she had scratched him. If there were bits of skin from Bob underneath her fingernails, it might mean that she had been fighting him off during an attack. But of course the ranger found no bits of skin there, and with good reason—the fatal shove had come so swiftly and unexpectedly that Donna had not had time to do anything.

Because of the winds it was impossible to fly in the National Park search-and-rescue helicopter that day. Lober and Herring had to spend all night in a lonely vigil with Donna Spangler's body. At 7:00 A.M. on April 12, despite gusty winds, Deputy Rye and Rangers Mike Weaver and Chris Fors flew to the scene of Donna Spangler's death. While aloft, Ranger Weaver videotaped the area and Deputy Rye began to snap still photos, but this aerial photography was short-lived. There were severe downdrafts and it was deemed prudent to land the helicopter.

Once they were on the ground, the three men hiked to the point where Donna fell off the trail. They reached this point at 7:55 A.M., and Deputy Rye began to record his impressions of the spot. He wrote: "The initial fall appeared to be approximately twenty-five to thirty feet where she landed on some rocks and then continued down a chute for a total distance of approximately 140 feet. The victim was visible from the point of the fall. A cream-colored hat was found at the point where the victim initially hit. At the base of the rock ledge at the beginning of the chute was this straw hat. Approximately thirty feet down the chute we found a broken pair of sunglasses and a watch band with no watch. Approximately ten feet further down, was one wool glove. Near the final resting place of the victim was another wool glove and a ski pole used as a walking stick."

For the next hour, Deputy Rye examined the items around Donna Spangler's body and took photographs. It wasn't until around 10:00 A.M. that she was placed in a body bag, slung by cable beneath the helicopter and choppered out to a helipad and placed in an ambulance. Then her body was driven to the morgue in Flagstaff, about sixty miles away.

While all of this was going on, Sergeant Osegueda had been talking to Bob Spangler. Bob told him that Donna had been taking Meclizine for vertigo. This medication had been prescribed by Dr. Boyd, her doctor in Durango.

That same day at 2:40 P.M. the autopsy of Donna Spangler was performed by Dr. Forrest Ritland with Sergeant Osegueda in attendance. In his notes Dr. Ritland reported that "the upper body is clothed in a pink t-shirt over tan bra. The lower body is clothed in purple-gray-yellow pants over white underwear. Gray and green hiking boots, gray socks and white socks are present on the feet. There are multiple tears on the clothing, more particularly the right pant leg. A red and white bandana is present around the neck.

"There are multiple recent abrasions and contusions on the body. These are shades of red-orange and pale blue-purple-green, respectively. There is a semiconfluent abrasion and contusion over the forehead with the small lacerations on right side measuring one and 2 centimeters. Ecchymosis is present around both eyelids.

"Abrasions are present over the nose and over both cheeks. Abrasions are present on the upper and lower lips and on the chin. Additional areas of abrasion contusions are present on the sides of the face. Abrasions and contusions along the left side of the jaw measure 1x3, 4x8 and 6x8 cm. Lacerations on the occiput measure 1x5 cm.

"There is a 4x6 cm contusion at the left base of the neck and there are contusions on the upper chest measuring 2x3 cm and 3x4 cm. Contusions on the left breast measure 2x2 cm."

The report went on to mention numerous lacerations and contusions all the way down Donna Spangler's body. "Manipulation of the torso shows multiple bilateral rib and sternum fractures with easy deformability over the entire chest. The head is abnormally mobile from the neck with associated fracture." All in all, the number of wounds showed just how violent her fall had been. There were several wounds serious enough to have caused death.

Forrest Ritland, M.D., wrote at the end of the report: "Cause of death: Multiple traumatic injuries. Manner of death: Accidental."

After Dr. Ritland's conclusion, Sergeant Osegueda wrote in his report: "As the result of follow-up investigation by Deputy Brett Rye which is consistent with medical examination, it has been determined that there appears to be no foul play and cause of death is accidental; therefore, this case will be reclassified to close. Disposition—Case closed, non-crime."

Bob Spangler was helped in his murder that year by the fact that there were numerous fatal falls around the Grand Canyon. In fact, 1993 was one of the worst years on record for accidental falls from the rim. At Cape Royal, German tourist Andreas Zimmerman, twenty-four, was jumping from one ledge to another when he lost his balance and fell four hundred feet to his death.

Within a couple of days, Lori Newcomb, thirty-one, walked far out on the edge to take a photo near the same spot. A rock crumbled under her feet and she fell 150 feet to her death.

Only one day later, James Merriman, fifty-one, a transient in the area, was leaping from rock to rock near Mather Point, trying to collect coins that tourists had thrown from the rim onto a ledge below. He was hamming it up for the tourists' cameras and yelled, "Watch this!" He tried jumping to a nearby rock ledge, missed, and tumbled 360 feet to his death.

But the most similar case to Donna Spangler's fatal fall that year occurred when Lawrence Jackson, twenty-four, was sitting with a friend near the Badger Overlook. The friend turned away for a moment. When he turned back, Jackson had vanished over the edge. Jackson had fallen hundreds of feet to his death. The friend had no idea what had happened. Jackson might have slipped, shifted his weight and become unbalanced or become dizzy. He was there one moment and gone the next.

If all these fatal falls at the Canyon could be accidental—then why not Donna's as well? After all, the Grand Canyon was a dangerous place.

After Donna's death Bob Spangler moved quickly. Within a very short time he had her remains cremated, just as he had done to Nancy, Susan and David. The cremation was done in Flagstaff, Arizona, before any of Donna's children arrived and could have a say in the matter. One relative was incensed by the quickness of the cremation and remarked later that cheap Bob had scooped Donna's ashes into an inexpensive plastic container. He grumbled that her ashes were barely cold before she was stuffed "into a cheap plastic tub." Once again there was no body that could be exhumed later for analysis.

Bernee Davey, Donna's daughter, remembered getting a phone call right after the "accident" from Bob, who was still at the Grand Canyon. She said later, "He sounded very upset and had a difficult time trying to talk to me."

When Bernee finally met Bob at Flagstaff, she said, "He was very quiet and closed in." She noted, however, that even though he did cry some, she never saw him break down. It was as if he were holding it all in.

The memorial service for Donna at the Spangler home in Durango was a farce as far as many people were concerned. And for all his methodical planning it was the one thing that Bob did not do well. At the memorial service Bob Spangler gave the eulogy. Donna's ex-husband, Wayne Sundling, later told the *Rocky Mountain News,* "He was quite different, unremorseful, it seemed. I couldn't bring myself to go back into Spangler's house after the service."

Marketing director Mark Schelper also noticed Bob's lack of emotion about the death of his wife.

He said, "Bob didn't seem to be upset at all. In fact, he was digging all the attention he got. It was like he was putting on a show. He liked being the star attraction."

KSRJ's Schelper told the *Durango Herald*, "He did a great eulogy. But he never cried at the funeral. He was so matter of fact. It was really weird. It just didn't feel right."

And Mark's wife was even more disturbed by the proceedings. She said, "There's something fishy going on here."

Joan McCabe, Donna's supervisor and friend at the Durango Sports Club, also noticed Bob's lack of emotion. She said, "We were all crying and sniffling during the service. But not Bob. I know that people grieve differently. But he didn't seem to be grieving at all. I began to wonder, what's going on here?"

One of the most skeptical people at the Spangler home that day was the neighbor from across the street who had first welcomed Bob to Durango after the big snowstorm. This man was originally from New York City and had a New Yorker's innate skepticism. As he watched Bob among the family and guests, seeking their attention, he noted Bob's complete absorption with himself. He seemed to have no grief for Donna.

The man turned to his wife and whispered, "I'll bet you he did it. He pushed her over the side."

Unfortunately, neither this man nor his wife ever went to the police with their suspicions. As time went on, Donna's death was chalked up as just one more tragedy in Bob Spangler's already tragic life. After all, wasn't the Grand Canyon a dangerous place and Donna prone to dizzy spells? Bob didn't take long in harping on these facts.

DJs rarely got to talk about bad things that happened in their lives at radio station KRSJ. But station manager John Mackley made an exception in Bob's case because he was so well liked. He let him report about the tragic loss of his wife on the air. In a brief announcement Bob told his audience how he had just lost his wonderful wife in a tragic accident at the Grand Canyon. To those who knew of the other tragedies in his life, it seemed totally unfair that he should have to suffer more. Some wondered how he could bear up under the strain. They were amazed at his resiliency and bravery in such times.

But Bob did occasionally act irrationally during this period, as if he were taunting anyone to catch him in his lies. A friend of Donna's named Sandy Brooks, who lived in Evergreen, Colorado, informed Bob that a memorial service was going to take place for Donna in Evergreen and that he was invited.

In fact, it was going to be more of a celebration of her life than a traditional memorial service. Donna's son Bruce said, "It was well understood by all her children and friends that her wishes were not to have any type of traditional funeral. She wanted to be cremated because she insisted our last memories of her not be that of a corpse. She wanted a champagne brunch and anyone who truly knew Mom, knew that was the most single appropriate thing to do. The message she wanted to send was, 'Don't mourn my death—celebrate my life.'"

Bob told Sandy Brooks that he would not attend. He said the celebration should be for her friends in Evergreen and that he had already conducted a memorial service in Durango. Brooks told Bob that she was really sorry that Donna was gone. He responded with a remark that surprised her. He said he had been receiving phone calls at the radio station from people he didn't know, expressing sympathy. He then told Brooks, "It's nice to know they appreciate my work."

Brooks thought that comment was a little odd, but it was nothing compared to what he said next. She told him that her husband had died and she knew he must feel very lonely in his big house in Durango without Donna. In reply Bob said, "Oh no, I have the dogs to keep me company."

Brooks was so incensed by this remark that she abruptly hung up the phone.

But for the most part, Bob Spangler watched what he said to others, and he made the most of the "accident" by contacting various news agencies about the dangers of hiking in the Canyon. On December 1, 1993, he was quoted in *USA Today* in a story headlined, AN EDGE OF TRAGEDY AMID CANYON MAJESTY. The story began by saying that the last time Robert Spangler saw his wife alive, he was setting up his camera and she was posing for one final snapshot at Grand Canyon National Park. He told them that she wasn't a very strong hiker. "I don't know," he said, "if she became unbalanced with her backpack or if she shuffled her feet or stepped on a rock that became loose. I turned around and she was gone. People that visit simply forget how spectacularly dangerous it can be."

The article went on to detail the deaths of six other people who had fallen in the Grand Canyon that year. This was as many deaths as the past three years combined. Park officials said they couldn't remember a worse year. All of this helped back up Bob's story of an accidental death.

Bob also spoke with a reporter on National Public Radio about the dangers of the Grand Canyon. He said, "In the course of my life I've hiked about eight hundred miles at the Canyon. We (Donna and Bob) were only maybe a couple of hundred yards up that trail when on one of those switchbacks came this beautiful sunrise. Easter sunrise, as a matter of fact. We decided to take one last picture back down the Canyon at the area we had been."

Bob was also presented on a short segment of a television program called *American Journal* in December 1993. He ran through his usual litany of facts about how the Grand Canyon was so dangerous. And then for one moment he stepped out from behind his mask of concern and sadness for Donna and showed his true nature. He became very animated and excited telling about how he had nearly fallen over the cliff himself on April 11, 1993. Anyone looking closely could see that he was not very concerned about the death of his wife at all. He had spoken of her in a very unemotional and almost monotone quality of voice. What he was really concerned about was his own close call. Everything always began and ended with Bob Spangler. The most important thing in his life was himself.

Bob was full of surprises that year and on December 30, 1993, fifteen years to the day since he murdered Nancy, Susan and David, he wrote a letter to his ex-wife, Sharon. It began by saying he wanted to wrap up the old year by giving her a gift. He said he'd been working on the letter all week thinking of nasty and angry things to say to her. But in the end he decided to keep all those comments out. Instead, he recalled a time in 1992 when they had spoken and he had said, "It would be nice to be nice, but I can't afford to be nice."

Nonetheless, he decided that since he was single again, and could afford to be generous, he would give her $10,000 in two installments: $5,000 in mid-1994 and $5,000 in mid-1995. He added that this was in no way an admission that he had "cheated, misled, defrauded or otherwise short-changed her in the divorce settlement." He told her she had signed her name to that document and gone along with its provisions and she couldn't whine about it now.

Bob said he realized that she had most of her cash tied up in real estate and was strapped for cash as far as everyday living expenses. He would make this onetime gift to help her out. But at the end he couldn't help putting in a few barbs. He told her the money wasn't as much as she thought she was owed, but it was better than nothing. And if she complained about it, that's exactly what he would give her—nothing. The last paragraph of the letter was particularly spiteful. Bob wrote: "I'm willing to be friends still, if you are, but not terribly close friends, okay? I'm sorry, but the negatives of your life have an unfortunate tendency to spill over on anyone nearby, which always brings me down, too. And I'm just not willing to risk my own life by getting too involved with your's [sic] again. Perhaps one day you'll find someone who doesn't come equipped with such a selfish attitude. Good luck."

Even more strangely, by July 1994 he was letting Sharon move back into his house in Durango as a paying housemate. It's not clear why Bob did this. Cynics who discovered later what he had done to his other spouses surmised it was a way to get her close, have her drop her guard and finally eliminate her permanently from his life. But the truth seems to be more complicated than that, as things generally were between Bob and Sharon. He found it very hard to sever all ties with her.

For her part, Sharon wrote a relative after moving into Bob's house on Oak Drive: "I'll stay here until I've had time to heal from all the harsh and sad events of the past half century." In the same letter she spoke of how she and Bob were going over her financial situation and he was giving her advice about mutual funds and money market accounts. She admitted it was all a moot point since most of her money was still tied up in her house in Pagaosa Springs. But she added, "Bob and I have enjoyable times studying and discussing the funds and as long as I can't actually do anything, the conversation is, so far, educational, stimulating and, I hope, harmless."

How harmless it was will never be known. When Sharon Cooper Spangler made that comment, she had less than five months to live. And despite all his protestations to the contrary, Bob Spangler always did benefit financially from the deaths of wives and ex-wives. If Sharon was out of the way, he wouldn't have to pay her the $5,000 he'd promised in mid-1995, or the $400 a month he had to pay her until 1997, and he would receive $20,000 stipulated in the divorce settlement if she died before him.

In 1994 Bob was feeling pretty smug that he had fooled everyone once again. He had murdered Donna right beneath the noses of the authorities and they thought it was accidental. The coroner's report even said so. And by October 1994 he was right in the middle of another mysterious death. Just how much he was involved in Sharon's suicide has never been proven. But one thing is certain, soon after she was dead, he was telling people different stories about the circumstances of her death just as he had done about the deaths of Nancy, Susan and David. To the authorities he told of how he had brought Sharon to the hospital as soon as he realized that she had taken the deadly mixture of pills and alcohol. But that's not what he told his close friend Jim Ohlman. Jim recounted later, "Within a couple of days of Sharon's death, Bob called me up to break the news. He said that he knew she was home because her car was in the driveway, and that on entering the house, noted that the door to her bedroom was closed. He said he didn't try to bother her at that time. Later, how much later he didn't say, he saw the memo taped onto the outside of her bedroom door. (The memo which supposedly said, 'I did it this time.')

"After reading it, he entered her room. The door was unlocked. He said he found Sharon lying on the bed, awake, and 'not with it.' He said they had some kind of conversation in her room. Sharon was on some kind of pretty potent medication, with two specific warnings to the effect that it was not to be taken with any form of alcohol or dairy product. Bob said there was an empty bottle of spirits on Sharon's dresser along with remains of a chunk of cheese. He also said that in his conversation with her, she very plainly told him what she had taken and that she had done enough research into the effects of mixing alcohol and dairy products with her medicine to be certain that the mixture and amount she had taken was more than enough to kill her.

"He took her out to his car and then drove her to the hospital. According to Bob, Sharon was awake, more or less lucid, and conversed with the doctors as she was being wheeled into the hospital in a wheelchair. They (the doctors) ran some tests on her and determined that they were too late to do anything to save her."

This last statement by Bob to Jim Ohlman is a curious one. Once again he decided to lie about something important and could be proven to be in contradiction to his assertion. The doctors did run tests on Sharon and determined that they might save her by using antidotes to the poison and did so with a battery of drugs and charcoal filtration treatment for the next twelve hours. Bob knew this, because he was there the whole time. Why he told this lie to Ohlman is not clear. Perhaps he just liked toying with the truth, and wanted to see how much he could get away with. Or perhaps the word "truth" was not part of his vocabulary. He often stretched it beyond the bounds of reason.

Bob did utter the words "Damn, I always knew she would do something stupid." These words may have been for the consumption of the medical staff that heard them, showing that Bob was indeed angry by her suicide. But the words were more true than he might have suspected, because the now-expired Sharon Cooper Spangler was about to turn his whole world upside down. Three dead wives and two dead children in less than sixteen years was one too many to ignore. The wheels of justice were a long time in coming, but the day that Sharon Cooper Spangler swallowed an overdose was the day they began to start turning. It was ironic in a way, the only wife he hadn't murdered, at least according to the story he would later tell authorities, would do Bob Spangler in, in the end.

Chapter 9

Glimpses of Deceit

For all his dexterity in eluding prosecution for his crimes, the fact of the matter was that Bob Spangler didn't know when to shut up. He liked basking in the glow of the attention as a tragic figure who had survived the deaths of his wives and children. In late October 1994 he contacted Bernee Davey, Donna's daughter, and told her, "Tragedy has struck once again. You recall I wrote you last May that my former wife, Sharon, might be renting a room here for a time as she sought to get her life resettled and under control. She did that, saying, incidentally, that she wished she could have met and become friends with your mother, who obviously was a very neat lady who taught me to be a much better person than Sharon remembered."

Bob went on to say that things had been going along pretty well for Sharon under his roof. He and Sharon got along much better as friends than they had as husband and wife. He related that Sharon had established a meaningful relationship with a man named Michael and that seemed to be progressing well.

Then he added, "Her long history of self-doubt, anxiety disease and clinical depression finally overwhelmed her. She took her own life with pills, dying in a hospital here Sunday morning, October 2."

Bob also contacted one of Donna's sons and had the gall to inquire if he would like to go on another hike in the Grand Canyon. He said that the fall colors would be very nice. A short time later, he wrote the son and said, "Thank you again for your call last month. I am pretty well convinced it had become just too painful for you to be in touch with me. And I could understand that perfectly. But talking with you always reminds me of your Mom because you were her favorite, and I hated losing that association."

Bob went on to say that he planned to take a batch of wildflower seeds to the Grand Canyon in the spring and scatter them at "Donna's Point." Donna's Point just happened to be the place where he had pushed her off the cliff. That he could write these things without a shred of remorse indicates just how vacant his conscience was. As Sharon had always said, "Bob could roll over and go to sleep like a baby. Nothing seemed to bother him."

But Donna's son was no fool. And he began to mull over the circumstances of his mother's death, the strange way Bob acted at the memorial service and the news that Sharon was now dead. He'd already been told by Bob that his first wife had killed the children and then herself. All of this, along with small inconsistencies about Donna's death, began to prey upon his mind. One of the things that irked him most was the way Bob had cremated Donna's remains so quickly after her death, without consulting her children. And the fact that Spangler did not have a celebration of her life with friends, but rather a somber memorial service that he presided over.

Even the final resting place of her ashes became somewhat of a mystery. Jim Ohlman, who was in touch with Spangler at the time, contended that her ashes may have ended up in different places. "In August 1994, he (Bob) mentioned burying Donna's ashes in two places, one along Paine Ridge in the La Plata Mountains. The other in the backyard. As for Sharon, he probably put most in the backyard. But I feel he also managed to slip an ounce or two into the Grand Canyon somewhere."

Bob only added fuel to the fire in this regard by his actions with Sharon's cousin Richard, who was the executor of her estate. Bob always claimed he didn't make money off his dead spouses, but that was not the case, and his legal battle with Sharon's cousin would prove just how far he was willing to go to earn even insubstantial amounts.

From the 1988 divorce settlement, signed by both Bob and Sharon, it was agreed that he would receive $20,000 from her estate if she died before him. Sharon's cousin, who lived in Florida, had to make numerous trips to Colorado to take care of her estate. In the process he ran up bills that came to $5,000. He charged this against the $20,000 Bob was to receive, leaving him with $15,000. But Bob wanted the full amount and took Sharon's cousin to court. Even though Bob had gained quite a lot by Sharon's death—the suspension of paying her $400 a month and giving her the $5,000 gift he'd promised for 1995—he still wanted every penny he could get.

In the end he won in the court battle and received the full $20,000. Sharon's cousin was so infuriated by the whole affair, he never wanted Bob Spangler's name mentioned in his presence again.

Bill Burnett, one of Donna's friends who had known her since the 1970s, was suspicious when he heard about Sharon Spangler's death. He was suspicious enough to phone the Coconino County Sheriff's Office Criminal Investigative Division in Arizona. Burnett's phone call was taken by Detective Lieutenant Rex Stermen. Burnett proceeded to tell him about Sharon's supposed suicide and the death of Nancy Spangler back in 1978. This caused enough concern in Lieutenant Stermen that he told a member of his unit, Detective Bruce Cornish, to look into the matter.

On November 4, 1994, Detective Cornish spoke with Bill Burnett on the telephone. Burnett said that Donna's death had always bothered him and he didn't think it was an accident. And now that Sharon was dead, all of the wives and ex-wives who had died around Bob Spangler was just too much to swallow. Burnett knew Donna's daughter, Bernee, and she had related Bob's letter to him about Sharon's suicide. More than anything else, this letter had spurred Burnett to call the Coconino County Sheriff's Office.

Burnett related to Detective Cornish that Bob had hiked nearly a thousand miles in the Grand Canyon over the years and knew a lot of its dangers. He also knew that Bob realized Donna had vertigo and was not a strong hiker. He said that Bob had no business taking Donna on that particular trail. Burnett did admit to Detective Cornish that he didn't know of any problems between Bob and Donna at the time of her death. He also didn't know if Bob ever collected any insurance money from her demise.

None of this was much to go on, but Detective Cornish decided to investigate the matter anyway. He phoned the Durango Police Department about Sharon's suicide, but they said they didn't have any records of a suicide in October 1994. Next he phoned the La Plata County Sheriff's Office. They did know about Sharon Spangler's death, but they told him they hadn't investigated the matter and that he should contact the La Plata County Coroner's Office for more information.

On November 7, Cornish spoke with Deputy Rye about what he had seen at the spot where Donna had fallen off the cliff at the Grand Canyon. Rye told him the area where Donna had been hiking was extremely rugged and there were numerous loose rocks at the location of her death. In his estimation it would have been very easy for someone to accidentally fall in that area.

Rye told Cornish that Bob Spangler was an experienced hiker and should have known better than to take Donna on that trail. He did, however, say there was a particular spot where Bob indicated he had set up his camera to take a photo, just as he had written in his report. It was a good place to take a photo with them in the foreground and the Canyon in the background. Rye also said he would not have picked the spot that Donna had fallen from to murder someone. At that spot it appeared to be only a twenty-five-foot to thirty-foot drop off the cliff. But there was a chute that couldn't be seen from an area at the bottom of the cliff and it descended at least another hundred feet. Even though the chute couldn't be seen from the trail, its presence is what definitely killed Donna Spangler.

What Deputy Rye may not have known was that Bob had hiked this very trail several times. He knew all about its terrain and may have even known about the rocky chute that descended below the Redwall, even if it couldn't be seen from "Donna's Point."

At around the same time that Detective Cornish began his investigation, Sharon Spangler's suicide popped up on the Arapahoe County Sheriff's Office "radar screen." This came about because Bill Burnett decided to call them as well about his suspicions. He talked to Sergeant Steve Curti in the Investigation Division. At 3:00 P.M. on November 4, 1994, Sergeant Curti made a very important phone call. He asked Investigator Paul Goodman to look into the death of Sharon Cooper Spangler. He knew there had always been suspicions about Bob Spangler's innocence concerning the deaths of Nancy, Susan, David and now Donna.

Investigator Goodman brought up some old files and discovered that Nancy, Susan and David had died on December 30, 1978, Donna Spangler on April 11, 1993, and Sharon Cooper Spangler on October 2, 1994. None of this was suspicious on the surface, except that they were all fairly young to be dying so suddenly from unnatural causes. On November 7, 1994, at about 10:00 A.M., Goodman contacted Detective Cornish in Arizona and filled him in on the details of the Nancy Spangler death case. Detective Cornish discussed a little about Donna's death and agreed to send Goodman a copy of his report. Cornish said Donna's case had been cleared in Coconino County and labeled an accidental fall. But it was now being reopened by his office and he was going to look into it. During their conversation Investigator Goodman told Cornish another interesting thing. He said that Bob Spangler had taken two polygraph tests in 1979 and had controlled his breathing. It could not be determined whether Spangler was being truthful or lying. When asked why he had controlled his breathing on the second test, Bob had replied, "Because I received training in public speaking and that's the way you're supposed to breathe when you're nervous."

Detective Cornish told Goodman that he'd contacted Investigator Larry Backer of La Plata County (where Durango was located) and wanted to know more details about Sharon's suicide. But so far he hadn't received a return call from him. Investigator Goodman thought it might be a good idea to contact Investigator Backer as well and he telephoned him on November 8. Backer told him that his department had not been notified at the time of Sharon's death and that Deputy Coroner Dick Mullen had done all the paperwork on Sharon and ruled it a suicide. That meant that the La Plata County Sheriff's Office had not become involved.

Investigator Goodman took on the old Spangler-Littleton case as a sort of fill-in, just something to be looked into in his spare time. He had plenty of other cases to work on in Arapahoe County and could not keep at it full-time. Nonetheless he was interested and a month later he contacted Investigator Scott Jackson in Durango, La Plata County. Jackson informed him that the coroner's report there indicated that Sharon had been suicidal before and often depressed. She had supposedly even talked to Dr. Boyd at the hospital indicating that she had taken a lethal dose of alcohol and pills. No sheriff's investigation had taken place and none was ongoing now.

On November 21, 1994, Detective Cornish spoke

with Donna's daughter, Bernee Davey. She told him about the letter she had received from Bob Spangler after Sharon's suicide. Bob told her in the letter that the suicide had occurred in part because of Sharon's problems with her boyfriend and her long history of mental illness. But he also twisted this story one more time, saying he couldn't awaken Sharon after he returned from his soccer game that day. This was in direct contradiction to his other story to Jim Ohlman that Sharon had been awake when he went into her room.

Bernee told Detective Cornish she wasn't sure if Bob had pushed her mother over the cliff at the Grand Canyon, but she did have questions about the circumstances. One of the things that bothered her was that Bob supposedly wore a hearing aid most of the time. But he had told her that when he hiked in the Grand Canyon, he never wore one. Bernee wondered if he wasn't wearing a hearing aid, how could he have heard Donna gasp or take a small breath before she tumbled over the side?

Detective Cornish called all four members of the group who had hiked on the Grand View Trail and kept crossing paths with Bob and Donna Spangler on April 10 and 11, 1993: Mark Stephen, Rick Morgan, Kevin O'Leary and Elizabeth Duncan. All of them told him things that had occurred that they thought were strange about Bob Spangler's actions on those dates. Mark Stephen told Cornish about Bob trying to keep tabs on all of them, especially where they were going to camp for the night of April 10. He even related, "Bob said, 'I'm keeping an eye on you.'"

Rick Morgan told Cornish, "If you were going to

harm someone, it would be a good spot. It would be out of the way and they would be alone."

Kevin O'Leary related Bob's curious remark right after they had exchanged addresses that he might need a new hiking partner in November, and if Kevin would like to be his partner. O'Leary thought this remark was way out of line considering that Bob's wife had just died a few hours before.

Detective Cornish contacted several of Donna's friends in the Durango and Evergreen areas. Some thought that the relationship between Bob and Donna had been just fine in 1993. But not everyone agreed with that assessment. Chief among the doubters was Sandy Brooks, who had known Donna in the Evergreen area and also knew that she was afraid of hiking in the Grand Canyon. She told Detective Cornish about her remark to Donna in April 1993, saying that she didn't have to go there if she was scared. But Donna indicated that she was going because Bob was so insistent.

In December 1994, Detective Cornish spoke to Donna's son Bruce Sundling. Bruce said that he hadn't seen his mother and Bob since Christmas 1992. He felt at that time that Bob controlled his mother's life and was very domineering. He realized that she had a hard time talking to Bob. She had told him that Bob was very set in his ways and didn't like change. Then she related that they didn't seem to have much in common.

Cornish asked Bruce if Bob owned a 35mm camera with an automatic timer. Bruce said he remembered such a camera and it did have an automatic timer. In fact, Bob had used it when he and Donna and Bob had gone on a hike in the Grand

Canyon in 1992. Bob had set the camera on a rock and had taken a photo of all three of them.

Detective Cornish spoke with Dr. Boyd in Durango and discovered the fact that he had been not only a physician to Donna Spangler, but to Sharon Spangler as well. For Donna he had prescribed Meclizine for vertigo and Prozac for depression.

All of these anecdotes were intriguing enough for Detective Cornish to pay Bob Spangler a visit at his Durango home on August 8, 1995. Bob was somewhat surprised by Cornish's unexpected visit, but didn't seem overly concerned when he let him into the house. They both sat down on separate couches and Bob seemed relaxed as they talked. Cornish asked him why he had taken Donna on such a dangerous trail, since he knew she wasn't such a good hiker. Bob replied, "The trail was wide enough to walk down and I didn't believe it was overly dangerous. Besides, we did go very slowly on the hike."

Cornish asked him what medication Donna had been taking. Bob answered that he didn't know she was taking any medication at all, except maybe for asthma. This was in direct contradiction to remarks he made to others and even in his newspaper remarks. Bob claimed not to know that Donna needed Meclizine for vertigo or that she even had vertigo.

Detective Cornish asked Bob about wearing a hearing aid. He said that he did have trouble hearing soft-spoken people but did not wear a hearing aid. Asked why he had camped at the illegal spot near the mine entrance on Horseshoe Mesa when he knew that was illegal, Bob answered, "We camped there to get a head start the next day. I knew it was illegal, but that was the reason."

Detective Cornish had already made preliminary

plans to have Bob tested on a polygraph at the San Juan County Sheriff's Office in Farmington, New Mexico. He now appraised Bob of that fact and told him it would be a good way of clearing his name of any suspicions people might be holding about Donna's death. The reaction from Bob Spangler was like nothing Detective Bruce Cornish had ever seen before. Almost immediately Bob jumped off the couch and began pacing the floor. He hyperventilated and muttered to himself, "Should I do it? Should I talk to him?"

Finally, with almost a wild look on his face, he explained to Detective Cornish that he had taken a polygraph test in 1979 because of the "tragedy" in Littleton, and it had been a horrible experience. He said he had hyperventilated then because he was so nervous.

Bob was certainly hyperventilating now and Cornish would comment later, "It was a very bizarre scene. I had never witnessed something like this before. I would have been less suspicious after visiting there if he hadn't acted in such a strange manner. But his actions were way off the chart."

Detective Cornish tried to allay Bob's fears about a polygraph test and told him that if he took one, he could tell Donna's kids the results and give them some peace of mind. This information about Donna's kids only seemed to make Bob more upset. Now he knew who had pointed Detective Cornish toward his door. Bob adamantly insisted he would not take a polygraph test for anyone, including Donna's children.

When Detective Cornish left that day, he had an overall impression of Bob Spangler as a man with something to hide.

Two weeks after Cornish's visit to Bob Spangler's home in Durango, Bernee Davey received a letter from Bob. He told her never to contact him again and he would not help her in any of her suspicions about the way Donna had died, nor would he help any of Donna's children ever again.

Three more months elapsed between Cornish's visit to Spangler's residence and Investigator Goodman's speaking at length with Dr. John Boyd of Durango about Sharon's suicide. Dr. Boyd told him that Sharon had said to him after being admitted on October 1, 1994, "I took an overdose," before she slipped into a coma. Dr. Boyd didn't seem to think the circumstances indicated foul play.

But Detective Cornish had been conducting his own investigation and had some interesting things to tell Goodman. He said that Donna Spangler's children felt that Bob had been in a rush to cremate her body. They also said that Donna had sold her house in Evergreen, Colorado, on Bob's insistence so they could both purchase the house in Durango. When it came time to draw up the deed on the Durango property, Bob had wanted it in his name only. He had only backed down when Donna stood her ground on this one issue. He grudgingly relented and both their names were included.

The biggest eye-opener of all was the family questioning why Bob had taken her to the Grand Canyon that fatal Easter week. He knew she suffered from vertigo and was not a strong hiker. She had even indicated her fears about the place to them and phoned each one of her children before leaving on the trip. It was as if she had a premonition that something bad would happen there. As with all the rumors swirling around Bob Spangler, there was no solid evidence. It was a combination of everything that made him look suspicious.

Investigator Goodman's caseload was heavy for the next five months and he only returned to the Spangler investigation after a long delay. But when he did, it was with a bang. He phoned Bob Spangler in Durango, Colorado, on April 14, 1995, and asked if Bob still owned the gun that had been used in a murder/suicide back in Littleton. Bob told Goodman that he had sold it after picking it up at the Arapahoe County Sheriff's Office when his name had been cleared.

Investigator Goodman asked him if he had copies of the autopsy reports on the deaths of Nancy, Susan and David. Bob said that he didn't.

Then Bob Spangler asked Investigator Goodman a question: "This all comes about because of Detective Cornish, I presume?"

Goodman cagily answered a question with a question: "Why would Detective Cornish of Coconino County, Arizona, be interested in an Arapahoe County, Colorado, case?"

Bob didn't answer the question. He abruptly changed the subject and tried eliciting information from Investigator Goodman, but Goodman wasn't playing that game and gave him nothing helpful.

Throughout the rest of 1995 Investigator Goodman tried getting information about Bob Spangler's financial records through various insurance companies and other companies to see if Bob had benefited from the deaths of his various wives. But because of the way the state financial laws were structured, he couldn't get any of the information he sought.

In early 1996 Investigator Goodman started working with Arapahoe County's new coroner, Dr.

Michael Doberson. It was a very frustrating time, since Goodman couldn't find any of the original autopsy reports and all of the other physical evidence from the Nancy, Susan and David Spangler case seemed to be missing as well. All the tissue samples that were normally held were never found. Whether they had been destroyed or lost in the intervening years, no one knew. But luckily for Goodman, Dr. Doberson was a good ally and became very interested in the Spangler case. Dr. Doberson was able to find some copies of the original coroner's investigative reports and toxicological reports on the victims.

In June 1996, Investigator Goodman provided Dr. Doberson with some crime scene photographs taken at the time of the deaths of Nancy, Susan and David Spangler. He asked Dr. Doberson to take a look at the photos and try to determine if all the deaths could have been homicides. If Dr. Doberson indicated that Nancy had indeed committed suicide, Goodman would drop the case and move on to something else.

Dr. Michael Doberson got right down to business. He said in his report: "At the request of Detective Paul Goodman of the Arapahoe County Sheriff's Office, I am receiving photographic evidence material from a case investigated by the Arapahoe County Coroner's Office on December 30, 1978. Very briefly, the case involves an apparent double homicide/suicide which occurred in Littleton, Colorado. The two homicide victims are named David A. Spangler (age 17) and Susan E. Spangler (age 15) and were found in their respective bedrooms with single gun shot wounds to the trunk. Their mother, Nancy Spangler (age 45) was found in the basement of the housed [*sic*] dead of an apparent self-inflicted gunshot wound to the head with an apparent typewritten note of suicidal intent nearby.

"The first photographs examined are a series of nine 8 x 10 colored photographs taken at the death scene in the basement. The first photograph shows Nancy Spangler slumped over to the right in a chair next to a wall in front of a typewriter. Photograph #2 shows a closeup of the deceased."

Dr. Doberson listed the other photographs and said of one of them, "The decedent's right hand is depicted in photograph #6, and is remarkable for a small amount of dried drops of blood over the dorsal surface of the hand and proximal fingers. The rest of the hand shows a moderate degree of rigor mortis including Tardieu spots."

In photograph #8 a close-up of Nancy Spangler's face was depicted. Doberson noted, "A moderate amount of dried blood over the right side of the face emanating from the mouth and nostrils. A roughly round wound of entrance is seen over the forehead slightly to the right of midline. Surrounding the wound and particularly apparently inferiorly, are a series of puncture red-brown to purple abrasions which extend outward to both eyebrows as well as over the left forehead. These injuries are consistent with stippling and suggest that the wound is of an intermediate range of fire rather than the typical contact gunshot wound seen in most self-inflicted gun shot wounds.

"A rough estimate of range of fire of this case would be from approximately two to eight inches. The intermediate range characteristics of the wound would make it atypical for a self-inflicted wound."

Dr. Doberson next discovered a group of photos

taken during Nancy Spangler's autopsy. Of these he wrote, "Photo #9 depicts a view into the occipital calavarium to basilar skull where a depressed fracture is seen from the interior surface. From the photograph, it is possible to estimate a direction of fire which appears to be front to back, and downward with a minimal lateral deviation." In other words, the gun was not held directly toward the forehead, but was slightly above and pointed downward. Once again this was outside the norm of most gunshot suicides.

In summation of his report Dr. Doberson wrote: "The most unusual feature of this case is the presence of an intermediate range. As noted above, self-inflicted gun shot wounds are typically of a contact nature. While the presence of an intermediate range gun shot wound does not rule out the possibility of suicide, it does allow one to entertain other possibilities (e.g. homicide). When viewed within the context of other circumstances for example, a neuromuscular condition from which Nancy Spangler suffered which resulted in weakness and unsteadiness, more questions regarding the manner of death arise. In any event, I believe these findings warrant further official investigation."

In essence, Dr. Michael Doberson gave Investigator Paul Goodman a green light to keep investigating Bob Spangler as the possible killer of his entire family in Littleton back in 1978. Goodman obtained an anatomically correct model of a human skull in August 1996. Using autopsy photographs that Dr. Doberson supplied, Goodman and senior lab technician Dick Hopkins determined the probable wound path for Nancy Spangler's fatal gunshot wound. A one-eighth diameter rod was placed through the skull to depict this path. A toy gun, similar to the actual .38 revolver, was installed on the rod to show placement, distance and angularity of the weapon.

To back up his claims, Dr. Doberson provided Investigator Goodman with a copy of *Sites of Suicidal Gunshot Wounds,* a study conducted by the King County, Washington, Medical Examiners Division. In the study it was revealed that out of 226 cases, firearms were used in 165. Of those 165, 82 percent of them were to the temple. Only 7 percent were to the frontal area of the head, where Nancy received her fatal wound. Furthermore, only 25 percent of the women studied used firearms to kill themselves. Women generally committed suicide by slashing their wrists or taking an overdose. And the few women who did kill themselves by guns, they usually did not shoot themselves in the head. They usually aimed for the heart. Most of them had not wanted to disfigure their faces in death. And to further show the irregularity of Nancy's wounds, almost no women held the gun at length to shoot themselves. Those who used guns generally pressed them against their bodies. Nancy holding the gun at some distance became even more improbable when it was recalled she had weakness in her right hand and could not hold a heavy object like a gun steadily.

In November 1996 Investigator Goodman met with Arapahoe County lab technician Diane Cloyd and Colorado Bureau of Investigations lab technicians Tom Griffith and Ted Ritter. After reviewing photographs, both Griffith and Ritter stated that they found the deaths of Nancy, Susan and David Spangler to be suspicious. One of the questions they had was how long a period of time would there have been between the wound to Nancy and her actual death.

Dr. Doberson mulled this question over and replied that he could not be certain how long it took Nancy to die from the time of the gunshot. In his opinion it was possible that she could have immediately become unconscious but still have moved for up to several minutes after being shot. And then he had a question of his own. He wanted to know why the original medical examiner, Dr. Wood, was so certain that the bruising on Nancy Spangler's right wrist was caused by her firing a powerful handgun. In Dr. Doberson's opinion the bruising was not caused by that at all. He told Investigator Goodman that he thought the bruising was actually Tardieu spots, which were caused by hemorrhaging of the minor blood vessels under Nancy's skin. Doberson explained this often occurred when blood rushed to a lower extremity in a person's body. In Nancy Spangler's case her right hand had fallen to the floor after she was shot. It was the lowest point of her body and blood had collected there. Dr. Doberson did not believe that Nancy had shot herself at all. Someone else had, and Investigator Paul Goodman had a good idea who that someone was.

Dr. Doberson had an expert back him up as far as the Tardieu spots went. He was forensic pathologist Dr. Dominic DiAmaio. Dr. DiAmaio's report cited numerous cases where a victim's limbs hanging over the side of a bed or a chair would collect Tardieu spots, and these spots developed two to four hours after death. This was right in the time frame in which Nancy Spangler's body was being photographed by investigators.

Bob Spangler was a fullback and captain on the best high school football team in Ames, Iowa, history.
(Yearbook photo)

BOB SPANGLER, *Fullback*

Bob Spangler (bottom row, center) was also a member of the Ames High School basketball team.
(Yearbook photo)

Nancy Stahlman, Bob Spangler's high school sweetheart, became his wife in 1955. *(Yearbook photo)*

Bob Spangler (third row, third from right) was in the Sigma Delta Chi fraternity at Iowa State. *(Yearbook photo)*

On December 30, 1978, Spangler murdered his entire family
in his home in Littleton, Colorado. *(Author's photo)*

Spangler shot his daughter
Susan, 15, in the heart.
(Yearbook photo)

When son David's wound
proved not to be fatal, Bob
smothered him to death with
a pillow. *(Yearbook photo)*

Spangler killed his family so he could marry Sharon Cooper. *(Courtesy of Jim and Janece Ohlman)*

While Nancy Spangler closed her eyes and waited for a surprise, Spangler shot her in the forehead. *(Courtesy of Arapahoe County Sheriff's Office)*

Bob Spangler used this pistol to kill his wife and children. He may have used the sock to try to cover up his fingerprints. *(Courtesy of Arapahoe County Sheriff's Office)*

... I may now that I've decided to do this? I found ... accident some time ago and couldn't help thinking ... I don't know why I didn't say anything. I feel ... We always argued about who'd have the kids. I will. ...'ll get along. You always have.

n.

Spangler typed this "suicide note" and tricked Nancy into signing it. *(Courtesy of Arapahoe County Sheriff's Office)*

Arapahoe County Sheriff's Investigator Paul Goodman never gave up in his quest to bring Bob Spangler to justice for killing his family.
(Courtesy of Paul Goodman)

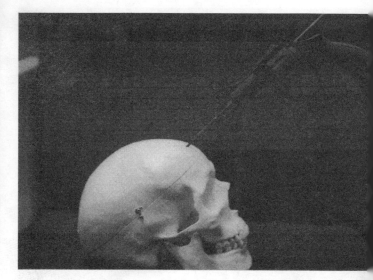

Using this toy pistol, Goodman determined the angle and distance from which Spangler shot his wife.
(Courtesy of Arapahoe County Sheriff's Office)

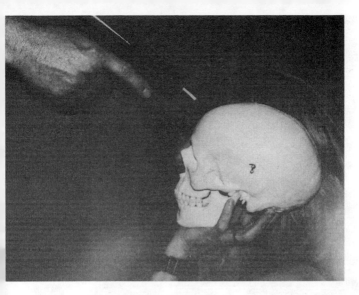

Goodman had a Sheriff's Office female technician pose
as Nancy Spangler to reenact the crime.
(Courtesy of Arapahoe County Sheriff's Office)

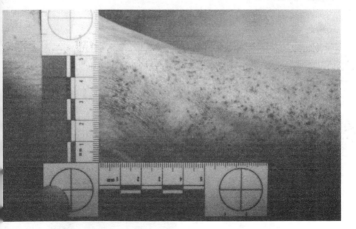

These tardieu spots on Nancy Spangler's wrist
were a key bit of evidence in her murder.
(Courtesy of Arapahoe County Sheriff's Office)

Sharon Spangler loved hiking in the Grand Canyon with Bob.
(Courtesy of Jim and Janece Ohlman)

Bob and Sharon Spangler and Jim and Janece Ohlman were all excellent hikers and backcountry adventurers.
(Courtesy of Jim and Janece Ohlman)

Bob Spangler became an avid hiker and amateur botanist and geologist in the Grand Canyon. *(Courtesy of Jim and Janece Ohlman)*

Spangler was fearless about heights, but endangered himself and others with his cavalier attitude about safety. *(Courtesy of Jim and Janece Ohlman)*

Donna Sundling, 56, married Bob Spangler on August 18, 1990, becoming his third wife. *(Courtesy of Bruce Sundling)*

Spangler bought this home in Durango, Colorado, with the help of wife Donna's money. When Sharon Cooper Spangler committed suicide here, it sparked intense police scrutiny of Bob. *(Author's photo)*

Bob Spangler pushed Donna Spangler over a cliff from this point on Easter Sunday, April 11, 1993. *(Courtesy of Coconino County Justice Center)*

Due to high winds, it was risky for a helicopter to transport Donna Spangler's body out of the Grand Canyon. *(Courtesy of Coconino County Justice Center)*

Donna fell 25 feet to the spot where her hat landed, then tumbled more than 100 feet to her death. *(Courtesy of Coconino County Justice Center)*

Bob Spangler covered Donna's face with a bandana and hiked to the Grand Canyon's South Rim to tell authorities about her "accident." *(Courtesy of Coconino County Justice Center)*

Spangler badgered law enforcement authorities to have them
return this diamond ring to him after he murdered Donna.
(Courtesy of Coconino County Justice Center)

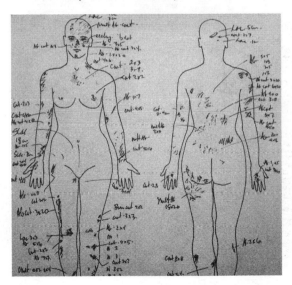

An autopsy sketch revealed the numerous injuries Donna
Spangler suffered after her fatal fall from the cliff.
(Courtesy of Coconino County Department of Health Services)

National Park Police Special Agent Bev Perry spearheaded the investigation of Donna Spangler's death. *(Courtesy of Bev Perry)*

On October 3, 2000, Bob Spangler was arrested for the murders of Nancy, Susan, David and Donna Spangler. Here, he is being led from a Grand Junction, Colorado, courthouse. *(Courtesy of Gretel Daugherty)*

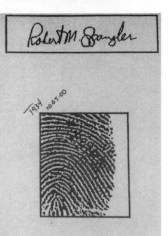

CURRENT INFORMATION

Spangler pleaded with the FBI that he not receive media attention
for his murders. His request was denied and his crimes
hit the newspapers and television airwaves.
(Courtesy of Federal Bureau of Investigation)

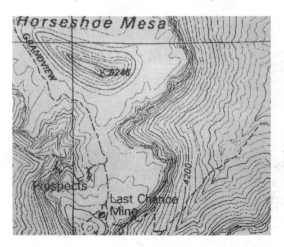

The FBI found this map in Bob Spangler's Grand Junction home.
It pinpointed the spot where he murdered Donna in 1993.
(Courtesy of Federal Bureau of Investigation)

Bob Spangler's children's grave rests on a knoll in
the Ames Municipal Cemetery. *(Author's photo)*

Nancy's grave, like those of her children, does not display
the name Spangler on her marker. It is a clear refutation of
Bob Spangler in their lives and deaths. *(Author's photo)*

It wasn't until April 1997 that Investigator Goodman interviewed a law enforcement officer who had actually been at the scene of the Spangler home in December 1978. This was Karen Beauchamp, who was now a detective with the Arapahoe County Sheriff's Office. She told him that Sergeant Marv Tucker and Lieutenant Les Murray were on the scene when she arrived. Her main job at the time had been searching the premises for any new clues. She recalled that Document Examiner Andrew Bradley had compared known typewritten samples from the typewriter recovered at the scene with the "suicide" note and Bradley had made a positive match between this note and the typewriter. He also compared known examples of Nancy Spangler's handwriting with the *N* signed on the suicide note. In Bradley's opinion, all were written by the same person. At this point Investigator Paul Goodman asked a question no one had asked before: "Was it Bob Spangler who gave Bradley the examples?"

"I don't know," Beauchamp replied.

She went on to say that even though Bob Spangler tested positive for gunshot residue and Nancy didn't, it was explainable. Colorado Bureau of Investigation experts had advised her that Bob could have handled the gun, as he said he did, and obtained levels of gunshot residue that would be traceable. There was no conclusion ever made whether Bob had fired the gun or not. The "suicide note" had looked so authentic that it had been the clincher.

Then Beauchamp told Goodman something that really piqued his interest. She said, "Jack Swanburg, the lab technician who ran the gunshot residue test, was a friend of Bob Spangler's." This was the first time Goodman had heard that.

Beauchamp ended by saying she always wanted to interview Bob Spangler about tire tracks in the snow of his driveway that were noticed on December 30, 1978. He had mentioned the trips he had taken with the car out of the driveway that morning. But the tire tracks indicated more trips than he had mentioned. If he was lying about this, what else was he lying about? Beauchamp said she never got the chance to interview Bob Spangler again.

After the final Colorado Bureau of Investigation report came in, back in 1979, Karen Beauchamp said she still had doubts about Bob Spangler's innocence. But Sergeant Ralph Severance of the Araphoe County Sheriff's Office ordered her to clear the case. The official conclusion was that Nancy Spangler had killed her children and then herself. Arapahoe County had plenty of other cases to deal with and wanted the Spangler case out of their hair.

A short time later, Goodman met with Agent Jim Alderden and his superior, Mark Wilson, of the Colorado Bureau of Investigation. After presenting his case about Bob Spangler's possible involvement, Wilson stated that he felt a further investigation was in order and that he would assign Agent Phil Wilson to help Goodman in his quest.

On May 8, 1997, Goodman interviewed Sergeant Marvin Tucker of the Arapahoe County Sheriff's Office about the Spangler case. Tucker had been there on December 30, 1978, and would never forget the scene. One thing he added to the already familiar story was that he and Coroner's Investigator Mark Hamilton had gone down into the basement after viewing the bodies of Susan and David Spangler. It was dark down there and the only dim lighting came from well-type windows. Hamilton had moved ahead of Tucker and nearly bumped into Nancy's body. When he saw it, Tucker said, Hamilton nearly jumped out of his shoes. No one had known of her presence up until that moment.

One thing always stuck in Marvin Tucker's memory that bothered him. He wanted to know why the pistol was several feet away from Nancy's body. That didn't seem natural to him. It was something that also bothered Investigator Goodman. And then there was the odd detail of a man's sock on the butt of the pistol. What possible reason could it have been there except to try and keep fingerprints off the pistol?

Much later on in the day of December 30, 1978, there was another occurrence that seemed strange to Sergeant Tucker. It was when Bob Spangler came home from his long journey around Denver and saw all the police activity at his home. Instead of being rattled by it all and the deaths of his entire family, Bob seemed to be very calm. Tucker said he thought: "He's a pretty good actor. There's something wrong here."

Sergeant Tucker contradicted Detective Karen Beauchamp in one regard. He said that she thought at the time that Bob Spangler was innocent; he and Lieutenant Les Murray did not. Tucker said he became aware after a while that there was intervention from up above to have the case cleared. He never found out who ordered it or why. All he knew was that it was closed and he thought it should have stayed open. He said that lab technician Dick Hopkins wasn't happy about the case being closed as well.

Then Tucker also recounted the story about lab technician Jack Swanburg and his relationship with Bob Spangler. There had always been something funny about that.

A week later, Goodman interviewed Jack Swanburg to get his side of the story. Swanburg told him that he had first met Bob Spangler in 1964 or 1965. At the time Spangler was doing public relations for the firm of Carl Byoir. Spangler was also an account executive there handling the Honeywell account. At that time Swanburg was employed by Honeywell in the Denver area.

Swanburg said that several times during the 1960s he would pick up Bob Spangler at Denver's Stapleton Airport and take him to the Honeywell Corporate Offices. Swanburg basically knew Bob in this capacity. Swanburg said he left Honeywell in the 1970s and became a lab technician for the Arapahoe County Sheriff's Office and he lost contact with Spangler.

Years later, he bumped into Bob Spangler while at a soccer game. By now, Bob and his family were living in Littleton, Colorado. Swanburg's son played soccer and Bob was a referee at the game. After that, he saw Spangler at several soccer games. Spangler was friendly and they chatted about old times, but it never developed into a close friendship.

The next time Swanburg saw Spangler was on the evening of December 30, 1978. He had gone to the lab to perform a gunshot residue test and was surprised to see that the man standing in his lab was Bob Spangler. This was a double surprise, since Swanburg had been in the murder home on South

Franklin Way that morning but did not know it was Bob's home or that the family killed was his. Swanburg must have been in some shock at the time. He told Goodman, "I don't remember completing the GSR Test on Spangler. But I must have."

A short time later that evening, Swanburg told his supervisor that he knew Bob Spangler. He talked about their prior relationship. His supervisor didn't think that was a problem. At some point Sergeant Ralph Severance asked Swanburg to try and get Bob Spangler to agree to take a polygraph test. Swanburg said he would try.

Swanburg then told Goodman that he knew Bob had spent at least one night at his home after the "suicide/homicide." He thought they had eaten a spaghetti dinner that night at his house. He added that he'd been given approval to have Bob stay at his home by his superiors. No one thought it was an unwise decision at the time. He also said that he and Bob did not discuss the circumstances of what had happened on South Franklin Way. Sometime that evening he convinced Bob to take a polygraph test, but when they showed up at the Arapahoe County Sheriff's Office to take it, Sergeant Severance wouldn't go through with it. He said that Bob Spangler was "too uptight" to take a test.

Swanburg said he never talked with Bob Spangler again after that. Within a short time the word was going around the Arapahoe County Sheriff's Office that Bob Spangler wasn't the victim of a tragedy but a suspect. Or as Swanburg put it: "A real hands-off person."

Jack Swanburg told Goodman that he began to have doubts about Bob Spangler's innocence at about that time. He had several unanswered questions which he jotted down.

1. Why was there a sock around the gun if it was suicide?
2. How did the gun get where it was found?
3. Were there problems with the gunshot residue test because of blood on Nancy's hands?
4. How many handwriting examples were compared to the suicide note and who furnished them?
5. What items were on the kitchen floor?
6. Was there ever a complete comparison of tire tracks?
7. Did the typewriter key strike indicate heavy handed or a light handed typist? In other words, did Nancy type differently than Bob?

From this interview Investigator Goodman concluded that Jack Swanburg had not helped Bob Spangler escape justice because of any kind of relationship they might have had. He concluded that it had merely been poor judgment on Swanburg's part to let Bob Spangler stay over his house after the murders.

By late spring 1997 Investigator Goodman was well on his way to putting together a case against Bob Spangler. And he was just about to have three other very important allies in his quest.

Chapter 10

The A Team

Paul Goodman phoned Investigator Bev Perry of the Criminal Investigation Unit, National Park Service Grand Canyon, about Bob Spangler in the spring of 1997. He'd gotten wind of the fact that Perry was conducting her own investigation of Spangler. Her investigation wasn't specifically about Spangler in the beginning. It was an overall investigation of suspicious fatal falls that had occurred at the Grand Canyon in recent years. And these investigations were handled by the National Park Police, an integral part of the National Park Service.

The general perception of rangers is of a friendly naturalist in a Smokey the Bear hat, leading people around on a nature hike. But someone had to protect not only the natural landscape but the visitors in the park as well. And these lawmen were the National Park Police. Paul Berkowitz, head of the National Park Police unit at the Grand Canyon, wrote the seminal book about national park and forestry officers, *U.S. Rangers: The Law of the Land.* He said, "It is the dual people and resource protection role performed by individuals or small groups of self sufficient law enforcement officers who 'range' over the vast tracts of public lands. I recall very early in my career viewing a large hand-carved wooden sign prominently displayed on the wall at the South Rim Ranger Station at the Grand Canyon National Park. The words eloquently and simply described the duties of Rangers:

To Protect the Park from the People.
To Protect the People from the Park.
To Protect the People from the People."

Initially the national parks had been patrolled and protected by the United States Cavalry. But in 1916 the National Park Service came into being and law enforcement rangers took over. They had to go beyond the prevalent myth that national parks were totally safe areas for the public away from city crime. In fact, the parks were also havens for dope smugglers and growers, psychopaths and gang members hiding from the law.

Berkowitz wrote a whole section on incidents involving deadly force used by rangers, starting in the very earliest days of the park service. Grand Canyon National Park was not immune to deadly force being used within its confines, right up through the period when the Spangler investigation started. In fact, Bev Perry was involved in an incident that happened right along the road that Bob Spangler had taken to murder his third wife. It began when the National Park Police got a warning that four members of the Gypsy Jokers, an outlaw motorcycle gang, were headed their way. At least one of the men had an outstanding felony warrant on him. These gang members were spotted by park rangers on the East Rim Drive. Told to pull over, they sped off instead and the chase began.

Roaring at speeds up to seventy miles an hour, the cyclists wove in and out of vacationing traffic on the narrow twisting road. The rangers kept right behind them. The bikers were seen trying to evade detection by pulling off onto a side road at Grandview Fire Tower. Cornered at the dead-end road at the rim of the Canyon, they were told to raise their hands and give up. Instead, one of them went for his saddlebag. While one ranger held a shotgun on the other three, a second ranger tackled the disobedient cyclist and pinned him to the ground. It was later discovered that this cyclist had a loaded Smith & Wesson .38-caliber pistol in his saddlebag.

Not long after this incident, it was recommended that the Grand Canyon National Park Police be issued long-distance OC spray containers, stun guns and a K-9 unit. The Grand Canyon may be a beautiful place, but it could also be a deadly place. As Paul Berkowitz wrote, "Every commissioned Ranger, Criminal Investigator and Special Agent of the National Park Service is charged with the duty of going in harm's way, where others may retreat. Ironically certain people view these parks, forests, recreation areas and public lands as places where they may completely abandon regard for laws that serve to regulate conduct."

Berkowitz broke down the groups of vacationers who visited Grand Canyon National Park into three groups: the Good, the Bad and the Ugly. The Good made up the majority of people who were there just to have a good time and obey the rules. The Bad were vacationers who made loud noise at night, drank too much and littered. They were more of an inconvenience than a danger. But the third group, the Ugly, were truly dangerous individuals. He said of them, "These people take greater risks and engage in far more daring, dangerous and threatening behavior. They believe that 'way out here' they can get away with anything. To them the pickin's are easy, the (non-law enforcement) rangers are a joke, and the real cops are few and far between."

Bob Spangler fell into Paul Berkowitz's category of the Ugly. He thought he could get away with murder at the park, but he would learn to his detriment that Bev Perry was a real cop. Perry had initially been a schoolteacher in DeKalb County, Georgia, but she was always so outdoor oriented that she quit her teaching job and became a recreation planner for the Georgia Department of Natural Resources. Good at snow skiing and kayaking, she eventually turned her love of wilderness into a career with the National Park Service. She initially became a seasonal ranger at Georgia's Chattahoochee River National Recreation Area.

Bev wasn't only interested in an outdoor job, she also found the field of law enforcement fascinating. In 1980 she was able to combine the two by becoming a law enforcement ranger at Kennesaw Mountain Battlefield National Historic Park. Completing a course in land management police training, she moved out West, first to Lake Mead in Nevada, then to Grand Canyon National Park.

As she recalled about this period, "During my time as a uniformed park ranger, I was a medic and member of the technical rescue team as well as a scuba diver and boat operator. It seems that death investigation and concerns for surviving family members have gone hand in hand with these interests and, all together, led me to reopening the Spangler case. I was the supervisory park ranger over the Back Country District at the time of Donna's death at the Grand Canyon. Based on an agreement between the park and the Coconino County Sheriff's Office at the time, the National Park Service role was limited to the initial response and recovery operation."

Then in 1995 Bev attended classes in the Criminal Investigation Training Program at the Federal Law Enforcement Center in Georgia. By the time she returned to the Grand Canyon in 1996, she was special agent criminal investigator Bev Perry. She noted that there were so many things about Donna Spangler's "accidental death" that were slightly atypical. None of them standing alone was enough to raise a red flag, but when put all together, they did give out a warning signal. There had been a rash of fatal falls in 1993, but they all occurred from one of the rims, except for Donna's death. Donna's fall was unusual because it came from within the inner canyon. And just the name Spangler raised Bev Perry's antenna a couple of notches. She knew that both Bob and Sharon Spangler were considered veterans in the tight-knit Grand Canyon hiking community. She had even met Sharon once at the Back Country Office and they had discussed Sharon's project of writing a book about trails on the South Rim. And Bev certainly knew Bob vicariously from Sharon's descriptions of him and his comments in *On Foot in the Grand Canyon*. From what she knew about him, it was unexpected that a hiking partner of his would end up dead on a backpacking trip.

Another signal was the park ranger folklore that

was making the rounds just then about Bob Spangler. It was told half in jest, half seriously among the rangers: Bob had given his wife a "Grand Canyon divorce." This was a term used to convey spouses who had conveniently pushed their mates over the side and then claimed it was an accident.

Nick Herring, one of the rangers who had first spotted Donna's body beneath the Redwall, even came up to Bev at one point and said, "Do you think he did it?"

She answered honestly, "I don't know."

Most of all, there was the spot of the "accident" on Horseshoe Mesa. On first glance it was an improbable spot for Bob to have murdered his wife. Why go to all the trouble of hiking that far and killing her there? Statistically, most fatal falls occurred from the rim. But as Bev Perry thought about it more, she decided it was a perfect spot for murder. From the vantage point of the promontory where Donna fell, Bob could have looked both up and down the trail to see if anyone else was in the vicinity. It was a seldom-used trail, especially at that time of day. And even if anyone had been in the area, the very nature of the spot would have made it difficult for them to see him as he pushed her over the side. It was a steep escarpment and the chance of anyone falling from there surviving was minimal at best. And even if they did survive, there were ways Bob could get down to make sure they didn't recover. The same would not be true of a push from one of the rims. The victim could fall to a ledge, survive the fall, and there would be no way for Bob to climb down and finish them off. All in all, Bev Perry decided it was a "smart place if you wanted to murder somebody."

Always curious about the death of Donna Spangler, Bev Perry asked her supervisor, Paul Berkowitz, if she could look more fully into the so-called "accident." Berkowitz had his own misgivings about Spangler and gave her his wholehearted approval. Bev's investigation got an added incentive when she eventually learned of Sharon Spangler's "suicide" at Bob Spangler's home in Durango, Colorado. As she said later, "We did not investigate Sharon's death, as we had no jurisdiction in that area. I do believe, however, that Bob at least manipulated Sharon to suicide. Interestingly, he was with her at the hospital the entire time from her admittance until death. Certainly, some of that time he would have been alone with her, and would have had opportunity to make sure her attempt was successful."

Bev still didn't know about the deaths of Nancy, Susan and David in Littleton back in 1978, but the deaths of Sharon and Donna were enough to make her really start feeling that something was amiss.

As time went on, Perry collected bits and pieces of information about Bob Spangler's activities. Just like Paul Goodman, she had other cases on the table, so she couldn't spend full-time on the Spangler case. However, the information she gathered was enough to make her want to learn more. She kept speculating about Bob Spangler's choice of a campsite on the night of April 10, 1993. He was enough of a Canyon veteran to know the site was illegal for camping purposes. And she wondered, why take a woman who had difficulty backpacking, trekking on the difficult Page Springs Trail? Bev knew that very few fatal falls at the Grand Canyon involved backpackers. They generally concerned the casual tourist who was goofing around at the rim or had imbibed too much alcohol. Donna Spangler did not fall into either of these categories.

Then there was Bob's unusual behavior at the Back Country Office when he reported the "accidental" death. He had stood patiently in line until his turn came and then calmly reported the matter. It certainly wasn't the demeanor of a distraught husband who had just lost his wife in a terrible accident.

The Spangler case was on the back burner for Bev Perry until a real turning point came in 1997. Just like Detective Bruce Cornish's phone call to Paul Goodman, Cornish's call to Investigator Bev Perry lit a fire under her case as well. Donna's children had been begging him to look further into the matter. He passed on to both Goodman and Perry what he had learned.

This phone call propelled Bev Perry's investigation of Bob Spangler from part-time status to full-time status. She also received a phone call from Paul Goodman about this time, and he filled her in about his investigation into the deaths of Nancy, Susan and David. This was a revelation to her and it added further incentive to investigate Spangler's Grand Canyon activities. There was definitely a pattern when it came to Bob's wives and children. They all died such unexpected deaths.

Goodman and Perry exchanged case files and promised to keep in touch with each other. Investigator Goodman related that he was having trouble getting the Arapahoe County District Attorney's Office to go forward in writing up a probable cause warrant against Bob Spangler. The prosecutor told him that the case was too old and had been closed by the Arapahoe County Sheriff's Office. Besides, almost all the physical evidence had either been lost or destroyed in the intervening years. The prosecutor thought that a case against Spangler would never hold up in court. Goodman was experiencing all the frustrations of gathering evidence on a case that might go nowhere in court in Colorado. It really rankled him that Bob Spangler might escape justice because so much of the original tangible evidence was either misplaced or destroyed.

Then Bev Perry had a bright idea. If Arapahoe County, Colorado, did not want to prosecute Bob Spangler, perhaps the federal court system would. It was just possible that Bob Spangler had murdered his wife, Donna, on federal land—Grand Canyon National Park. All the evidence Paul Goodman had been collecting would not go to waste. In fact, it would help strengthen Bev Perry's own case with a list of prior bad acts. Investigator Goodman said he was willing to go this route. Anything was better than letting Bob Spangler escape justice. If they couldn't get him for murdering Nancy, Susan and David, then they'd get him for Donna.

Bev Perry was in luck as far as the federal angle went. She approached the local FBI office in Flagstaff, Arizona, for help in the matter. As it turned out, the office was now headed by a new regime, one willing to work with other agencies. This had not always been the case in the old FBI. They tended to guard their secrets carefully, ride rough shod over local agencies and take all the credit when a conviction came. But the new head of the Flagstaff office, C. McDermitt, instituted a policy of cooperation in his district. He had been in the FBI's Behaviorial Science Unit, and the information Bev Perry gave him about Spangler intrigued him.

A supremely important meeting took place in

the Flagstaff FBI office in early January 1998. Paul Goodman was there to present his facts, as well as Detective Cornish and Investigator Bev Perry. McDermitt listened to all they had to say and agreed that the accusations they brought against Bob Spangler had enough merit to get the FBI involved. After presenting his facts, Detective Cornish said that Coconino County would not become involved in the investigation. His office was mainly concerned about expenses in a cold case that might go nowhere. Goodman and Perry, though, were in it for the long haul.

McDermitt decided to add one more component to the mix, and his decision was a good one. He said he would assign a new FBI agent to the area to help Goodman and Perry coordinate their efforts and lend backing of the FBI's resources. He couldn't have picked a better man for the job: Special Agent Leonard "Lenny" Johns.

Lenny Johns was an Air Force Academy grad before becoming an FBI agent. He convened sessions with McDermitt and they decided to charge Bob Spangler with a white-collar crime, wire and mail fraud scheme. The reason they took this approach was that they surmised Bob had somehow benefited financially from the deaths of his various wives.

Since Arapahoe County wasn't going to prosecute on the Littleton murders, something else had to be found concerning the death of Donna Spangler. All the team members knew that the case would have to be well documented and airtight. There was very little physical evidence left to bring into court. They would have to gather so much circumstantial evidence against Bob Spangler that he would plainly see they had him dead to rights and that it would be in his best interests to confess and cut a deal. In effect, they had to play a high-stakes poker game no matter what cards they held, and bluff Spangler into folding his own hand that he had played so well for so long.

This problem of tracking Bob Spangler's financial angle was mulled over by McDermitt and Lenny Johns. The case with Donna especially stuck out in this regard. He had made her sell her Evergreen home and put the proceeds into the Durango home, and after she died, that home was his alone. But McDermitt and Johns weren't excluding Sharon from the mix. Special Agent Lenny Johns wrote in an initial brief: "Sharon Spangler died of an alleged drug overdose. She was found by Robert Spangler and taken to the hospital where she subsequently died. It is presumed that, due to the frequency and suspicious circumstances surrounding the deaths of Spangler's wives, an investigation should be instituted regarding the possibility of insurance fraud, mail fraud and fraud by wire."

As coordinator of the team, Special Agent Lenny Johns assigned Goodman and Perry special tasks to perform and areas of investigation. Goodman would concentrate on the Littleton details and Bev Perry on the Grand Canyon. And very early on, Bev Perry made one very important request. She touted the hard work and success of former Coconino County prosecutor Camille Bibles, who had just become a prosecutor for the United States Federal Court, Phoenix. She said that Camille Bibles, assistant United States attorney (AUSA), would be an excellent choice to head the judicial angle of this case as it developed. Lenny Johns spoke with Bibles and agreed. He even wrote down in a memo: "Camille Bibles was a county prosecutor here and well-liked by law enforcement. Bev Perry strongly advocates Bibles."

Camille Bibles might have taken a very different path from being a prosecutor if not for a colleague in Coconino County. She had majored in zoology and her prelaw work was as an instructor teaching outdoor skills, such as rock climbing, backpacking, caving and paddling. She fully intended to work in law protecting the wild areas of America, but she was drawn into criminal law by a Coconino County prosecutor who wanted to capitalize on her background in biology. He was working on a case that involved a man who had killed his pregnant girlfriend, and he wanted Bibles to help him because of her background in biology. It was the John George case, and her testimony helped convict him and eventually send him to the gas chamber.

As Camille said later, "The minute I hit the courtroom, I knew that it was home for me and I have never looked back. My biology background was a huge benefit in prosecuting violent cases."

Her next criminal case concerned the first use of DNA allowed in court in Arizona. It dealt with a man that had the proximate last name as her own, Richard Lynn Bible. She handled the scientific forensic evidence in the case and went on to specialize in violent crime prosecution. She even did a stint as chief deputy in the district attorney's office. But she realized her real love was in the courtroom and that she just wanted to prosecute and not deal with administrative duties.

From that point on, her prosecutorial career ran the gamut. She successfully prosecuted an Apache

County man for killing an endangered Mexican gray wolf; she prosecuted men who had attempted killing police officers, and gang members who had tried to murder a Phoenix prosecutor; she prosecuted Judy and Donald Booty, who had tortured their two-year-old toddler to death.

One of the most troubling cases Bibles tackled was against Todd Lee Smith, who had murdered an elderly vacationing couple not far from the Grand Canyon. Smith was a violent drug abuser who threatened to cut off his own mother's fingers, one by one, if she didn't cash bad checks for him. When vacationers Clarence and Elaine Tannehill pulled into a campground near Smith's home in August 1995, he broke into their trailer, beat them, slit their throats and robbed them. He was eventually caught and arrested.

Calling Smith remorseless and depraved, Camille Bibles successfully sought and received a death penalty conviction against him in May 1997. It sickened her that violent individuals such as Smith would use the Grand Canyon area as a scene of murder. As she related, "In my free time, I explored the outdoors, and the Grand Canyon is a favorite, special place for me. I have hiked its interior many, many times. It was one of the places that I sought for balance against the horrors that I saw at work."

Once she came on board as a team member amassing evidence against Bob Spangler, she saw within him a new and different desecration of the Canyon she loved. She said later, "Bob Spangler used the Grand Canyon, a place that is one of America's cathedrals, as a murder weapon."

* * *

The remarkable thing about the four members of the investigative team—Paul Goodman, Bev Perry, Lenny Johns and Camille Bibles—was how well they all worked together. Law enforcement and judicial personnel do not always mesh with members of other agencies. Territorial lines come into play and egos can be easily bruised. Right from the beginning, however, there was none of that with these four. They all had a common goal and they worked toward it without fanfare or posturing. The goal was to bring Bob Spangler to justice and stop him before he could murder anyone else.

Each of the members of the team brought special characteristics to the table that complemented the others. Paul Goodman was thorough and had a gift for interviewing. Camille Bibles was tireless in putting all the information together for its future use in court. Lenny Johns was a good coordinator, able to assign tasks to the others that needed to be performed in their own areas. And Bev Perry was the spark plug to prod the others on when things bogged down.

One of the main reasons for having the FBI involved was because of their deep pockets. This was one of the reasons that Coconino County had decided not to come on board. They weren't sure there would be a payoff for all the money and time spent on a case where the suspected murders were years old. The FBI also had resources that the other agencies just could not match. Investigator Goodman wrote in one report about this aspect of the investigation: "The US Attorneys Office made arrangements for psychological assistance about the perpetrator throughout the investigation. Each agency left the meeting with a list of items to be completed." Lenny Johns was typically the man who would make up the list and set a time frame for its implementation. He realized, as did the others, they all had other cases to take care of as well as the Spangler case. In fact, some of these were much more pressing than the Spangler case.

As the investigation got well under way, a very curious thing happened in 1998. Bob Spangler, who loved Durango, suddenly decided to leave the area. In a letter to the editor of Durango's *Herald,* Bob wrote a piece headlined AN END TO COUNTRY MUSIC MORNINGS. He said that it had been a terrific seven years in Durango, playing country music. And he thanked all his friends for making his stay in the area so satisfying.

He thanked all his loyal listeners, and then he wrote something interesting as far as the investigators were concerned. Bob said, "Everything is fine. I've had no problems. But there are new opportunities I want to pursue in Pennsylvania. So I'm off to a new life there. God Bless. Bob Spangler."

Mark Schelper, KRSJ marketing director, was stunned by this sudden revelation from Bob. He knew that Bob was pretty heavily involved with a woman who lived in a nearby suburban complex. They had been dating fairly intensively for some time, even though they were very different personalities, according to Schelper. "But they were an item," he added.

And Schelper knew that Bob was enthralled with the Grand Canyon. He told Bob, "You love Durango and this area. And what about all your hikes in the Grand Canyon? You'll be so far away."

Bob looked at him and calmly replied, "You grow out of things, sometimes. And move on."

Much later, Mark Schelper would think, "Yeah, grow out of things like wives and families and move on."

At this point Schelper began to wonder if Bob Spangler had indeed murdered Donna at the Grand Canyon. He already knew the rumors going around the radio station. This sudden move seemed to give them credence. And Mark wondered if there was a police investigation going on that precipitated Spangler's sudden move.

But the investigators knew something that Mark Schelper didn't. The "new opportunity" Bob wanted to pursue in Pennsylvania was a woman. A woman who now had to be protected if things got out of hand.

Bob had met this woman in a chat room on the Internet. They exchanged numerous messages and both liked what they were reading about the other. She was about Bob's age, and in the lexicon of the investigative team, she would become "the Pennsylvania Woman." She was given a geographical identity to conceal her real name.

Bob was so enamored with this woman that he decided to sell his house in Durango and move to Pennsylvania. As Bev Perry later said, "She and Spangler met in the chat room and everything was great over the Internet. Then one day he suddenly showed up, uninvited, on her doorstep. It really freaked her out. Here was this man who literally popped out of nowhere. He was very pushy right from the start and wanted to move in with her. He told her he wanted to get married right away. This was all too much for her. I think she glimpsed something from his dark side. She wasn't like the other women he had steamrolled. She was feisty and able to stand up for herself. She eventually told him to get lost."

Paul Goodman added, "They may have seemed compatible over the Internet, but they weren't at all in person. She was a night owl and he was not. There were more differences between them than similarities. It didn't take him long to leave the area."

Having made a fool of himself on this foray for romance, Bob Spangler could hardly go back to Durango after telling everyone of his great "new opportunity" in Pennsylvania. Instead, he gravitated to Grand Junction, Colorado, in the northwestern part of the state, about two hundred miles north of Durango. And there was method to his madness of moving there. He later told a friend, "There's a lot of divorced, single women in Grand Junction." Bob fully intended to find himself one.

On January 27, 1999, Special Agent Johns held a teleconference with all the other members of the team as they sat by their phones in their respective offices. The case had taken on such vast logistical distances that Goodman was sitting in mid-Colorado, Bev Perry at the Grand Canyon, Camille Bibles in mid-Arizona and Lenny Johns in Flagstaff, Arizona. Johns told the others he was seeking a mail cover through the United States Postal Service and would be working on a federal subpoena in getting Bob Spangler's financial records. He hoped to have better luck than Paul Goodman had in obtaining these documents. If he could follow the money trail, he might be able to discover how much Bob benefited by the death of each wife.

By May 1999 there was also a new plan of surveillance. It was learned that Bob Spangler had applied for a permit to hike in the backcountry of

Grand Canyon National Park that summer and Special Agent Lenny Johns and the others wanted to watch him as he moved through the Canyon. They surmised they might discover something useful while he was there.

In a memo dated May 17, Lenny Johns wrote the Phoenix FBI office, "Case agent requests that the following agents (names deleted) be approved for holiday pay, lodging and per diem to accommodate the surveillance of Spangler in the Grand Canyon." Johns added, "Assistance is required because there may be opportunity for a chance to contact Spangler on the hiking trail and at camp sites that he plans to overnight. Special Agent (name deleted) will be paired up with a female Park Service Special Agent to hike into the Canyon and do close surveillance, possibly contacting Spangler to gain personal information from him. Case agent will prepare a list of topics to discuss with Spangler. Should this opportunity arise, Special Agents (names deleted) will assist other Park Service Agents with surveillance of Spangler along the rim of the Canyon and at his hotel room."

National Parks investigator Bev Perry was also conducting her own surveillance that year. And she went one step further. Bob Spangler was on friendly terms with one particular backcountry park ranger who often issued him permits for backpacking in the inner canyon. She wanted this ranger to chat with Bob and gather any information he could from him. Since Bob was taking new dates on Canyon hikes, it was always in the back of the team's mind that the women might be in some danger if things somehow went wrong as they had in the past. This had to be prevented at all costs.

Another means of keeping tabs on Bob was by soliciting information from his friends and former coworkers. One of the FBI reports covered comments a hiking colleague of Bob's made to another Grand Canyon veteran around this time: "I hiked from Cremation Canyon to Indian Garden on the Tonto Trail with (name deleted), an acquaintance of Bob Spangler. He said he knows Spangler and stayed with him at his home in Durango. I don't recall when he said this took place. According to (name deleted) Spangler told him that Sharon and he had been living together at Spangler's home and Sharon had her own room. According to this acquaintance, Spangler told him that Sharon was terminally ill and was taking numerous medications. I don't recall if a particular disease was mentioned. Later Spangler returned home one day and saw a note on Sharon's door. He went inside and found her dead."

Once again Bob was changing stories, just as he had done about how Nancy, Susan and David had died. To some people in Grand Junction he was now telling the familiar stories that his children were killed by Nancy, and to others that they had died in a car accident. And now he was telling this person that Sharon had been terminally ill before committing suicide. The team members wondered just how much Bob had helped her become "terminal."

The FBI went so far as to monitor a Web site that had been set up as a memorial to Sharon Spangler. This Web site was put together by an outdoor enthusiast who knew Sharon well. It wasn't clear if he knew anything about Donna's death, but he did know about Sharon's suicide because of an e-mail

Bob had sent him, and he passed the news along to other Grand Canyon stalwarts.

The Web site was called, "In Memory of Sharon Spangler," and both it and Bob's response added new insights into Sharon and Bob's lives. The Web host had written: "There are good days and bad days and this week I encountered another one of those dreaded bad ones. The episode began when I received an e mail from a guy named Bob Spangler, who's [*sic*] name did not register and I just let the memo sit in my box for awhile. When I finally started to read the memo a few hours later I was shocked. Oh, you're that Bob Spangler, Sharon's husband!"

The Web host wrote that he was first "psyched" because Sharon's book, *On Foot in the Grand Canyon,* had inspired his first real backpack trip into the Grand Canyon. He had always wanted to meet Sharon and he thought that Bob's e-mail was bringing him a step closer to that reality.

Then he learned from Bob that Sharon had died back in October 1994. He said that in that instant he realized that all his hopes were dashed. "I had hoped to meet Sharon someday and sometimes wondered if I would ever run into her and Bob somewhere in the depths of the Canyon." He expressed how it would have been wonderful to sit down and exchange Canyon stories with her. After Bob's e-mail he knew this would never happen and decided to construct the Sharon Spangler memorial Web site.

The Web host asked Bob to contribute a short biography about Sharon and add it to the site. What Bob wrote about the woman who had committed suicide in his home was very revealing.

He began that he'd first met Sharon in 1976 when he'd needed an assistant in Denver and she walked through the door. He said that she was the obvious choice in a large field of candidates. Bob told about how they had become friends and eventually married (omitting all references to his first wife, Nancy, and his children). He said that after a long motorcycle tour of the West Coast in 1979, which was their honeymoon trip, Sharon had suggested a hike in the Grand Canyon on the way back to Colorado. They took the hike and he had been in love with the place ever since.

Bob told of Sharon's childhood in St. Louis and eventual career as a Grand Canyon author. He added that Sharon was much more than that in her "too brief lifetime." She was a teacher, dog trainer, yoga instructor, stock broker's assistant and recipient of a degree in communications. But he believed her greatest contribution was introducing so many people to the wonders of hiking in the Grand Canyon. He spoke of how she had planned to write a second book about trails into the Canyon from the North Rim, but it was never meant to be.

Bob wrote: "I have continued to hike the canyon, delighting especially in communicating with other afficianados and helping newcomers get started. I love guiding first timers and experiencing their thanks and joy as Sharon and I first experienced it all those years ago. I miss her very much. What a wonderful, talented, creative woman was Sharon Spangler, one of the Grand Canyon's most eloquent friends."

In response to the memorial site, e-mails and comments came in from around the nation. One person wrote, "Your tribute left me with tears about to spill despite my reading it while at work. I too have shared those dreams of sitting on a limestone shelf, low in the Canyon, trading stories with her."

Another man from North Carolina wrote, "I just caught your tribute to Sharon Spangler and was stunned also to learn of her death. Such an energetic articulate and apparently devoted worshiper of the outdoors isn't supposed to die so early. We envision such perceptive people as having a degree of immortality, something that seems only natural for one who communes with nature so regularly, so peacefully, so harmoniously."

The man went on to say that he had given Sharon's book to his wife to read as an introduction to hiking the Canyon. His wife was not a strong backpacker and was fearful of hiking in the Grand Canyon. In some ways she sounded just like Donna Spangler, and it was ironic that the man had given her a book that was associated with Bob Spangler. What was even more chilling was the fact that occasionally Bob would leave messages on the Web site. The man wrote to the site's owner, "Please forward my appreciation to Bob Spangler for sharing his thoughts."

The FBI kept close watch on this Web site to see what other thoughts Bob Spangler might have about Sharon or Donna. He was always full of inconsistencies, but every so often he let the truth leak out.

During this period Special Agent Johns took a very close look at Bob Spangler's written statement that he had produced for the National Park Service right after Donna's "accidental" death on April 11, 1993. Johns wrote several comments right on a copy of Bob's statement, outlining his thoughts about certain sections. Where Bob wrote, "I positioned Donna" (at the promontory), Special Agent

Johns wrote above it in bold print, **"Admits physically adjusted her."**

Spangler's statement: And turned to mount
the camera.

Johns' comment: *Doesn't* **say moved away to
mount.**

Spangler's statement: I looked over the edge
and saw her some 200 feet below.

Johns' comment: **He's right there. Doesn't
move. Doesn't race.**

Spangler's statement: I dropped my pack and
ran back down the trail.

Johns' comment: **He now hurries.**

Spangler's statement: There was no pulse, her
legs were badly broken.

Johns' comment: **She no longer has a name.
No horror, no grief. Emotion missing.**

Spangler's statement: I carried her pack up to
where I'd dropped mine and for some
reason tossed it up behind some bushes
and walked out.

Johns' comment: **Cavalier action. What's the
meaning of this? Abrupt ending.**

Special Agent Lenny Johns also took a closer
look at Bob Spangler's written statement he had
given the Arapahoe County Sheriff's Office in 1979
after the deaths of Nancy, Susan and David. Once
again Johns made comments in relation to certain
passages of Spangler's statements.

Spangler's statement: I told my wife.

Johns' comment: **Only time he used the word
"wife."**

Spangler's statement: Nancy indicated.

Johns' comment: **She's no longer his "wife."**

Spangler's statement: I recall seeing a neighbor whose dog was out by the curb.

Johns' comment: **Opening door for an alibi.**

Spangler's statement: I just started repeating, "Oh, my God. Jesus!"

Johns' comment: **Thinks this is what someone who cares would say.**

Spangler's statement: I didn't even think of the children at the time.

Johns' comment: **No regrets. Never says he misses them.**

Special Agent Johns also compiled a list of questions and comments about various aspects of the deaths of Nancy, Donna and Sharon Spangler. Many of them covered old ground, but a few were new variations on the theme.

Concerning Nancy, he wrote:

1. Nancy's blouse had no powder pattern on it.
2. Nancy's hand would cramp and she could not write with it. Robert often filled out checks and Nancy signed them.
3. No identifiable latent prints were developed on the typewriter. No latent prints were found on the pen or note. Distinct wipe marks were developed and photographed on the typewriter.

Concerning Donna, he observed:

1. Donna walked with two cross-country ski poles for balance.

2.   Bob collected Social Security survivor ben-
     efits from death of Donna, as well as $8,000
     from a mutual fund, not to mention the
     house.

Concerning Sharon, he wondered:

1.   What toxic levels of what drugs were in her
     bloodstream?
2.   Who was the source of the drugs?
3.   Bob no longer had to pay $400 a month
     until July 1, 1997. A total of $12,800.

Such odd statements in Bob's reports and lack of
grief on his behalf led Lenny Johns to ask for an
FBI profiler to be assigned to the case. Special
Agent Johns contacted Bev Perry, Paul Goodman
and Camille Bibles in a teleconference to discuss
this suggestion. He knew he would need their cooperation for the possibility of a profiler's
assistance. Each one of them would have to provide
information and their own insights about Bob
Spangler for this to work.

All three of the others agreed this was worth pursuing. Investigator Paul Goodman went so far as to
prepare a multimedia presentation about Spangler
for the profiler. They well knew that all the FBI profilers were terribly busy and turned down about 80
percent of the prospective cases sent their way by
outside agencies. But they also knew that Bob Spangler was not your run-of-the-mill killer. He was
well-spoken, educated and able to hide his crimes
for a lengthy period of time. They were certain that
Spangler would pique the interest of the National

Center for the Analysis of Violent Crime (NCAVC), at Quantico, Virginia.

Arguably, the first profiler was a Manhattan psychiatrist named James Brussel in the 1950s. He worked on a case concerning "the Mad Bomber," who was planting bombs around the New York City area. Over the course of years the police were getting nowhere on tracking down the bomber. In frustration, a Manhattan police lieutenant suggested they use the services of Brussel.

Brussel looked at crime scene photographs, along with notes and letters from the bomber. After careful analysis he suggested that the person behind the bombings was probably a single, heavyset, middle-aged man living with a female relative. He also said the man was probably a Roman Catholic and had been a former Con Edison employee. He suggested this last item because the first two bombs had been set on Con Edison property. When police finally arrested George Metesky as the Mad Bomber, all of Brussel's predictions came true. Metesky fit all the categories.

It took a while for law enforcement agencies to accept profilers as anything more than a modern sort of witch doctor. By the 1960s the FBI began a prototype profiling unit and by 1972 it became the Behavioral Science Unit. The unit painted a broad picture of suspects by keying in on probable areas of gender, age, race, economic status, residence, education and family background.

Still somewhat of a stepchild within the FBI, the unit got a huge boost when Agent John Douglas became head of the FBI's Investigative Support Unit. One of the chief tools he developed was the art of the interview. He said that the profiles he created were accrued by interviewing serial killers and other violent offenders to see how they thought. Over the years he interviewed the likes of Charles Manson, Sirhan Sirhan, Richard Speck, John Wayne Gacy, James Earl Ray and David Berkowitz. He told reporters, "You have to try and walk in the shoes of the people who perpetrate the crimes. You do that by really rubbing shoulders with them."

Douglas and his colleagues veered away from strictly psychological terms when describing suspects. They no longer used words like "paranoid," "schizophrenic" or "psychopath." Instead, they created their own lexicon with words describing serial killers as "organized" or "disorganized." As Douglas told an audience at a seminar, "I'm interested in behavior. I'm interested in knowing what these people are made of, and what makes them target a certain victim."

By the 1990s, in the cases that the FBI profilers took a look at, they were correct about 80 percent of the time in their assessments of individuals who were eventually caught and arrested. And by the time Special Agent Lenny Johns's investigative team was asking for FBI profiling help, the unit was now known as Criminal Investigative Analysts of the National Center for the Analysis of Violent Crime. They were headquartered in Quantico, Virginia. And though the entire unit contained only thirty individuals, and received over a thousand requests from law enforcement agencies, the Spangler team was right about one thing. The NCAVC was indeed interested in the Spangler case and took it on for analysis. The profiler who got the Spangler case at Quantico was Agent Gerry Downes. He was good at his job and had a well-respected reputation within the unit for the accuracy of his assessments.

Gerry Downes received copies of the investigators' case work, including written letters and statements by Bob Spangler. As Bev Perry said later, "We also provided details we learned about Bob's life in general, what we believed was important to him and what was not." By this means Gerry Downes was able to build up a profile about Bob Spangler concerning his psyche and habits.

With all of this information and profiling help, Bev Perry said, "We were closing the circle tighter and tighter around Bob Spangler."

One thing the investigators became aware of about Spangler after his Pennsylvania foray was that he was trolling, via the Internet, for new female companions. And this practice really intensified once he was in Grand Junction, Colorado. The one fear in the back of the team member's minds was that he'd find a companion and make her a new wife. Once they were married to him, wives of Bob Spangler did not have a long life expectancy.

Chapter 11

Ladies' Man

One common thread in Bob Spangler's life was that he didn't like living alone. He may have grown tired of women that he didn't find appealing anymore and found unconventional ways of making them disappear from his life, but the fact of the matter was that he always needed one around. The problem was that they were exciting for a while but slowly lost their appeal. Then they had to be disposed of.

One theme about Bob Spangler held true in Grand Junction as it had in Durango, and that was that Bob was perceived as a good neighbor. A couple who lived to the right of him on Applewood Street, John and Joyce Williams, certainly ascribed to this perception. Joyce said, "He was a friendly neighbor. He always said hi. He jogged a lot in the neighborhood. He seemed very active and fit. A nice gentleman with a nicely groomed beard. His appearance was always very neat and he kept a clean house and yard."

John added that Bob had a wry sense of humor and twinkle in his eye when he told a joke. "They weren't the belly-laugh kind, but very dry. Almost sarcastic, but funny."

Both Williamses noted that Bob was friendly with the boys across the street and tried to get them to join a soccer league. "He was a ref," Joyce said, "and I heard he was good at it."

Since Joyce knew that Bob was single—just what lies he told her about his former spouses is not clear—she planned to set him up with one of her single-woman friends. She decided she would invite Bob to dinner and the woman too. Just a casual affair and see if they clicked. But for some reason it never came off. Later, when she found out about the "real Bob," she thanked her lucky stars that the dinner never happened.

Bob probably would have welcomed the dinner. He was definitely cruising the Internet for single women in Grand Junction at the time. In fact, it was almost becoming an obsession with him. In this new town he was no longer a local celebrity as a DJ as he had been in Durango. Bob Spangler turned more and more to the Internet for love and companionship. He might have been more circumspect in this activity if he'd known the FBI would eventually use these e-mails against him. But without this knowledge Bob Spangler plunged right into the dating game. A lot of the names of the women he was contacting via the Internet have been blacked out in the FBI reports, to protect their privacy, but what he had to say to them came through loud and clear. Never one to shy away from touting his own athleticism, despite the fact that he was now sixty-six years old, Bob constantly tried steering his new prospects toward backpack trips. Especially to the Grand Canyon.

In an e-mail dated April 4, 1999, Bob wrote to one prospective partner and hiker who was to go on a trip with him, "Ya know so far as sharing gear is concerned, about the only things we'll have in common are a stove and water filter. Everything else is personal and pretty much unshared—food, clothing, ground cloth. Oh we can pass trail mix back and forth. I don't think it will be too much of a risk to set out with high hopes and a gallon or so of water apiece in the packs."

The next day, he e-mailed a male friend about what he'd like to do for the coming year. Since the next year was 2000, and there were Y2K concerns in 1999, Bob alluded to a Y2K Web site on the Internet. He told of a man who wanted to move to Australia, set up a Y2K community and fill it with nice-looking eligible women. Bob wrote, "You'd have to tell him you have a friend (me) who wants to come along."

But Bob didn't move to Australia. Instead, he picked up the threads of a romance with a woman in Colorado who had enticed him for months. The only problem was she had so far seen their relationship as being just friends while he wanted it to go to another level. Since her name has been blacked out on the e-mails by the FBI, it's not clear if she was the woman in Durango whom Mark Schelper knew about, or one who lived closer to Grand Junction. (Most indications are that she lived near Grand Junction and the timeline seems to fit that supposition.) What is clear is how much he wanted her, and she took on the nickname of "the Lady," an acknowledgment of just how much he wanted her more than any other. Bob told her, "Can you stand being peppered with attentiveness both aurally (telephone) and visually (computer) like this? Or is it all just a bit much?"

He was indeed constantly phoning and e-mailing her, and he soon related: "You have only yourself to blame, of course, what with encouraging a communicative gentleman such as myself to become attached to you, not to mention being such a delightfully bright, cheerful, intelligent, beautiful, good humored, well spoken, active, capable individual whose warm outgoing personality is pure pleasure to experience. Given such circumstances, how could such intense interest NOT be aroused and sustained?"

It was interesting for the FBI to monitor these activities as far as Bob's social life went, but they were also concerned in his e-mails about Grand Canyon treks he was planning on taking. They were aware that every so often there would be a moment of truth in Bob's statements—a moment when he came out behind the gentlemanly mask and admitted something he generally kept hidden. But there was another purpose for this surveillance as well. If Bob took some female companion on a hike and she somehow just happened to have an "accident," they wanted to know about it right away.

Bob also had to submit a request to the park service for a trip into the backcountry of the Grand Canyon, and it was a good way to know when he was going there and with whom for surveillance purposes. On April 22, 1999, Bob e-mailed a friend about an upcoming hike. "We're on to Boucher [Trail] Sunday, over to Hermit—Monday, Monument—Tuesday, and out on Wednesday. No doubt we will head immediately for our room at the Yavapai [Lodge] for showering and the general task of preparing to reenter civilization."

But the main purpose of Bob's e-mails during this period was to keep in touch with the Lady and find new female companionship, most likely without her knowledge. As for the Lady, he told her that he wouldn't be able to talk to her for a week because of the upcoming hike. He said that hadn't happened since January. He related that he fully expected to enjoy the hike, but that he would miss her. Then he mentioned that he really anticipated the hike they would take together in the Canyon later that year. "I will have you all to myself in the Canyon," he wrote. "You are an exceptional individual."

He laid on all the flattery once more. "You're bright, strong, just over flowing with endearing characteristics. You are a joy to be with. It feels good just being near you, talking, touching occasionally, laughing together. In these brief months you've become immensely important to me. I'm so glad we met. I'm confident fate has good things in store for us."

When it came to the Lady, Bob acted more like a lovesick teenager than a sixty-six-year-old man. Because she wouldn't give herself to him fully, she became his ideal woman. She was the treasure he could not quite obtain. It spurred on his romantic notions about her. He would sign off on the e-mails with "Love, affection, admiration, appreciation and all that good stuff."

In May of that year, Bob couldn't help crowing about his part in a search-and-rescue mission in the Grand Canyon while he was on a trek with a male companion. These kinds of episodes always got his juices going. It concerned a young man who was unfamiliar with the trails of the Canyon and had gone astray. As Bob related to an acquaintance, "He got good and lost, ran out of food, tried to find a way up a side canyon and started dropping his stuff. I was so wrapped up in this missing person case I completely forgot to get us squared away (for an upcoming hike)."

Bob had been hiking with another man from California when they stumbled across someone's pack and other gear that had been abandoned in a side canyon. Bob found the hiker's permit and discovered the young man was completely in the wrong area from the one he had designated. Even worse, the hiker was scheduled to have been out of the Canyon a week before. This was no joke. Year after year novice hikers died of dehydration in the inner canyon.

Bob said, "When we found his pack and clothing dumped along a side canyon, we assumed the worst."

Bob dug into the man's pack and came up with a billfold. Inside he saw the man's driver's license and one more thing, the phone number of the young man's mother. With this bit of information, Bob and his companion began a trek to reach a ranger before it was too late for the young man. It's hard to know exactly what Bob felt in this instance. He may have felt compassion for the lost hiker and even a sense of concern. But what also comes through in the rest of his statements is how much he dug the role he was now playing, that of rescuer. He managed to contact a ranger named Bil (correct spelling) Vandergriff and fill him in on the circumstances of the lost hiker. He told a friend later, "I spent a couple of hours talking to the ranger about the incident." He said the ranger was kind enough to phone him at home with word that they'd called the young man's mother. Bob related, "They learned he was just fine. He'd gotten out with the help of another hiker and gone home without bothering to tell anyone." Then Bob added that the young man never wanted to set foot in the Grand Canyon again.

Ranger Bil Vandergriff had taken the original report from Bob Spangler, and as Bev Perry recounted: "We decided to use this to our advantage. Interestingly, Spangler seemed to make a connection with the gear he found and his son David who had been murdered. There was some artwork in a journal which apparently reminded him of some drawings David used to do. More important to me at the time was I saw this incident as a way to initiate a contact with Spangler that would seem appropriate to him. I was out of the park at the time of the report, learning about it only after Spangler had already returned to Grand Junction. Ranger Vandergriff knew about the larger investigation and let me know about it immediately upon my return.

"Spangler's report of finding this property and his expressed concern for the owner was appropriate and frankly appreciated. But my interest in contacting Spangler was to learn the identity of a woman friend I had seen him hiking with during a surveillance of his departure from the Hermit Trailhead during a hike some months prior. Since Spangler seemed genuinely interested in the welfare of the missing hiker, I decided to have Ranger Vandergriff call him and let him know we'd located the young man and thank him for making the report. I thought this would be a welcomed call and that he'd be pleased to know the outcome. From this opening, I wanted Bil to engage Spangler in conversation about hiking, and if not volunteered, to make a reference to his woman friend by name. I picked the name 'Jennifer' for him to use as it was the name of a co-worker easily remembered and explained as to where the name came from. Our hope was to be corrected by Bob and get the actual name of his friend. I wanted to know who she was for two reasons. One, she was someone we needed to eventually interview and two, she was potentially at risk. A motivation for me in this case always included concern for the next woman who got involved with him, especially if they married him.

"The call went well initially, with Bob being friendly and quite appreciative that we'd taken the time to call and let him know the outcome of the search. However, he seemed to have already gotten past any sentimental references to his son David. When Bil dropped the name Jennifer, I think we got a glimpse of the killer Bob. His voice went very flat and cold in tone, saying simply, 'I never told you her name.' Bob at some level seemed to recognize how he sounded and brought his charm back almost instantly. It was obvious he didn't like us prying into his life, but must have concluded it was a harmless comment on Bil's part and that his response was too abrupt. He never actually told Bil her name, but he gave the initials of her nickname and enough about her work that we were able to identify her through Detective Goodman's contacts in Grand Junction. I listened to the entire conversation but did not talk to Bob at all."

Bob would have been less enthused about all his e-mails going back and forth if he'd known just how much they would eventually help the investigators keep track of his activities. During one e-mail he said he was going to ref some soccer matches in the Grand Junction area and then go down to the Virgin Islands with his brother for a couple of weeks. While there, he'd try some snorkeling and stop off in the Appalachians on the way back to try kayaking and visit friends.

Once Bob was back in the Grand Junction area, he spoke of fixing up his new home on Applewood Street: "I've finished refurbishing my home here with a new roof, new carpeting, new paint everywhere inside and out. I'll get some perennial plants planted now and then sit back and enjoy everything."

But Bob was too restless just to sit back and enjoy things on his own. He wanted a female companion and he kept up a multifront war in that regard. He would keep on cajoling the Lady to be with him. And he would troll for prospective new feminine company via the Internet.

As far as the Lady went, the much anticipated Grand Canyon trip with her did not take place. Sullenly Bob wrote a friend, "Bad news. One darn thing after another. My relationship with her seems to get better or worse at unpredictable times. Anyway, we are experiencing a noteworthy flare-up at present and she decided to cancel the Grand Canyon trip."

Later, they must have patched things up because Bob related that he and the woman were going to take a trip to the Virgin Islands. But his ego was still bruised and he sarcastically wrote: "The choices

came down to which of the two events she wanted
to do most, and that turns out, surprise!, two weeks
worth of water fun instead of a short week of
desert/canyon."

Another flare-up must have occurred before the
end of June 1999 with the Lady. He told her, "It's
no fun to conclude something that seemed so
promising, but really isn't. There's no apparent reason why it isn't."

He mentioned that if he wasn't on top of her
"every day by phone or in person, things might
change for the better." He hoped they would eventually be more than just friends. "At least it's worthy
of further exploration," he said. "It's no secret how
I felt about you from day one. You knocked me off
my feet. Damn, I really don't like this! I suppose
we'll survive. But I'd much prefer surviving together instead of apart."

He then told her he wouldn't bother or call her
so often, but he'd always be there for her if she
changed her mind about their relationship.

Perhaps to take his mind off her, Bob hiked in
the Grand Canyon again with some companions.
And he gloated about his athletic abilities compared to theirs. In a message to a friend he wrote:
"I guess I've been doing this so long I've just become unable to see the trails as others do. They
don't seem all that difficult or demanding to me,
while my trail mates are gasping and having real
trouble. We saw a bighorn on the cliffs and a huge
grand daddy rattlesnake with about 14 or so rattles.
Very exciting."

Bob may have enjoyed the Canyon hike, but his
thoughts were never far from the Lady. He soon
forgot his promise not to bother her and was soon

e-mailing her once again, pestering her about their relationship. "Are you still wondering about trying to figure out what happened to us? Surely yes. Couldn't very well invest six whole months and not spend at least a few days at the end analyzing what on earth went wrong."

He wanted to know when she first felt things weren't working out. He dwelled on her rejection of him. In the past it was he who had decided when a relationship was over. The fact that a woman was rejecting him was unbearable.

He told her, "I try to imagine what there is about us, about our relationship, about me during those months, that would, if not turn you off, at least fail to turn you on. I think pretty much everything else on my part was there."

And then he described himself as attentive, undemanding, humorous, eager to please, kind, considerate, always available, always interested and optimistic. He asked her what was missing. In Bob Spangler's estimation of himself he was a paragon of virtue and ought to be irresistible to her.

Later, he asked, "What do you think the other men in your life had or did that created a sexual attractiveness I have clearly been unable to project?"

He said that at first he thought it might have been because they started going out so soon after she had broken up with another man, but then he reminded her that at that time she said she wanted a new relationship. This certainly wasn't turning out to be the relationship Bob wanted. In the past, when he went after someone, he usually got her. He was always driven to attain his goal, whether it be a tough hike in the Grand Canyon, climbing a rock wall or obtaining a woman.

Bob implored her by saying, "If you ask me, we are two pretty neat people who deserve to be in love, somewhere, somehow, with someone. Friendship is not bad; in fact, it is great. But I want that and love too. And so do you, I know."

Bob wouldn't give up on the subject. Rejection was just too painful for him and perhaps it harkened back to his dark fears of being adopted. After all, if his own mother had rejected him, what did that say about other women? Rejection meant loss of control. Rejection dredged up painful thoughts that perhaps at heart he really wasn't worthy of being loved.

He contacted the Lady again soon thereafter with the questions "Is there still a chance? Any likelihood or even a faint possibility?"

For one brief moment he looked at things as they really were and wrote, "I suppose not. If the chemistry isn't there, if the magic hasn't occurred, somehow I have a hard time imagining a turnaround." But in almost the next breath he said, "Still, pretty nearly anything is possible."

Bob was a man who knew the meaning of possibilities. If he could make his entire family disappear so that he could have the woman he wanted at the time, then anything did seem possible.

Even more than the woman in Pennsylvania, the Lady had really gotten under his skin. It only spurred him on to obtain what he couldn't have. And here he deviated from many other killers. For other serial killers, they often murdered the people they couldn't have, out of sheer frustration and anger. But not Bob. He first wanted the object of his desires. It was only after a woman became mundane and lost her magic, he would turn murderous. When she was his wife and had a financial hold over him, it only upped the stakes.

Bob's continued promises not to bug her were soon broken by a new e-mail. He wrote: "It just didn't evolve into a romance, and why on the earth not? Shoulda, coulda, mighta, oughta. But didn't. Damn!"

And then he turned to pop psychology to help him in his battle to win her over. He told her he had recently read *Men Are from Mars, Women Are from Venus*. He reiterated what the author said, that sometimes there was no particular reason why certain men and certain women didn't click. These individuals hadn't done anything wrong, they were perfectly nice people, but they just weren't the right one for the other. He asked her, "Is that your feeling?"

He said he understood this concept, but there was a huge gap between Bob's understanding the concept and accepting it. He pulled a line right out of the book when he told her, "In the meantime I can be your male Diane companion, whenever you need/want company."

Perhaps it was this rejection by her that propelled Bob to try something that he hadn't done before. He applied for and got a small role in a dinner theater production of *Annie* in Grand Junction. Speaking of the rehearsals, he told a friend later, "I got one of the multiple parts, which include such things as a homeless person in a Hooverville, a member of Roosevelt's cabinet, etc. Still new to the trade to warrant starring parts, but even on this small scale the new experience is extremely interesting to me."

The rejection by the Lady also made Bob troll in

the Internet dating waters at an increased rate, all while he still begged her to patch up the relationship. Bob contacted a new woman in a nearby Colorado town and told her that someone would have to look to James Michener's book *Hawaii* to understand her name's derivations. (She apparently had an exotic name.) He said her name was strikingly beautiful and distinctive of the islands. He asked her if her name had any further holistic meaning.

He also was not shy in telling her that they were meant to meet—why else had he seen her ad a week after it was supposed to have been pulled from the site? From her description and narrative, he told her she was witty, impish, intelligent and had all the qualities he admired immensely. He really laid it on thick for a woman he had never met. He added that she was strong, independent, capable and no doubt brimming with other qualities. He told her she was utterly delightful.

Then Bob described himself, and he must have been feeling some desperation at this point. He gave away more about his early life than usual. Bob said he had grown up in Iowa, had taken an early retirement years before and that Grand Junction was an excellent place to live. He also told her that he had followed job opportunities to New York, Minneapolis, then back to New York, where he'd started a second career in public relations. Without any irony he told her, with full knowledge of the murders he had committed, "There are many, many details and life events laced through those years."

Bob wanted to know why she had picked the small town of Telluride, Colorado, to live after having inhabited cities on both the East and West Coasts. He admitted that "there's a great appreciation of holism there, but surely if that had been most important, you'd have chosen something like Sedona, Arizona."

Then surprisingly for Bob, he tweaked her about this in a negative way. He said, "Perhaps there was some life event there that kept you away?"

Subconciously, perhaps he was thinking of his own "unpleasant life events" that kept him on the move away from cities where he had committed murders.

Bob told her that life for him was good, and would be even better with someone to share it with.

At some point he contacted the Telluride woman and said, "Chemistry is the key ingredient. We can exchange further data at a distance or do it in person. If you have a day or so to spare sometime soon, I could drive to Telluride and we could walk a trail or two while checking out one another's auras and attitudes."

In retrospect it was amazing to watch Bob Spangler in his chameleon act, becoming whatever he thought the woman in the ad or over the Internet may have wanted to hear. In this instance he was becoming "New Age Bob," speaking of holism and auras. In another instance he could be "Sophisticate Bob" or "Athletic Outdoorsman Bob." He would say whatever he thought the woman wanted to hear just to get a relationship going.

He told the Telluride woman, "I'm a sooner than later kind of person, and we should get together soon."

Unfortunately for Bob, he was too late with the Telluride woman. She told him that she'd just found someone new and "struck it rich." But as a kind of sop she added that she had a good friend who might like going out with him.

Bob was irked by her response, but was so desperate that he swallowed his pride and contacted the Telluride woman's friend. He e-mailed this friend and said, "If you really aren't interested, just say so. I'll not pester you. But your friend in Telluride didn't feel I was the worst sort of person you could be in touch with."

Once again he went into a litany of stories about his younger years and added, "I'm outdoorsy and athletic. I enjoy hiking, biking, swimming, and tennis." And it must have come into play that she liked skiing, because Bob said that he liked skiing as well. This was in direct contradiction of all his comments to Donna that he didn't like skiing and was worried that it would hurt his knees or ankles. But back then he had a woman he didn't want anymore. Now he had to say anything to win a new one.

Bob told the new prospect that he was 6', weighed 170 pounds, and was "incredibly healthy and fit. I'm reasonably well-to-do, but interested in sharing that well-to-doedness with someone."

It's not clear if he sent out another e-mail a few days later to this same woman or someone else. After all, he was searching the singles papers and cruising the singles sites on the Internet pretty steadily at this point. But most likely it was to the Lady. It had all the earmarks of his persona as "Helpful Caring Bob." He said, "You've been hurt before? Don't want to take a chance on being hurt again? You won't be baby. I believe this is why we found each other, so we could help one another bury the pain of previous failures through a partnership based on faith, trust and love."

It's almost surreal hearing these words pour out of Bob Spangler's mouth. He was so devoid of a normal person's conscience that he felt no irony, no shame, in talking about a relationship based on faith and trust. What trust would the woman have had if he'd calmly explained that he'd murdered his first family and third wife? But thoughts of guilt or remorse never entered his mind. The murders had been as antiseptic as he could make them. They were never in the heat of passion. They were cold and calculated in the extreme. He could tell his listeners on radio station KRSJ, "Women are to be cherished," and then push his wife, Donna, over a cliff. He could tell his listeners that "women are special," after putting a bullet in Nancy's brain.

Once again he brought up the old refrain, friends are important, but nothing compared to lovers. He asked her to please open her heart to him: "Please let me love you for the rest of your life."

It was a strange double life Bob Spangler was leading that year. He was imploring the Lady to share the rest of her life with him, while actively sending out e-mails to new prospective female companions. It was just one more instance of how he could compartmentalize things. The Lady was in one compartment. All the rest were in another. That it should cause him sleepless nights was a very remote probability. Sharon, after all, had said he would roll over, after the most grueling hike, and fall asleep immediately. It's the innocent man who can do this. Or one who has no innocence.

But the strain showed itself in other areas, and in July 1999 Bob took a very unusual step for him. Always disdainful of the haunted places in his past, he suddenly told the Lady that he was taking a road trip back to Iowa. As he said, "Suddenly got the urge to check my roots in Iowa. I'll be in touch the instant I get back."

Bob apparently enjoyed his trip to Iowa very much. He told an old high school chum there that he'd been visiting friends and places he knew in his youth—especially Ames High School, where he'd known his glory days on the football field. Then Bob said that he was looking forward to their fiftieth high school reunion in 2001. He didn't mention if he'd gone to the cemetery in Ames to look at the graves of his wife and children. If he had, its hard to know what emotions he would have felt. Bob always distanced himself from that event. He may have half believed all the lies he'd been telling about their demise: Nancy had killed the children; they had died in a car wreck; David had died of a drug overdose. He had told so many lies he couldn't even keep track of them. Even if he admitted to himself that he had done the killing, he viewed it more as a necessity at the time rather than actual murder. Bob compartmentalized things so well, the killings to him were just one more thing on a list of things to do: go to the grocery store, get gasoline for the car, kill the family. These all had equal weight of importance.

When Bob did get back to Grand Junction, it wasn't his ladylove that he first e-mailed, as promised. Instead, it was someone new who apparently had answered one of his queries on the Internet while he was gone. He told her, "You need a sympathetic soul with whom to relax and exchange tales of what's been happening in your life.

Like to go for a walk, have coffee, have lunch together, sit in the park and watch kayakers?"

Bob was moving in all directions now. He agreed to meet this new woman in a small town near the ski resort of Snowmass, Colorado. He told her she would recognize him because "I'll be wearing shorts, sandals, and a t shirt, but you'll recognize most readily the neatly trimmed white beard beneath a not-nearly-as-furry head. More than likely we'll be the two people most obviously scanning the lunch scene for someone else."

So how strange it was that within a few days of this meeting, Bob was telling another friend about his ties with the Lady. He related they'd already said all the appropriate words about things not working out and splitting being the best for the both of them; they needed to get on with their lives. But in the next breath he was still holding out hope that things would turn around.

Bob said, "She's the best thing that ever came down my pike. Maybe one of these days one of us will come to our senses and realize we have something too good to mess up. I mean, how many people get married and never get around to being friends? We have the friendship part down in spades."

Spurred on by his hopes and dreams, he met with the Lady once again, only to run up against the same brick wall. Never one to give up easily, he told her, "I think it's pretty much a case of us looking at the same situation, but seeing things through different eyes. You seem to be seeing a situation so good the way it is, you don't want to risk changing anything for fear of damaging what you have. I see a situation that has been absolutely wonderful, but seems stalled now and in danger of serious damage if we don't advance. To me a loving relationship advances through friendship to include physical intimacy as an integral part of the relationship."

If Bob was so loyal to her, what was he doing the next day e-mailing another woman he had just met? Obviously, it was the compartmentalization in effect once more—that he was deceiving the Lady about his undying love never crossed his mind.

To the new woman, most likely the one he met near Snowmass, he said, "Conversations flowed easily, personalities seemed to compliment, physical deformities weren't apparent. A couple of hours slipped by rather quickly and pleasantly. I liked being with you."

Bob was playing both sides against the middle by now. He wanted the Lady, but if that didn't work out, he would take what he could get. One thing he didn't like was living alone in his nice home on Applewood Street in Grand Junction.

Bob was soon telling a male friend, one who apparently had a new lady friend, "May one hope that you prove at least as efficient when it comes to recommending a woman friend for me. As you're aware, we dote on [women] with spirit, intelligence, humor, attitude, energy, good looks, high hopes. Are affectionate, easy to be with, enjoyable companion, friend/buddy/lover/soulmate type of woman."

And there it all was in a nutshell. The image of the perfect woman and mate for Bob Spangler. All of this had the yearning for a goddess, not a person of flesh and blood. His standards were extremely high when it came to a woman, and when he first fell for one, he would project those qualities onto her. But after the magic began to fade and he saw her for what she really was, only human, then she had to die and be replaced by some new quest. For a while Sharon had embodied those qualities in his mind and Nancy had to die so Bob could obtain his fantasy woman. But when Sharon grew old, she was dropped for a new vision of perfection. When Donna was no longer his "dream girl," she had to be eliminated as well to clear the field for whoever might come along next. In Bob's mind he deserved such a woman. After all, he had called himself "attentive, undemanding, humorous, eager to please, kind, considerate, always available, always interested and optimistic." A remarkable man such as himself obviously deserved a remarkable woman.

There was something else going on as well. In the very deep dark center of Bob Spangler was a hole that he could not fill. On one level he believed all the "public relations" hyperbole he had invented about himself. And part of it was true. He was athletic, had a dry sense of humor, was an accomplished actor and conversationalist. But all the hikes in the Grand Canyon, all the rock climbing and ovations on stage, could not fill that hole. Perhaps it was the blackness of knowing that he had been rejected at birth, and to fill the void he yearned for the ideal woman to prove that he was lovable and worthwhile.

In an e-mail in late August 1999 Bob replied to someone on the Internet with unusually smutty comments for him. He generally played the gentlemanly type. But here he said, "The allusion of your massage therapist oiling you out of your sandals left me smiling. I've never experienced massage by a pro for anything, let alone all over. Or is all over the criterion for relaxing any tightness anywhere?"

He brought up one more thing that he had never done. This person had mentioned having been hypnotized. Bob swore vehemently that he would never be hypnotized, and with good reason. He knew that if he was hypnotized, all the dark secrets that he kept inside might come tumbling out. There was no way he was going to expose those to anyone. If he was afraid of being polygraphed, this went double for hypnosis.

But Bob Spangler was more adventurous in another area. For the upcoming production of *Annie* he would have to shave off his beard. He told a friend, "I really am kind of curious to see what I look like after all these years."

In an e-mail to a male friend in the Grand Junction area in that same time period, he was smutty once again. His friend was in the dating game as well and jokingly remarked about living on "Pussy Ridge." Bob replied, "I really get off on your sense of humor."

It was something near the end of this particular e-mail that had unforeseen and dire consequences, not only for Bob but also for the woman he mentioned there. He told the friend that he'd recently gone to a breakfast for singles held by a group called Connections, in Grand Junction. He'd never had much luck there, but went anyway with the off chance that he might get lucky someday. Bob happened to look down the table and made eye contact with a new woman he'd never seen before. Bob told his friend, "Instant interest from her signaled a pool party at her home later that day. Then hiking, biking, walking, talking and telephoning back and forth. Voila, we have what appears to be the start of a significant attachment. Quite unexpected, but very pleasant."

The woman's name was Judith "Judy" Hilty and she lived not far away from Bob in Grand Junction.

Bob elaborated to another friend about his first meeting with Judy. "I glanced down the table and there was this woman I'd never seen before, apparently arrived a little late, who looked very interesting. And she was looking back at me with what seemed to me similar interest. Hmm, I thought to myself. Isn't this interesting?"

Soon he was crowing to friends about the attributes of Judy Hilty. Only days before he had been pining as usual about the Lady. He had once called her, "delightfully bright, cheerful, intelligent, beautiful, good humored, well spoken, active and a capable individual." Now all of that was forgotten, as if she had never existed. He could shuffle the compartments of his love life around like a master magician, making one appear while the other disappeared.

Now he was telling friends all about Judy. He said, "It was even more of an instant connection than I (and the Lady) experienced, but with all the romantic elements that always were missing with her, present in abundance, for both of us. We've spent considerable time marveling at the intensity of our mutual feelings."

Bob told of the hot days spent in her swimming pool and the cool nights spent in his hot tub. He said they were checking out the local movie, theater, restaurant and jazz scene. He also said they were on the same wavelength on just about everything.

Only days later he was telling another friend, "Ever hear the song 'Everything's Coming Up Roses'? The incredible Spangler luck seems to be holding in the female department. Down one month, only to spring back up the next. The new kid on the block and I are really cooking. An instant and simultaneous item."

He added that within a short time she was staying at his house, and he was spending even more time at hers. That was because he was helping her with fix-it projects around her house. Then he added, "Ah, love! Ain't it wonderful?"

Amidst all this lovey-dovey romance, an incident happened to show the other side of Bob Spangler for a moment. Of course Judy Hilty never saw it happen. A friend, who thought he was doing Bob a favor, signed him up to receive messages from an Internet service called Mailbits. This service sent him quotes, jokes and other material via e-mails. Bob was incensed and sent the friend an e-mail titled "WARNING! Do not EVER send my name or address to ANYONE. I am quite upset. PAY ATTENTION TO THIS!"

Soon thereafter he put his mask back on and became "Friendly Uncle Bob." In an e-mail to one of his nephews, he wrote, "The [Lady] has passed into another realm. However, another even nicer lady has appeared who is not only a strong hiker but has quickly become a romantic attachment in my life." Her name was Judy Hilty.

He mentioned how in the coming spring he planned to take Judy on a long backpack trip in the Grand Canyon from Elves Chasm along the Tonto Trail. Their hike would take them right past Horseshoe Mesa and the spot where he had pushed

Donna off the cliff. He had once called this locale, Donna's Point. The place where he told her son that he would scatter wildflower seeds in her memory. Now it was just a footnote in his past.

Bob also talked about his acting abilities. He said, "I'm having an excellent time being an actor in a dinner theater production of *Annie*. Singing, dancing, emoting. Lots of fun."

He entitled this e-mail "The New Me."

But, in fact, it was the same old Bob, scrambling for new adventures and new romance. He was either in the dumps about some relationship gone bad or on a new high. At present it was all blue skies and roses. In November 1999 he told a friend about his relationship with Judy: "We thoroughly enjoy each other's company. Doesn't feel at all like raging hormones of some new or lustful attachment; just wonderfully naturally, unhurriedly, inevitably, and most pleasantly RIGHT. We aren't quite living together yet, but spending an inordinately large amount of time in each other's company."

He told how he was helping Judy at her home, doing numerous projects. He said they were having so much fun doing this that they were seriously thinking of shopping around for fixer-uppers to purchase, renovate them and resell. They didn't plan this as a money-making scheme. Rather, they'd do it because they enjoyed it so much. Bob said, "It's been a spectacularly successful and enjoyable liaison." Then he added if they made some money at it, all the better.

Amidst his new life with Judy, Bob got another whiff of nostalgia about his high school days in Ames, Iowa, when an old teammate sent him a book he had just written about their undefeated season. Bob gushed in his praise about the book, telling the team-mate, "You've done a remarkable job of recalling days of our youth; the town, the atmosphere and most of all what it was like during the unforgettable fall of 1950. I was absolutely transported back in time. To a better time, wasn't it?"

Bob told his old teammate that it was interesting seeing those scenes recounted by someone else who had been on the field. Of course, he said, he had been so mixed up in the action that he never got an overall view of what was happening. And then he bragged, "As a professional writer, myself, I'm quite impressed by your obvious skill and talent for storytelling."

Just how writing a few public-relations papers or e-mail correspondence made Bob Spangler a professional writer, he didn't say.

Even though Bob was stirred by the recollection of past glory and called it a "better time," the fact was he was having the time of his life in the present with Judy. At heart he was not a man to dwell on the past—not on the Ames of the 1950s or the murders of Nancy, Susan and David or the death of Donna. He was always looking to the future. Life was going to be better than it had ever been. True happiness was just over the horizon.

Bob was having such a good time, in fact, that he made a decision as the new year of 2000 approached that was unheard of just a short time before. He wrote a friend: "I guess I'll be dropping out of sports and pursue a new partnership opportunity. After 23 years of basketball officiating, and 25 years in soccer, this is no small decision."

Refereeing and coaching had defined in part who he was for so many years. And now he was willing to drop it all by going into partnership with Judy in fixing up old houses, living in them as they did the work, then selling them for a profit. They would work their way from one house to another, never having to worry about a roof over their heads.

Bob was about as happy as he had ever been in the spring of 2000. He would have been a lot less happy if he'd known that the team of investigators was tracking his every move. He couldn't start a new project or take a hike in the Grand Canyon without them knowing about it. He couldn't find a new lady friend without them knowing that as well. Bit by bit they were pulling all the loose threads together and amassing an immense amount of data to confront Bob with at some point. Their plan was to put it all together and have Camille Bibles present it to a grand jury sometime in early 2001. Then they would arrest him.

Two major things, however, happened in the summer of 2000 that changed everything. One concerned the investigators' ongoing efforts of contacting people who had known Bob in various areas where he had lived. And the other happened because of something Bob did himself. Taken together, these two developments made the investigators move with new speed and determination. They were not only worried about making their case, they were worried about what Bob Spangler might do to his new love, Judy Hilty.

Chapter 12

The Shadow of Death

All spring and summer of 2000 Special Agent Lenny Johns had been sending subjectology questionnaires based on NCAVC data to friends and colleagues of Bob Spangler. The area these were sent to covered the gamut from Iowa to Denver, Grand Junction, Durango and the Grand Canyon. The questions posed came directly from what the profiler thought might be important to the case. Always in the back of Lenny Johns's mind was the thought that there never would be a "smoking gun." There would have to be an overwhelming amount of circumstantial evidence that would compel Bob Spangler into a confession in hopes of making a deal with the United States Attorney's Office. The questionnaires were one more means of collecting that circumstantial evidence.

The FBI questionnaires sent to the Durango area were especially helpful in adding bits and pieces of information about Bob. One person commented that Bob left the Durango area suddenly in 1998, and the man wondered if it had something to do with Donna's death. He had always been uneasy about the Grand Canyon "accident" and noticed that Bob didn't seem to grieve very much about Donna. This man wondered if there was an investigation going on, one that Bob had gotten wind of in 1998 just before he left an area that he loved.

But the most important lead in the Durango area came from a woman who had worked with Bob Spangler at the Four Corners Broadcasting Company. She had been a news director/reporter while Bob was a DJ there. The FBI already knew this woman very well and had contacted her on numerous occasions in the past on a case that had nothing to do with Spangler. In an incredible bit of coincidence, this woman's former boyfriend was Jason McVean, one of the infamous "Four Corners Fugitives" who had killed a Cortez policeman in May 1998 and sparked one of the wildest shoot-outs and largest manhunts in American history. The woman was Linda Wallace and it is impossible to tell of her connection to the FBI and Bob Spangler without a short history of Jason McVean and the Four Corners Fugitives.

Linda Wallace had considered her handsome, rugged boyfriend, McVean, to be a "tender, caring partner." He always seemed upbeat, in love with the outdoors and her. Linda Wallace couldn't have imagined in her wildest dreams what McVean and two other men would do on May 29, 1998. How much McVean was a survivalist and into the militia craze that was sweeping the nation at that time is a matter of debate. He did have many survival skills and a certain amount of dislike and mistrust of the federal government, filtered through his views about Ruby Ridge and Waco. But McVean's friend Robert Mason was definitely a militia-type guy and had a grudge against the IRS, which was billing him for $1,500 that he didn't think he owed them.

For whatever reason, Mason, McVean and a friend named Alan Pilon stole a water truck from an oil field parking lot near Ignacio, Colorado, at 11:30 A.M. on May 28, 1998. The next morning at 9:24 A.M., Cortez police officer Dale Claxton spotted the three men in the stolen truck and began following them. The truck pulled over and stopped just outside the Cortez city limits. Before Claxton even got out of his squad car, one of the three men walked toward him and opened up with an automatic weapon. Claxton died almost immediately in a hail of gunfire.

After killing Claxton, the three men sped off down the road for several miles and commandered a flatbed truck at gunpoint. Just then Montezuma County sheriff's deputy, Jason Bishop pulled up looking for the water truck. As Bishop drove alongside, one man on the back of the flatbed truck opened up on him. Bishop was wounded in the back of the head, lost consciousness and crashed his vehicle.

The three desperate men now raced off in the flatbed truck and saw a Colorado State patrol car coming their way. The man on the back of the flatbed truck fired with his automatic weapon. Patrolman Steve Keller wasn't hit, but his squad car was riddled with bullets and put out of commission. Seconds later, Cortez police sergeant Sue Betts arrived on the scene and was fired at as well. Up ahead of the flatbed, Deputy Todd Martin was waiting with a shotgun. But before he had a chance to fire, the man on the flatbed and a passenger opened up on him, and Martin received serious wounds to the elbow and knee.

Montezuma County officer Jim Wynes was nearby and rushed to give aid to Martin, while State Trooper Keller, whose vehicle was out of commission, ran up and jumped into Martin's squad car. Despite already having been fired upon, he gave chase in the cruiser.

As Keller was in hot pursuit, county sheriff's officers Lendol Lawrence, Terry Steele and Joey Chavez were approaching from the other direction. The fugitives sprayed all three sheriff's vehicles with automatic fire before the officers could set up an effective roadblock. Luckily, none of the officers were hit.

There were four cruisers on the fugitive's tail now. It is estimated that since their first shots at Officer Claxton, the gunmen had fired over five hundred rounds of ammo in the space of just a few minutes. And the pursuit was far from over.

At the intersection of U.S. Highway 160 and Road G, the gunmen shot at a passenger vehicle and roadside Dumpster. The vehicle and Dumpster spun into the intersection, creating a traffic jam and in the confusion the gunmen were able to shake their pursuers. They disappeared up McElmo Canyon, doubled back on Pleasant View Road and headed for Hovenweep National Monument in Utah.

Hovenweep Monument superintendent Art Hutchinson happened to be listening to the police scanner at the time and worried about the visitors in his park. He rushed to close the main gate, but just before he reached it, the flatbed roared into view and sprayed his vehicle with fire. Hutchinson wasn't hit, but his vehicle was, and it bounced off the road and into a ditch. The flatbed

continued on and headed up into rugged Cross
Canyon.

In Cross Canyon the gunmen abandoned the
flatbed and covered it with brush to hide it from detection. Then they took off on foot into the twisted
and brush-covered terrain. It wasn't until 1:00 P.M.
that law officers discovered the abandoned flatbed
and knew the gunmen were on foot. They also
knew that all three men were heavily armed and
not afraid to die fighting.

Over the next few days, the manhunt involved
more than five hundred searchers from fifty different
law enforcement agencies. There were eighteen he-
licopters, Navajo trackers and even search dog teams
and mounted posses. The FBI became heavily involved in the case as well. It was one of the largest
manhunts ever seen in the American West.

But Cross Creek was ideal for desperate men to
hide out in and move under cover. The terrain was
tortuous and covered with thick brush that men
could crawl under. It wasn't until June 4 that one of
the gunmen surfaced from cover on the banks of
the San Juan River near Bluff, Utah. A social worker
named Steve Wilcox was sitting at a picnic area
near the river, eating his lunch. Something he did
must have spooked Robert Mason. Mason fired at
him and Wilcox took off running. He soon spread
the alarm and San Juan County sheriff's deputy
Kelly Bradford arrived on the scene. He was peer-
ing over a bluff for the gunman when the deputy
was shot several times. The fact that he was wearing
a bulletproof vest probably saved his life.

As the search teams rushed to the area, they
found out who this gunman was. They stumbled
upon the body of Robert Mason, who had appar-

ently shot himself in the head rather than be taken alive. There were several pipe bombs scattered around his body.

The search now reached a frenzy. The entire town of Bluff, population three hundred, was evacuated, and all kayak trips on the San Juan River were stopped. Law enforcement teams scoured the hills, mesas and river area around Bluff for McVean and Pilon. But these two seemed to have disappeared into thin air.

Seventeen months later, a group of Navajo deer hunters stumbled upon a skeleton near Tin Cup Mesa. Forensic lab technicians proved it was the skeletal remains of Pilon. He had suffered a broken ankle and a gunshot wound to the forehead, but the gunshot wound only added to the mystery. From the angle of the wound it was apparent that Pilon had not shot himself. Had McVean done it because Pilon asked him to? Or did McVean do it because Pilon was slowing him down because of the broken ankle?

As for McVean himself, he became the stuff of legends. He never has been found. Several theories surfaced about what happened to him. One is that he escaped the area soon after the major shoot-out and has been underground ever since in some other part of the country. The second theory is that someone in the Bluff area offered him a safe house and he stayed there until things cooled down, then made his escape. The third theory is that he died somewhere in the backcountry and his body or skeleton may never be found.

Whatever happened to her former boyfriend, Jason McVean, Linda Wallace became a very important person to the FBI in the Four Corners Fugitive case. They wanted to know everything she could tell them about McVean. They also wanted to know if he ever contacted her after September 29, 1998. They kept in touch with her over the years, and when Special Agent Lenny Johns learned that she was a close friend of Bob Spangler's, there was a whole new round of FBI dealings with Linda Wallace.

During the whole Four Corners Fugitive situation, Bob had lent a sympathetic ear to Wallace. Wallace later told a *Denver Post* reporter, "Bob was real sympathetic. I remember some intense hugs. He just didn't seem to have much insight into [the situation]. But I went to him for comfort over Jason McVean being wanted for murder."

Linda Wallace knew quite a bit about Bob Spangler because of her association with him in Four Corners Broadcasting. She even went up to Grand Junction to visit him at his beautiful new home on Applewood Street. This was before he had met Judy Hilty or the FBI started asking her questions about Spangler. Linda and Bob talked about all the tragedies in his life and how Donna had fallen off the cliff at the Grand Canyon. Wallace noticed a photo of Bob and his first family sitting on the mantelpiece. They were all gathered around a Christmas tree back in the 1970s. She asked about the photo and he said his first family had all died in an auto accident in the Denver area. And then he added a familiar wrinkle to an old lie. He said he had been driving the vehicle and was the only survivor. This added to the sympathy that Wallace gave him and he lapped it up.

Bob mentioned to her about Sharon dying of an overdose in his house in Durango back in 1994. Wallace asked him how he had dealt with all these tragedies in his life. Bob answered, "I had to find it within me to deal with it."

Linda Wallace went on to tell the *Denver Post* reporter about one of her trips to Bob's house, where he was "very friendly and flirty. His house struck me as palatial. He told me he made a killing on his Durango home." It was an interesting phrase on his part. It really had been a killing—a killing of his wife Donna, who had sunk a lot of her own money into that Durango home.

Wallace continued, "There were photos of the Grand Canyon everywhere. On the walls and on the shelves."

Wallace did not visit Spangler's home again after early 1999, but she kept in touch with him by telephone and letters, even though these began to peter off after he met Judy. Then out of the blue she received a letter from him dated August 18, 2000. It was a letter that had great consequences, not only for her but Bob Spangler as well.

The letter started out sympathizing with her about her sick dog, but then Bob said he had news that would make the news "about her doggy" pale by comparison. He wrote: "I learned on August 12th that a totally unexpected and incurable combination of lung cancer and brain lesions has sneaked out of nowhere and probably will end my life sometime in the next few months."

He told her that six months was a guesstimate of how long he had to live. It all seemed strange to him, since he looked and felt just fine at present. Spangler told her that doctors planned to treat him as quickly and gently as one could hope with a couple weeks of radiation to stabilize the swelling on his brain and relieve the pressure. He said, "All

things considered, I can probably drop off at the
end quickly and with little difficulty."

Bob said he had only begun to notice symptoms
the month before. He had trouble with his eyesight
and found it difficult to concentrate. He began to
forget his lines at the little theater. He and Judy
thought this might have been from working hard
seven days a week on the fixer-upper they had
bought. He had been enjoying the work until the
previous month when suddenly it all became too
much. Bob said it had become evident that something was wrong, and that's what led him to go to
the doctor for a checkup.

Bob continued, "None of them (the doctors) has
evinced the slightest doubt from day one. Apparently this is one of those breakout cancers that grow
quietly years and years, showing no symptoms, not
debilitating you in any apparent way, until suddenly
you reach a magic plateau beyond which everything goes downhill quickly."

Then Bob told her to write or call anytime. He
said he'd spend the last year with Judy, his dearest
friend, companion, love and spousal equivalent.

Bob ended by saying, "I wish there was more I
could say, more we could do, but the show seems to
be ending rather sooner than expected. We face it
with as much equanimity as possible. Goodby and
good luck in whatever awaits us all."

Linda Wallace later told the *Denver Post* reporter
that after reading this, "I just burst into tears."

Bob wrote a similar letter to his old hiking
friends, the Ohlmans. Much of the letter had the
same ingredients, but he added a few more lines to
them. He said, "An unexpected voice from the past,
which will sort of get us on to wrapping up our

whole association. Begun all those years ago with you guys at the old train station depot with an odd-ball woman (Sharon) who had an idea she could write a hiking book, and wound up with us enjoying some incredible adventures that I wouldn't have missed for anything."

Then Bob told them about his inoperable cancer. He closed by saying, "Thanks for being such wonderful friends to Sharon and me. There was a lot of bad things between the two of us (him and Sharon). But so much more good. I cherish the memories."

Bob told neighbors, friends and fellow actors at Grand Junction's Cabaret Theater about his cancer as well. From all of them he elicited responses of shock and sadness. Strangely enough, he spoke of his own death in the same manner he had spoken of the deaths of Nancy, Susan, David, Sharon and Donna. It was as if he were looking at it from afar and speaking with dispassion. He dug the sympathy he got, but he never cried and moaned about his fate. It wasn't exactly bravery, but it wasn't fear either. Bob had always lived in a world of his own devising, and cancer was just one more factor in it.

Those around him acted in a much more emotional manner than he did. The actors at the Cabaret Theater put on a benefit dinner for him. One neighbor in the Applecrest Subdivision, Lillie Lockman, later told a *Denver Post* reporter, "I returned a gift of apples from his tree by baking him an apple pie after learning of his incurable cancer."

From everywhere he turned in Grand Junction, Bob Spangler elicited the sympathy and concern he always craved, but his letter to Linda Wallace elicited one more thing he never could have imagined. She was in constant contact with the FBI, and after she read his letter, she struggled with her conscience about what to tell them. On one hand, she wanted the FBI to just "leave him alone and let him die in peace." On the other hand, if what they were implying was true, the gentle Bob Spangler she knew had killed his wives and children. In the end Linda Wallace showed Special Agent Lenny Johns the "cancer letter."

This letter, and one more crucial event on September 1, 2000, set off alarm bells amongst all the investigators. Bob Spangler and Judith Hilty were married on September 1, at the courthouse in Grand Junction. With two witnesses, and no minister or justice of the peace in attendance, they legally performed the marriage ceremony themselves. As a court clerk wrote later, "This was the only paperwork required by the county to get married." As a wedding gift to Judy, Bob did something very unexpected. He signed over his house on Applewood Street to her. The man who had always been taking money and property from women, after he had murdered them, was giving some property back to a woman. The only problem was, there was blood money tied up in that house. Much of the proceeds to buy it had come from the sale of the Durango home, a home for which Donna had paid a substantial amount. But possibly because of the cancer, Bob was in an expansive mood, and he gave his new bride what he could. Or cynics would say later he was just trying to hide his assets from others. It was no secret that by now he despised Donna Spangler's children. He blamed them for putting Detective Cornish onto him in the first place back in 1994.

With the knowledge that Bob Spangler had terminal cancer, and had married again, the investigators called an emergency meeting on how to deal with the situation. On one hand, it opened up new and unexpected possibilities. Bob just might be in the mood to confess, knowing that he had such a short time left. On the other hand, Bob was at his most dangerous when he was married. What if he grew angry at Judy one day because of his failing mental capacity? He had dealt severely with wives in the past who displeased him. All the team members were now concerned about Judy's safety.

The Veterans Administration Medical Center in Grand Junction informed Special Agent Lenny Johns that they had no record of Bob Spangler as a patient. On some level Johns must have wondered if the "cancer letter" was just one more of Bob Spangler's tricks. But a week later, St. Mary's Regional Medical Center confirmed that Spangler indeed had cancer and was scheduled to start radiation treatment the following week. Lenny Johns knew it was time to act.

Johns contacted the Grand Junction Police Department about possible use of their interview room for a talk with Spangler. The Grand Junction Police Department told him that all their offices were being renovated and out of use. Johns next contacted the Mesa County Sheriff's Office about using their interview room. Mesa County Sheriff's Office agreed to his request and told him it would be open to him if needed.

Meanwhile, AUSA Camille Bibles was drawing up her complaint against Robert Merlin Spangler for presentation to a grand jury earlier than expected. With all the information she had gathered from

Bev Perry, Lenny Johns and Paul Goodman, she arranged a presentation about everything they knew so far about Bob Spangler.

In her paper Bibles wrote extensively about the death of Donna Spangler and even about Sharon Spangler's suspicious suicide. She really keyed in on Donna's fear of heights, her vertigo and the way Bob had cajoled her into going on the Easter weekend hike at the Grand Canyon. Then she wrote: "At request of Grand Canyon National Park Investigator and the Arapahoe County Sheriff's Office Investigator, an investigation into these matters was opened by the Flagstaff Resident Agency of the FBI. Through meetings with the National Center for the Analysis of Violent Crime, Special Agent Johns was provided with a questionnaire to be distributed to several people who know/knew Robert Spangler. One of these individuals participating in the questionnaire received a letter from Spangler indicating that Spangler was suffering from terminal cancer with a life expectancy of only a few months.

"In view of Robert Spangler's terminal condition, and in the hope of a confession in his waning days of life, the United States Attorney's Office, National Parks Service, Arapahoe County Sheriff's Office and the FBI are in concurrence that the next logical step in the investigation is the immediate interview of Robert Spangler. It has been approved for Special Agent Johns to travel to Colorado to participate in the interview. Assistant United States Attorney Camille Bibles, Detective Paul Goodman and Special Agent Bev Perry are meeting in Grand Junction, Colorado, on September 13, 2000, to initiate the interview with Robert Spangler. AUSA

Bibles and Investigator Bev Perry will not participate in the interview.

"It is requested that SAC authority be granted to
electronically record the interview of Robert Spangler via video tape and/or audio tape. Detective
Goodman has advised Special Agent Johns that it is
the policy of Arapahoe County Sheriff's Office to
video tape interviews, and that the Arapahoe
County Attorney has specifically requested any interview of Robert Spangler be video taped.

"More importantly, this matter is unique. Robert
Spangler is the sole and strong suspect in three bru-
tal homicides and two very suspicious deaths. He
was the last person to see his two wives alive. He
quarreled with his first wife just before her murder and that of her children.

"There is minimal physical evidence regarding
the murders of Nancy Spangler and her children.
What evidence exists brings strong suspicion on
Robert Spangler, but is far from conclusive. While
there is also strong reason to suspect Robert Spangler in the deaths of his other two wives, due to the
benefit to him by their deaths, no evidence exists
that he caused their deaths. Robert Spangler benefited by the death of Sharon by way of termination
of alimony payments he was making to her, the collection of Social Security survivor benefits from her
death, and $20,000 from her estate—a condition of
their divorce should she proceed [sic] him in
death. By Donna's death, a failing relationship was
ended at a time when Robert was believed to be involved in an affair with another woman.

"The driving force for any criminal charges
against Robert Spangler and the primary evidence
at trial, can only be a confession by Spangler. AUSA

Bibles has committed to pursuing charges against Robert Spangler should he confess, regardless of his medical condition. However, AUSA Bibles is concerned that he could attempt to use his state of mind, regarding treatment of his brain cancer, as a reason to suppress any admissions he may make. Therefore, AUSA Bibles has opined that having the interview video taped would preserve Spangler's statements and clearly and definitely reflect his state of mind without question."

To make sure that Bob Spangler would actually be in Grand Junction when all four of the team members arrived, a request was made by Special Agent Lenny Johns for FBI surveillance of Spangler's activities. He wrote FBI Headquarters in Denver: "Request for Grand Junction, Colorado Regional Agent to conduct a logical investigation to determine if Robert Spangler will be in the local area on September 13, 2000, to be interviewed. It is understood by the case agent that this may be difficult to do without tipping off Spangler and caution should be used to ensure that this does not happen."

FBI surveillance of Bob and Judy Spangler's vehicles began on September 8, 2000. The local agent reported a 1993 red Subaru in the driveway on Cannell Avenue, where Bob and Judy were staying. He also noticed Bob and Judy take a short hike in nearby Colorado National Monument. This surveillance served a dual purpose. It not only kept tabs on Bob but allowed the agent to see just what effects the cancer was having on his physical abilities. On all the days subsequent to September 13, the agent kept up the surveillance on Bob and Judy Spangler. Both Bob and Judy's vehicles were in the

driveway when Paul Goodman, Bev Perry, Lenny
Johns and Camille Bibles arrived in Grand Junction
on September 13, 2000.

As they all pulled into the parking lot of the Mesa
County Sheriff's Office on that date, they all knew
one thing. If they couldn't convince Bob Spangler
to confess, he would probably die before he was
ever brought to justice. The full stories about the
deaths of Nancy, Susan, David, Donna and Sharon
would never be known. But Lenny Johns and Paul
Goodman had a couple of aces up their sleeves.
They were good interviewers and profiler Gerry
Downes had given them some key tips on how to
approach Bob Spangler. There was only one question now: who was more wily, the profiler or the
profiled?

Chapter 13

"You've Got Your Serial."

Paul Goodman wrote in his notebook that he met Bev Perry, Lenny Johns and Camille Bibles at the Grand Junction FBI Office at 2:05 P.M. on September 13, 2000. Also present were Special Agent Ron Baker of the FBI and Grand Junction police detective Amy Cryman. They put in a telephone call to Gerry Downes at the FBI profiling unit in the Washington, DC, area for one more strategy session about how best to interview Bob Spangler. There was already a consensus amongst the investigators that Bob Spangler was a psychopath. The phrase they commonly used about him was "It's all about Bob." The advice they received now from Downes was to play off his super-size ego.

The strategy session went on longer than expected and the investigators decided to put off contacting Bob Spangler until the next day. Goodman, Johns, Perry and Bibles didn't show up to Spangler's door until 1:00 P.M. on September 14. They figuratively crossed their fingers. All their years of hard work came down to this moment. Investigator Goodman later said, "We just knocked at his door. He didn't seem surprised. He didn't seem like he was expecting us either. There was no reaction. It was like 'Oh, hello.'"

Interestingly enough, there was a ploy in effect on the investigators' part at this initial meeting. It was Investigator Goodman who introduced himself to Bob and showed his credentials. Lenny Johns did not speak at all or identify who he was. That would come later.

Taking the lead, Goodman asked Bob to come down to the Mesa County Sheriff's Office for an interview. Bob agreed to go with them but said they would have to give him a ride, since he was now having difficulty driving because of his cancer and Judy wasn't at home at the time. They agreed and transported Bob down to the sheriff's office.

Once Bob Spangler and the investigators reached the Mesa County Sheriff's Office, he was treated to an inventive piece of stage work. Spangler had always prided himself on being a good actor, but he now got a bit of his own medicine handed back to him. According to Bev Perry, in order "to enhance that moment, per Downes's suggestions and with the help of both Mesa County Sheriff's Office and Grand Junction Police Department personnel, we created a busy scene of investigators working on boxes of material and signs directing personnel to a room occupied by the 'Spangler Task Force.' Bob saw all this activity on his way to the interview room. There was a combination of using his ego and his need to control the situation. Revealing all of this to him in that way would help set up the appeal to his ego as to how he could help us, and particularly FBI profilers understand such crimes. It was deemed pointless to appeal to any moral justification which was unlikely to impress him."

The videotape in the interview room started rolling at 1:40 P.M. Bob Spangler looked relaxed as he sat in a chair across from Paul Goodman and Lenny Johns. Goodman introduced himself as a detective with the Arapahoe County Sheriff's Office and said that his investigation had started after the phone call from Detective Cornish from Coconino County, Arizona. He then said, "I'd like to introduce my partner, Special Agent Lenny Johns of the FBI."

Until that moment Spangler had no idea who Johns was. He momentarily looked surprised and then pleased that the FBI found him important enough to be investigating him. This was the reaction that Goodman and Johns had hoped for.

Lenny Johns told Bob, "I've been working with Paul on this situation for a couple of years now. We knew about your condition and we thought it was important to come and talk to you at this time."

Spangler replied, "Okay. Well, I don't have much longer."

Johns said, "Who knows. God is in control and there's always miracles. I don't know if you have belief in that at all."

Spangler looked dubious about God's intervention and replied, "Things happen. So you kinda go with what's most likely to happen." And then he added, "I haven't regretted a thing."

If Goodman and Johns were stunned by this admission that Spangler didn't regret anything that he'd done in his life, including multiple murders, they didn't show it. Instead, they explained to Bob the current investigation that was taking place by them and Perry and Bibles as well. They said the investigation was covering the deaths of Nancy, Susan, David, Donna and Sharon. They also explained that there was a grand jury in session conducted by Camille Bibles, as well as one being conducted by Arapahoe County on the deaths in Littleton.

Bob Spangler initially told his standard lies and covered the same old ground with them about how all these deaths occurred and that he had nothing to do with them. But Special Agent Johns assured him they weren't buying those stories anymore and it was only a matter of time before the grand jury indicted him for some or all of the deaths.

Bob still stalled for a while. He talked about the death of his first family on South Franklin Way and how he spent the night with lab technician Jack Swanburg. He talked about how he had obtained an attorney on that case and how his name was eventually cleared. Then he said something odd about the deaths of Nancy, Susan and David. He told Goodman and Johns, "Even though I grieved for them, I didn't grieve long enough for them."

Bob began to talk about Sharon and said that he'd married her too soon after the deaths of his family. He stated that this probably caused problems in his marriage to Sharon. Then he added, "I compartmentalize things and don't live in the past."

He told them that he had nothing to do with Sharon's death. He had returned home early from a soccer game on October 1, 1994, to find a sign on the door that said, "I've done it this time." Bob recalled, "She was upset that I found her."

About Donna he said, "Marrying her was a mistake. She got jealous and angry if I even talked to a female neighbor." By the end of their marriage he said he didn't feel any love for her. He said she didn't trust him or appear to be very happy. He also said that he knew Donna feared the Grand Canyon, but she must have "sucked it up" to go with him on the 1993 Easter weekend hike. He concluded by saying it was not a special marriage or strong relationship, but he proclaimed his innocence once again, saying that she had accidentally fallen off the cliff as he reported.

Bob Spangler and Lenny Johns and Paul Goodman went round and round. Johns and Goodman were both great interviewers. One would take the lead and then the other. It wasn't a good cop/bad cop routine. It was just different styles. Bev Perry later said, "They both had great techniques. They knew how to make people open up. There needed to be a rapport between the interviewers and the interviewee. I think Lenny made some really good choices early on and throughout the interview."

Paul Goodman, for the most part, had done a great deal of homework about Bob Spangler and knew the facts of the case forward and backward. He had a keen recollection of details and Johns recalled one incident during the interview where Goodman corrected Spangler about a vehicle he owned back in the 1970s. Johns said, "Spangler got a funny look on his face when he realized that Goodman was right and he was wrong. It showed him just how much Paul knew about him." And Johns added about Goodman, "He knew just when to jump in and when to be quiet. He was a great interviewer. Spangler seemed to trust him."

For his own part, Lenny Johns liked to interview "by the seat of his pants," as he put it. He didn't like to overprep and said that doing so could be counterproductive. Later, Johns recalled, "I wanted to see where the conversation with Bob Spangler would go. Let it flow naturally, but always with some direction in mind."

Whatever they said to Bob Spangler, it slowly seemed to work. At some point just before 3:00 P.M., Bob began to realize that they knew a lot more about him and his activities than he thought they did. A little after 3:00 P.M. Bob asked Goodman and Johns an important question, "What can you do for me?"

It was the first sign he was about to break. His comment had all the implications that he had indeed done something wrong and wanted to make a deal. He added one more key phrase: "This information is going to be hard on Judy."

It had been Bev Perry's job to contact Judy Spangler that day. Bev had monitored the first portion of the interview with Bob on September 14 and then went with a Grand Junction police detective to find Judy. They initially contacted her at work and escorted her to her home. They not only told her how the interview was going but also about all their suspicions about what Bob had done to two of his wives and both of his children.

Bev Perry said later, "I characterized our interview with Judy as something like an interview of a domestic-violence victim combined with a death notification. It truly turned her world upside down as we told her of our investigation, our belief that Bob was a murderer and our concern for her welfare. We were with her pretty much the entire time Bob's first interview was going on. We also went to their home, where she gave us a handgun for safekeeping. However, she was insistent on seeing Bob. We gave her a ride to the Mesa County Sheriff's Office, where Bob was.

"Paul Goodman told me later, Bob was originally quite mad when he was told that agents were already talking with Judy at the end of his interview. But once they were reunited at the Mesa County Sheriff's Office and Judy told him that she had been treated kindly, he seemed okay with it. I talked with both of them a little prior to their departure that day."

Realizing that Judy might be the key for Bob opening up completely, they allowed him to see her in private in another room at 3:40 P.M. Bob and Judy had their conference and afterward he indicated they wanted to go home to discuss things more fully. The investigators agreed this might be a good idea and escorted Bob back to Judy's vehicle. Just before they drove away, Goodman said to Bob, "I really want to hear from you."

"I know you do," Bob replied.

There was an intense discussion between Bob and Judy that night. It is not exactly clear what he told her, but it seemed to run in the vein of Spangler telling Judy about the deaths of his first wife and family and of Donna, but not the details of him murdering them. Apparently, he was still fudging the facts about how deeply he was involved. This was particularly true about Donna.

On September 15, 2000, at 7:20 A.M., Bob Spangler gave Special Agent Lenny Johns a phone call. He suggested they meet once again at the Mesa County Sheriff's Office after breakfast. At 8:50 A.M. both Lenny Johns and Paul Goodman went into the interview room with Bob and Judy Spangler. Bob said he wanted her there. As Bob spoke, with the videotape rolling, Lenny Johns jotted down free-form notes on a scratch pad. It was both a way for him to think about what was going on, but it was also a rough chronology of events as they occurred.

Bob started by saying that he needed more information from Johns and Goodman and that he was thinking of cooperating on the Littleton case. He reiterated that there was no case at the Grand Canyon, since he hadn't done anything wrong there. Lenny Johns wrote down on the scratch pad: 8:48 A.M.—Consider co-op, Littleton. No way, says, Arizona case/if brought up would be admission prima facie."

Bob continued that in reference to the Littleton case, if there was a grand jury, then there probably was enough evidence to indict him.

Johns wrote: 8:51 A.M.—"Believes will be indicted."

Then Bob added that he could see they were not already in a position to arrest him or they would have done so. He asked what kind of incentive they might give him if he cooperated.

They said they were willing to talk about it.

An interesting exchange between Lenny Johns and Bob Spangler occurred soon thereafter.

Johns wrote: 8:52 A.M.—"Bob said, 'You can't hold us.' I replied, 'You're a stone cold killer and you know it. Go ahead.'"

Bob must have been taken aback by Special Agent Lenny Johns's adamant accusation of him. He gave a half smile and said that he would like to talk to an FBI profiler. He thought that would be interesting.

By 9:00 A.M. they were all still talking about the possibility of Bob talking to a profiler, and the difference between the Littleton case (state) and Grand Canyon case (federal). This went on until

9:30 A.M. when Bob had just about decided to give up information on the Littleton case. But first he wanted something in return. What he wanted was a thirty-day grace period before there was an arrest so he could put his affairs in order and take one last trip to the Grand Canyon.

At this point Paul Goodman and Camille Bibles left the room. Bibles was ready to give up this concession on her part, but they needed to know how the Arapahoe County District Attorney's Office felt on the Littleton case. Goodman phoned District Attorney Robert Chappel and discussed the matter. After a few minutes he had his answer. Arapahoe County would go along with Bob Spangler's demand if he gave a full confession.

The moment of truth for Bob Spangler came on September 15, 2000, at 9:49 A.M. At last he began to tell the truth about what really had happened that cold winter's day of December 30, 1978, in Littleton, Colorado.

Paul Goodman said, "Let's start with the night before. I understand there was an argument that night between you and Nancy."

Bob answered, "Nancy and I had separated, for whatever time it was. And I was enamored with Sharon. About the end of the year I wanted to get back with Nancy. At some point I thought, 'This isn't gonna work.' I didn't want to be with her. Obviously, she was upset. And properly so. She asked, 'Why on earth did you come back if you just wanted to break it off again?'"

And then Spangler's thoughts drifted ahead to his ability to do the crime. He said, "A lot of stuff your profilers will be fascinated with, and I will be fascinated to hear from them, is because a lot of it is as if you reached a decision to take their lives, but without any remorse. As if a curtain dropped and I'm not really involved (long pause). I have no idea why I was capable of such a thing. I asked myself afterward, 'How in hell was I capable of doing that?' And yet, having made the decision, I simply followed through on it."

Goodman: So, you got up early that morning. . . . Were you up before Nancy?

Spangler: Yeah, it was a simple matter to persuade her to come down to the basement.

Goodman: At that point, did you already have the gun in your possession?

Spangler: After I bought it, I shot off four or five rounds to make sure it would work. This was premeditated. I think I had taken the gun down into the basement the night before.

Goodman: So how did you talk Nancy into coming down into the basement?

Spangler: It was after Christmas. I told her, "Come here. Sit quietly. Close your eyes."

Goodman: And she did that? She sat quietly?

Spangler: Yes.

Goodman: What were your next actions?

Spangler: I got the gun. Put it to her head. And shot her. It was easier than divorce. Many times afterward I thought, "How could I do that?" It was my nature, I guess. Something in me that allows me to take myself apart from whatever is

happening. Like standing on the outside and watching. I make a decision
and carry through on it. (He shook his
head in bewilderment.) I really don't
understand how on earth I could have
done that. (He laughed.) It was so utterly incorrect.

Goodman: The note that was found. When
did you type that?

Spangler: I don't know. Day before. Something like that.

Goodman: That was her initial on it?

Spangler: Yes.

Goodman: How did you get her initial on it?

Spangler: Christmas was here. I just got her
to sign her initial. It was already typed
out. I put a piece of paper over it and
had her sign it.

Goodman: Was it that morning?

Spangler: I can't tell you. It could have
been days before.

Goodman: Did you make any adjustments
with the typewriter? Did you wipe it
down?

Spangler: I don't think so.

Goodman: So you've got her in the basement. You retrieve the gun and shot
her. What did you do next?

Spangler: (Long pause) I left the gun on
the floor. Wait. That can't be. Because
the next step was to shoot David and
Susan. And this was simply a matter of
me being enamored with Sharon. I
thought at the time it would be easier
than divorce. And she was not a chil-

dren person. The only thing I can come up with is that it seemed like a good idea at the time.

Bob said he went upstairs and found Susan sleeping in her bed. She never heard him as he approached, gun in hand. He moved close and shot her in the back. The bullet went through her body. He said, "I shot her in the heart. I believe that's what the coroner's report said."

There was one last task to perform. He went to David's room and indicated that it was harder than killing Nancy or Susan. He said he couldn't move forward for a close shot. He stood six to eight feet away and fired.

Goodman noticed that Bob was very dispassionate when talking about murdering Nancy and Susan. When he spoke of David, though, his voice changed and he became more upset. He had always been closer to David, and Goodman wondered if Bob's hand shook as he shot his son.

The shot was not fatal. David woke up in absolute shock at being wounded by his father. Bob said, "I ended up smothering him with a pillow. He couldn't fend me off because he was in total shock."

Bob added that he didn't shoot David again because that was not his plan of how Nancy would have shot the children, each once, and then herself.

At this point Bob Spangler turned directly toward Goodman and Johns and asked, "Why was I capable of such a thing?"

He seemed to have no answer to that question.

Bob continued that after murdering David he returned to the basement and dropped the pistol near Nancy. Then he said he grabbed his coat, climbed over the fence and walked around, just as he'd said in the initial police report. It was cold outside, so he went back to the house, got in his car and drove away. He drove around all day in Denver, had a hamburger at a Burger King and went to watch *The Lord of the Rings* at the movie theater on University Avenue. He said when he returned home, he fully expected to be the one to "discover" the bodies and call the police about the tragedy.

Timothy Trevithick disrupted his plan, however, when he climbed through the basement window and found the bodies. In some ways this worked out even better for Bob. As he approached the house that day, he was met by Arapahoe County sheriff's officers. They asked him a few questions and then told him to sit in his car. While he was sitting there, he watched as the bodies of his family were brought out on stretchers, placed in the ambulances and taken away. Then he was taken to the sheriff's office for questioning.

Goodman asked Bob why he had placed a sock on the butt of the pistol. Bob replied he had no recollection of doing so. Then Goodman asked him if he wore gloves when he fired the weapon. Bob answered that he knew he was wearing gloves later, but he threw them away in a Dumpster sometime that day. The gloves he eventually gave to the police were a different pair.

Goodman also wanted to know about Bob's conversation with lab technician Jack Swanburg that night. Bob said he remembered being over his house, but they never discussed the case. The one thing they did discuss was the possibility that he might take a polygraph test.

Then in a kind of halfhearted explanation for

the murders Bob said, "I'm different. I'm adopted. Don't know how it could have happened. I'm not normal. But I am not a serial killer."

Lenny Johns raised his eyebrows at that.

Around 10:17 A.M. Special Agent Lenny Johns clued in Bob on how the prosecution might proceed. One thing that he and the others knew—and Bob didn't—was that the federal case with Camille Bibles was taking the lead against Spangler for the murder of Donna. The Arapahoe County case was far behind and might never get off the ground before Bob died of cancer. But so far, Bob Spangler had not given one shred of evidence against himself on the death of Donna Spangler. If he didn't, everything they were doing might become academic because he would die first.

It was at this point that Lenny Johns and Bev Perry really came to the fore. They both knew Bob Spangler well at this point and deduced what might be very important to him. Some kind of bargain could be struck if he would give up information on the murder of Donna Spangler. Johns reiterated that if Spangler cooperated fully on all cases, he could probably be permitted to visit the Grand Canyon one last time. It was also apparent that Bob Spangler was adamant that none of Donna's children get any proceeds from the sale of his house on Applewood when that went through.

Bev Perry said later, "I was in the room pretty early on. I think the time I spent with Judy the first day (September 14) was helpful in overcoming Bob's resistance to talking about the murder of Donna at Grand Canyon National Park. After his confession to the 1978 Littleton murders, there was a two-part appeal. My part was directed at Judy as much as Bob, as I believed she could influence Bob at that moment in time and that she could relate to someone caring about what happened to their mother. It was important to convince Bob that we would not come after him or his estate if he confessed. Bob was determined to control his money even after his death. And he did not want any of the money going to Donna's kids.

"As for the Grand Canyon, Bob and Judy had already planned and obtained Grand Canyon backcountry permits for a trip in October. They were planning to do what is the Royal Arch Route."

But the real prize for Spangler, in Lenny Johns's estimation, was that Bob wanted to talk to an FBI profiler to find out why "he was different." Johns dangled this prize in front of Spangler and used a small ruse of his own. He said that no FBI profiler was going to talk to him if he only claimed the murders of three people. There needed to be a fourth. He had to be determined to be a serial killer. The murders of his family on South Franklin Way had only been a mass murder, Johns told him. Not a serial case. If he didn't give up the fact that he'd murdered Donna at the Grand Canyon, he could forget about ever talking to an FBI profiler.

Bob turned to Judy and quietly discussed the matter. At 10:30 A.M. he turned back to Lenny Johns and said, "You've got your serial."

And then he added that they were giving him credit for one too many. He said he'd killed Nancy, Susan, David and Donna, but not Sharon. Bob commented that she'd really committed suicide as he stated. But then, only hours before he'd stated he'd had nothing to do with Donna's death. He could only be believed up to a point.

Bob explained that he'd been unhappy in his marriage to Donna, but there was no real plan in place to kill her on the early part of the Easter week hike. In fact, he didn't reach a decision about it until the morning of April 11, 1993, the fourth anniversary of their meeting.

Bob seemed most relaxed discussing the Grand Canyon crime with Bev Perry. He knew she was a Grand Canyon veteran and admired her for it. She asked him, "Did she (Donna) want to go on the hike?"

Spangler: I don't know. I guess. I think this was another case of her going on a hike because she knew how much the Canyon meant to me.

Perry: Were you having arguments at the time?

Spangler: No. It was just not a good marriage. I learned after we were married she seemed to have a lifelong jealousy. A lack of trust. This became more abundantly apparent as time went by. I was also in a physical condition, and I don't know what brought it on . . . age, or what is now very popular, erectile dysfunction. So, I wasn't interested in a sex life with her. But no arguments. No fights.

Perry: How was the hike in?

Spangler: Long. Especially in terms of time, because Donna was not a strong hiker. We stayed at the mine to get a jump start on the next day (he had a quizzical look on his face). I must have been thinking about it at that point (snaps fingers as if having a revelation). I must have been thinking of it, for it to suddenly pop out like that. Clearly, the decision to kill her was reached the next morning.

Perry: Before you left your camp?

Spangler: No. We did start up that trail that goes up the side. And I had to be thinking, "Either now or never." There is not any place farther up for a fatal accident to occur on the rest of the trail. Oh, it could, but you wouldn't be certain of the results. And thanks to my nature, I was capable of doing it. The place where she stopped was fairly vertical. And she was not a big woman, so she was no match for me.

Then in a matter-of-fact manner he asked Perry, "You've been to the site?"

Bev Perry answered, "Yes."

Spangler asked, "It's what, one hundred and thirty, two hundred feet down?"

Bev said, "We measured it. It's one hundred and forty feet."

Spangler then recalled his emotions right after pushing her over the edge. And he became very animated about his own close call with death. "I can remember leaning forward to look over the edge and nearly fell over. All that weight of the pack. It was a very close thing. After Donna's death, I began to notice I couldn't go places that I could before. Suddenly I became aware of heights and the real danger that exists in the Canyon."

Bev Perry noticed how dispassionate Bob was while talking about the murder of Donna, but how excited he became while recounting his own near miss. It was all about Bob as usual. As he had done about the murder of Nancy, once again he commented, "It was easier than divorce."

At this point Paul Goodman backtracked and asked why he had killed Nancy, Susan and David. Bob answered, "I'm a selfish person. I was looking for the easy way out and they stood in the way of my relationship with Sharon."

Just before the interview was over, Lenny Johns asked Bob, "After getting this off your chest, do you feel good about talking about it now?"

Bob Spangler shrugged and said, "I don't know. I'm interested in talking to your profilers. Whether they come to any kind of speculation as to why or how I'm capable of compartmentalizing and doing something like that. I mean, most people are incapable of doing it. You might think it, you might want to, but barring being in the midst of a fight, I don't think most people are capable of simply saying, 'Well, I guess I'm gonna do this,' and then do it for God's sake."

Then after a long pause he added, "I'm different. I think I'm interesting. I'm not your average everyday person. I'm adopted. I have no idea who my parents were. What my background is, or what the gene pool might have been. Whether that has anything to do with it, I don't know. Maybe later some epiphany will occur."

At this point Lenny Johns emphatically said, "I can tell you one thing, it is not normal to be capable of what you did."

Bob slapped the table with his hand and said, "I believe that!"

Johns continued, "I see in you an interest to be evaluated and to find out what makes you—you. If I was in your shoes, I would want to do that. The thing that makes you a serial killer, that makes you different from us, we have a mechanism that makes us go, 'I'm gonna kill that son of a bitch!' But then we let it go. But you don't have that mechanism."

At around 11:20 A.M. the interview was over and both Bob and Judy Spangler left the Mesa County Sheriff's Office with the understanding that he would be arrested after a thirty-day grace period. He would have time to wrap up his affairs, but he could not recant on any of the promises he made. He was to cooperate fully with authorities about the murders. Besides the complaint already going forward in the federal grand jury, another one was soon drawn up by Paul Goodman concerning the Littleton case.

Goodman wrote: "Based on the aforementioned, the Affiant respectfully requests a warrant of arrest for Spangler, Robert Merlin, for the charge of Murder in the First Degree. Three Counts." The arrest, as agreed upon, would not take place immediately.

In this interim Bev Perry was busy talking with Bob and Judy Spangler about their planned hike in the Grand Canyon. As Perry recalled later, "I expressed my concerns about their trip and choice of hikes. My tone and approach was that of a backcountry ranger concerned about search-and-rescue issues on that very difficult hike and how unpredictable were changes in his physical health. Actually, what I said was very sincere from those perspectives. I didn't think either one of them would have believed any sort of ruse. They were both too experienced and, in Bob's case, knew the Canyon too well."

But Bob had his own ideas about how things should be run, and the deal was in place for less than three days before Bob Spangler started trying to tinker with it. Always one who wanted to have the upper hand and be in control of events, he sent two remarkable letters to Special Agent Lenny Johns. The first letter was dated September 18, 2000. It began: "There's an issue I have to raise before meeting and talking with your profilers. It's extremely important to me. The issue is publicity. I don't want to disillusion all the people I've known who consider me an exemplary person, one they admire, respect and love. I cannot see the necessity of that."

He told Johns that the public was hardly "aching" to hear about him. He said he wasn't a serial killer the public was aware of. Not some guy who collected homeless people, gays or blacks to be murdered. In fact, the public had no reason to fear him and shouldn't become aware of him through the media. He told Johns that his arrest and confession wouldn't persuade one potential or current serial killer from doing what he felt he had to do. He said the deterrence factor would be zero.

Bob went on to say that the only reason the FBI would release publicity about him was to polish their own image: "A chance to brag about how good you are. But you'd be doing that at the expense of those innocent people who believe in me, admire and respect me, think of me as the embodiment of what a human being should be."

He asked why these people should be punished,

why their memories of him should be tarnished, since he was going to die soon anyway. He wondered how such publicity could benefit society sufficiently to outweigh the pain and suffering these individuals would feel about him.

Bob listed all the things he was giving the investigators "free of charge," as he put it. First, there was a confession on a couple of cases that may have never seen the inside of a courtroom. Second, there was a promise by him to work closely with profilers, holding back nothing. Third, the cancer would kill him soon, so they wouldn't have to wade through eight years of appeals connected with most murder cases. On this last point about the terminal cancer, he asked rhetorically, "God's retribution, hmmm?"

Bob said, "In other words your [*sic*] getting a free ride on this. I'm making it incredibly easy on you. Isn't that enough? Reassure me, please."

Obviously from the response he got, Bob Spangler wasn't reassured. The timing of his second letter, and a comment that he made in it, makes it evident that he was ready to break off the "deal" if all his demands weren't accepted. He wanted to call the shots, and there were some shots the investigators were not willing to make.

Bob's letter dated September 20, 2000, was just as remarkable in its own way as the first one. He really didn't see himself as a serial killer. He was an "exemplary human being" in his own estimation. Someone whom people admired and respected. And now he felt persecuted because the investigators were going to release information to the media the way they did about all criminals. Whether Bob Spangler liked it or not, he did live in a democracy where the First Amendment was still in place and criminal activities were reported in newspapers. He decided to ignore that fact.

Bob wrote to Lenny Johns in his letter of September 20 (a letter meant for public distribution): "If you're reading this, it means the FBI and/or Arapahoe County Sheriff's Office in Colorado have deliberately lied to me in order to gain my cooperation and brag about themselves. Here's the story."

He told of killing his family in Littleton and murdering Donna at the Grand Canyon. He said he wouldn't give the rationale for why he had done those things. "Suffice it to say," he added, "they occurred."

He surmised that the law enforcement agents didn't have an airtight case against him or they would have already arrested him. They had to come angling to him for a confession. He added, "They said they knew I was a serial killer and threatened serious federal grand jury indictment consequences if I didn't agree to work with their profilers." But he said he countered with the fact that his death by cancer was a lot more serious than any grand jury indictments they might throw at him.

"The imminent death angle was everything," he explained. "Had I not an absolute death sentence (due to cancer), I very likely would have decided to make them go to court and try to prove what they hadn't been able to prove up to then. My reputation with friends was outstanding and I say without hesitation, well deserved."

Then he added that he really was two separate people: "I'd say about 99.9 percent qualified as an eminently admirable human being, a good friend, able mentor, solid role model and pretty much all around good guy. But in two days out of nearly 68 years I was a killer."

Bob asked if the fact that he was a killer canceled out all the good aspects of his life. He said that his friends and sports associates had nothing but praise and respect for his abilities. He wondered why there must be "heartache for innocent people by exposing their idol's feet of clay."

Bob supposed the only reason the FBI and Arapahoe County was doing this was because they were being stupid bureaucrats who did everything by the book. Then he lashed out, "The FBI's promise to me, its reputation for trust and integrity, be damned."

Bob wondered if the profilers had learned much about him from his confession on videotape. He said he supposed he had a mind that allowed him to kill. "It requires a singular focus in committing the actual crime, quite cold-bloodedly." But he argued the acts were separate from the rest of his life. He said that afterward he suffered all the sorrow and grief of his dead family, as if someone else had done the murders. "As I write this I cannot understand how I was capable of such irrational and violent acts."

Then Bob admitted something interesting. He said he had written this particular letter even before the first one before because he did not believe that the investigators would stick to their deal (though he failed to admit that they had never promised there would be no media exposure on the case). He said he decided to go ahead with the confession, even though he didn't trust them, mainly because he was interested in talking to an FBI profiler about the "black side of my life."

He stated, "One hopes they (the investigators)

feel a little chagrin for being caught in their lie to gain my help."

Bob closed with a remark that they did not know the real him. The other part of his life, the killer, he said was only 1 percent of his makeup. It was somehow not even associated with who he really was. Bob wrote: "My real self is quite real, quite honest and quite worthy of respect. I am sorry and ashamed that this second life you weren't aware of ever existed. I was terribly wrong. And I am also dying. That's my story. Goodbye and God bless all of you. Robert M. Spangler—Confessed Murderer."

With the issuance of this letter to Lenny Johns, Bob Spangler in effect told him that all deals were off. He wouldn't cooperate with them anymore and they could do their best to bring him to trial.

There is further evidence that Bob Spangler was not going to cooperate with authorities no matter what. According to Camille Bibles's point of view: "There was a good plan in place and we did have the profilers on their way to the Canyon." In fact, the profilers were going to talk with him on the South Rim. But Bob was right about one thing. None of the authorities were going to let him hike down off the rim with Judy. As Bev Perry said later, "We were going to let him come to the park for a visit. Even speak with FBI profilers. We never felt we could let them hike in the Canyon. The risk to Judy was unacceptable. We planned to make the arrest before any planned hike. But he backed out of his arrangements, which negated our good-faith efforts to address his concerns about the time he needed prior to being taken into custody. All of that ended when Spangler contacted Lenny and said he didn't want to go to the Canyon anymore and didn't want to work with us, to a large degree, because I think he knew he wouldn't be coming home. At that point Lenny and I headed to Grand Junction; Paul Goodman, who was on his way to the Canyon, diverted to Grand Junction; and Camille went straight to Phoenix."

In fact, there was real concern now amongst the investigators about what Bob Spangler's next move might be. Lenny Johns wondered if he might try pulling a "suicide by cop." In other words, provoke a confrontation while being arrested so that the police would have to shoot him. By this means he would put the onus on the police for shooting "poor cancer-stricken Bob Spangler."

There was also the concern that he might, in a fit of anger, kill Judy, his new wife. Or in a twist of the Littleton scenario, he might kill her and then himself. After all, what did he have to lose? He was a dead man anyway.

Bev Perry was so concerned for Judy Spangler's safety that she had phoned her every day after the confession of September 15, saying it might be wise if she left the house and stayed with friends. Judy replied she was not afraid of Bob. She said she knew he was telling the truth about killing the others, but he had changed. She didn't believe he would harm her.

If all deals were off on Bob's part, so was any chance the investigators would give him a chance to go to the Grand Canyon for one last camping trip. There was no way the investigators were going to let him near the edge, especially with Judy around. It was too convenient a spot for a homicide/suicide.

Camille Bibles sped up the grand jury indictment process against Bob Spangler while the investigators went into a prearrest mode. Close tabs were kept on Bob, in case he should try and make a run for it. Special Agent Lenny Johns scratched down several items on his notepad that would be important when the arrest came and things needed to be done soon after the arrest. In uppercase letters he wrote down on the pad, as far as the upcoming arrest went, "CAUTION!"

One of the interesting notations on his pad was about how Bob did everything he could to try and control the situation. Johns thought it might be useful to try and deflate Bob's estimation of himself, force him to see that events were running past his ability to control them and make him more compliant. He was apt to be less dangerous to everyone around him, including himself, if he felt the reins of power were out of his grasp. Johns wrote, "Show him he can't win. He's a child serial killer. Investigate past him. Overwhelm him."

And Special Agent Johns began compiling a list of all the things he wanted on a search warrant when it came time to implement it. He wanted all three homes in Grand Junction owned by Bob Spangler—the one on Applewood, the one on Hill and the one they lived in on Cannell—to be searched and certain items seized. This would go a long way in adding to Camille Bibles's ammunition when it came time for trial.

Johns also wrote a letter to his superiors asking that every phone he used be installed with a recording device. He wrote, "I authorize Special Agents (names deleted) of the Federal Bureau of Investigation, to install a recording device on any telephone utilized by me for the purpose of recording conversations I may have with Robert M. Spangler."

Johns wanted all his conversations on tapes so that Spangler could not later say he had been threatened, lied to or made certain deals by Johns.

By the evening of October 2, 2000, Camille Bibles had what she had been looking forward to for so long. It was an indictment by the grand jury. The foreperson signed off on the statement, which began, "On or about April 11, 1993, in the District of Arizona, within the confines of Grand Canyon National Park, Robert Merlin Spangler did, with premeditation and malice aforethought, kill and murder Donna Sundling Spangler."

The arrest was to take place the next day in Grand Junction by law enforcement officers. The question on everyone's mind: would Bob Spangler attempt to kill them, kill himself or kill his wife?

Chapter 14

"I'm Not Afraid of Bob."

The investigators were taking no chances on the morning of October 3, 2000, when they moved into position to arrest Bob Spangler at his home on Cannell Avenue in Grand Junction. An FBI report showed that the team wore protective gear, identifying clothing, body armor, and carried pepper spray, flex cuffs and handguns. There was a check mark on the report next to an item called "The FBI Policy of Deadly Force." It read: "Agents may use deadly force only when necessary, that is, when the agent has a reasonable belief that subject of such force poses an imminent threat of danger of death or serious physical injury to the agent or another person."

Street side security was placed in the hands of Grand Junction police officers as well as around the surrounding area. An EMS ambulance was on call just in case there were any injuries. And Special Agent Lenny Johns let the others know that he wanted to let Bob Spangler come out of the house on his own, but under no circumstances was he to be allowed back into the house once he'd come out. He was deemed to be too much of a threat to himself if he did so, and to Judy as well.

At 1:15 P.M. everything was in place and it was now up to Bob Spangler how things would proceed. He really had nothing to lose if he shot it out with the officers. Bob played it by the book, though, cognizant of the fact that an arrest did not make a conviction. He was still cocky and sure of himself and determined to beat the rap, even though he had given away so much in his confession. He still had a few tricks up his sleeve.

Bob was angry at the FBI, when he left the house, was handcuffed and then placed in a squad car. To his mind, they had broken their agreement. He had been promised a last trip to the Grand Canyon. He was going to the federal courthouse in Grand Junction instead.

As Camille Bibles remembered, "Moments after the arrest warrant was issued, Lenny had Spangler in custody and I was in a phone conference call with Donna's children. They had no idea what was going on until that call, and I felt strongly that they needed to be told as soon as possible."

At the Federal Building in Grand Junction, Bob had an initial appearance before United States magistrate judge James Robb. AUSA Camille Bibles presented the charges against Spangler. The whole thing took only a few minutes.

After the initial appearance Bob was transported to the Mesa County Sheriff's Office Detention Facility. He was fingerprinted, had his mug shot taken and was placed behind bars. A short while later, he received some medication for his cancer, delivered from his home.

The following day, Special Agent Johns filled out a

form asking for a search warrant on all the homes owned by Bob and Judy Spangler in Grand Junction. These included the house lived in by Bob on Applewood Street before he met Judy, the house currently lived in by the two on Cannell Avenue and the fixer-upper on Hill Avenue. Special Agent Johns gave Judge Robb a detailed summary of the case against Spangler that covered all the information they knew about him. He also said that on the day of the video-taped interview, Bob had expressed concern to Judy about the files on his computer that pertained to his numerous hikes in the Grand Canyon. With this in mind, Special Agent Johns told Judge Robb that the files should be seized and searched, since they might reveal criminal activity Spangler had been involved in at the Canyon. He backed up his concern by quoting from FBI profiler Gerry Downes of the NCAVC about the habits of serial killers. "After discussion with Downes of general facts on this matter, it appears that Robert Merlin Spangler is capable of planning and committing aforementioned criminal activity. The experience and research of the NCAVC has determined that these types of individuals have a tendency to both obtain and keep personal items from their victims. Typically, retained items may include clothing of the victims and other personal items such as photographs, personal identification cards and jewelry. These items are sometimes maintained by the offender for their personal gratification. Accordingly, these items are generally kept hidden by the offender in an area they feel is safe and secure. Your affiant submits that there is probable cause to believe Robert Merlin Spangler has stored newspaper clippings, journals, videotapes, audiotapes, correspondence and maps relating to Grand Canyon hikes. Your affiant further submits that there is probable cause to believe that there is electronic mail stored on Robert Merlin Spangler's computer."

Receiving a search warrant from Judge Robb, Special Agent Johns methodically wrote down the way he wanted to approach the search of the various homes around Grand Junction. He wrote: "First Priority—Applewood Street. This is Bob's house. It is the residence he bought when he moved to Grand Junction from Durango. It's where he lived prior to moving in with Judith Hilty. Bob maintains a fax machine at this address. Bob keeps records of his past hikes at this residence.

"Second Priority—Home on Cannell Avenue. This is current residence of both Bob Spangler and Judy Spangler. Their computer is at this residence.

"Third Priority—Home on Hill Avenue. It's the remodeled house. Bob Spangler was in this house most of the afternoon of September 28, 2000."

For some reason the plan did not work out quite as expected. The house on Cannell Avenue was searched first, not second. But as the search proceeded, Special Agent Johns kept a running timeline of items as they were seized.

Cannell Avenue Residence:

1:15 PM—Denver map and four large family photograph albums.
1:35 PM—Robert Spangler's last will and testament.
1:38 PM—Folder with confession statements.
1:50 PM—Grand Canyon hiking folder.
1:53 PM—Maps where Bob's ashes are to be placed in Grand Canyon.

2:10 PM—Mutual fund and other financial
    documents.
2:15 PM—Floppy disk labeled Grand Canyon.
2:51 PM—Property ownership paperwork.
2:53 PM—Copy of article on 1978 deaths.
3:20 PM—Dell Pentium II CPU.
3:23 PM—Hardcopies of e mails made by Bob
    Spangler.
3:50 PM—Bag of shredded paper from waste-
    basket.
3:50 PM—Deceased family members identity
    papers.

The search and seizure team next moved to the
house owned by Bob Spangler on Applewood
Street.

5:12 PM—Grand Canyon photographs.
5:14 PM—Grand Canyon video tapes.
5:15 PM—Donna, Sharon and Bob's Journals.
5:15 PM—Compaq Presario CPU.
5:19 PM—Miscellaneous photos.

The last house searched was the fixer-upper on
Hill Avenue and it revealed one very interesting
item.

6:45 PM—Book, <u>Final Exit</u>, found in closet.

This book started a debate amongst the investigators about its possible use. The book was written by
Derek Humphry and it told how a person might
commit suicide. But it also went into detail about
how a person might make a suicide look like a death
from natural causes. There were several underlined

passages. It was wondered if Bob planned to use this book to commit suicide, or had he used it to mask that of Sharon Spangler back in 1994? After all, he was the last one in the room with her when she died. Had he helped her die? It was already known that he was no novice at rigging a homicide to look like a suicide. As Bev Perry later said, "The so-called note that Sharon had written before her suicide had all the earmarks of 'Bobspeak.'"

Whatever the case about Sharon Spangler, there were more pressing matters at the present. Bob Spangler had a detention hearing on October 6, 2000, at 9:00 A.M. before the United States magistrate judge James Robb. Camille Bibles was there for the United States Attorney's Office and court-appointed defense attorney William Kain represented Bob Spangler. The entire proceedings lasted only eight minutes.

During that time friends of Judy Spangler sat around her in the front row, giving her moral support. When Bob Spangler entered the courtroom, he winked at Judy and seemed almost chipper that morning. However, there were others in the courtroom who were not there to support Judy or Bob. They were Donna's children, and they looked with loathing upon the man who had killed their mother.

According to the *Grand Junction Daily Sentinel*, "Relatives of his third wife, Donna Sundling, filled half the front row of the courtroom in the Wayne Aspinall Federal Building." The newspaper also stated that Bob made no statements but conferred frequently with his lawyer. Bob was particularly mortified at having to wear a standard jail issue jumpsuit during the proceedings.

During the brief proceedings defense counsel Kain said they would waive an identity challenge. Bob

Spangler was remanded over to the custody of a United States marshal for transportation to a cell in Denver before proceeding to the District of Arizona.

William Kain had only a short statement written by Bob to present to a few reporters stationed at the courthouse. It read: "He says he has cooperated with the FBI at all stages of the investigation. He has been diagnosed with terminal brain cancer. And he has only a few months to live."

When a reporter asked if Spangler had indicated any remorse for the killings, Kain answered he was not authorized to say anything more.

Judy Spangler said even less to reporters as she left the courthouse, surrounded by friends. She called out to the newsmen, only once, saying, "I'm not afraid of Bob!"

What started out that day as a trickle of media attention, soon turned into a flood, just as Bob Spangler had worried it would. Several large newspapers in Colorado and Arizona were picking up the story, as well as local radio and television stations. Headlines above the articles said such things as: MAN HELD IN DEATHS OF 2 WIVES AND 2 KIDS; CONFESSED KILLER TO BE SENT TO ARIZONA FOR TRIAL; FORMER DEEJAY SUSPECTED OF KILLING WIVES, and even from as far away as Ames, Iowa, the newspaper stated: FORMER AMES MAN ADMITS TO KILLINGS.

The news about Bob Spangler's arrest spread outward in all directions—shocking friends, family and associates, and touching even former law enforcement agents. Some of the friends and neighbors were thoroughly stunned by the news. To them, Bob always had been the perfect neighbor and perfect friend, just as he claimed to be. Donna Christensen, a neighbor on South Franklin Way in Littleton, told a *Denver Post* reporter, "I'm flabbergasted. Oh, you're kidding. We had always heard that she (Nancy) had killed the children and then herself. I remember it happened during a football game, and everybody was very surprised after the game to find these yellow barricades around."

Joyce Williams of Grand Junction, who lived next door to Bob on Applewood Street, said, "He's the kind of person you always wanted for a neighbor. This is just terrible."

Laurie Lacy of Grand Junction, who helped Bob officiate soccer games, told the *Denver Post*, "After we found out, we all compared notes about all those deaths. He told us all different stories about how his kids had died."

In fact, Spangler had told some referees that his first wife committed suicide after his daughter had died of a drug overdose and his son was killed in a car accident. He told Lacy's husband that both children had died in a car accident. And he'd told some people at the theater group that his first wife died of cancer.

One person from the theater group told a reporter, "I don't know why we didn't compare stories. I guess we didn't want to talk about it."

He might well have asked why Bob made up so many different stories of how his first family had died. Methodical in so many things, he seemed to make up stories about their deaths on the spur of the moment.

One of the people who worked with Bob at the Grand Junction little theater told the reporter for the *Daily Sentinel* that Spangler had been preparing for an upcoming role in *Joseph and the Amazing Technicolor Dreamcoat*. As the newspaper pointed out,

"It's a musical about the biblical tale of a man left to die by his brothers, but miraculously survives."

Down in Durango, Coby Weigert, superintendent of recreation for the city, remembered Bob Spangler as a certified soccer referee. He told the *Durango Herald* that Bob was a dependable employee and knowledgeable referee who always took time to explain to children why he made a certain call during a game. Weigert said, "It's kind of shocking news if this truly holds up. I never thought it would have happened, just based on his demeanor at work."

John Mackley, who knew Bob at radio station KRSJ, told the *Durango Herald,* "He was a private man, and he seemed saddened to have lost his wife, Donna." Mackley also spoke of Bob's strong opinions about domestic violence. "I remember some of his shows and Bob really pouring out his heart to the listeners about how he had gone through it. He was quite an actor."

Then Mackley admitted that after Donna's accident at the Grand Canyon he and others had a fleeting moment when they no longer believed Bob's story. "It just didn't feel right," he said.

In fact, there were a lot of people around Durango who didn't believe Bob Spangler's stories. Cindy Marquardt, who knew Bob in Durango, told the *Rocky Mountain News,* "There were grisly jokes going around, rumors that he pushed his wife over the cliff."

Ward Holmes, former general manager of Four Corners Broadcasting, told the *Denver Post,* "Rumors of foul play by Spangler after 1993 began to spread. Not everyone was shocked to hear he confessed."

Speaking to the *Durango Herald,* Holmes added, "I'm just glad he came clean, and if there is an afterlife, I hope he finds some kind of peace there. Because I know he's very ill."

John Mackley picked up on this theme by saying that he was sorry Spangler chose the life that he had: "He could have genuinely been a good person instead of pretending to be a good person."

Of course the people affected the most by Bob Spangler's confession and arrest were the surviving family members related to Nancy and Donna. Donna Sundling Spangler's ex-husband, Wayne Sundling, told the *Rocky Mountain News,* "The word 'endearing' gets used a lot in the news stories about him. It seemed like he was always described as a great soccer coach. He called his marriage to Donna a mistake. That it was easier than divorce. Her life was anything but a mistake. He was just a predator on the loose. This has really hurt my children."

Donna's children were only in their thirties when Bob Spangler killed their mother. He'd even had the gall to tell one of her sons after her death that he planned to take a hike back to "Donna's Point" and plant wildflowers there in her memory. All of them hoped that he lived long enough to face justice on earth and not just on some more ethereal plane. They also were in the planning stages of doing one more thing that Bob had feared: sue him and his estate, after he died, in civil court to get back some of the money that Donna had sunk into their Durango home—the very home he'd said he'd made a killing on.

The relatives of Nancy Spangler felt just as angry about what Bob Spangler had done. In some ways, even more so. He had not only murdered her, he had heaped the onus of being a "suicide" and "child killer" upon her, even though she was innocent of both. Her memory had been tainted for twenty-eight years.

Nancy's stepsister, Cathy, hoped that the court proceedings would restore some of Nancy's good name. It was as if he had killed her twice. First in the flesh, then her reputation.

Martha Winter, Nancy's cousin, told the *Rocky Mountain News*, "I've had all the emotions. Fury, frustration, grief. I loved Nancy."

Especially painful to Martha were the allegations that Nancy had turned the gun on her children and then herself. "That was very hard. You want the world to know she was an innocent person. I wish the generation before me could have known the truth. I wish her mom could have known. That my dad could have known."

Nancy's own mother, Manzella Fitch, had died the year before Bob Spangler confessed, going to her grave not knowing that Nancy was innocent of homicide/suicide. But she'd always had her suspicions about Bob's role in the tragedy. And so did Martha Winter. When she saw Bob at Manzella Fitch's funeral, she told him, "I never want to see or hear from you again."

Perhaps the one most affected by the news was Nancy's stepbrother, David Fitch. He told the *Rocky Mountain News* reporter that he struggled for years with the homicide/suicide that Nancy had supposedly committed. Over time he began to suspect Bob Spangler. He didn't think his sister was capable of such an act, and he wondered how petite Nancy could have overpowered her strong, tall son. He added, "I just couldn't believe Bob's second wife died accidentally. People who believe that, I've got some swampland to sell them."

David brought up something else that was in the back of other family members' minds as well. It was the investigation that had been conducted in Littleton in 1978. Fitch wondered if perhaps Bob had been arrested back then, he might never have met Donna Sundling and could not murder her.

In point of fact, the 1978 Arapahoe County Sheriff's Office investigation of Bob Spangler had not been handled well. True, forensic procedures were more primitive then and there was, after all, that "suicide note." But even with these facts, there was more that could have been done on the case.

Neither Marvin Tucker nor Karen Beauchamp chose to talk with reporters after the news of Bob Spangler's arrest broke. But one person did, and he took his lumps, admitting that his part in the initial investigation had been less than sterling. He was lab technician Jack Swanburg.

Swanburg told the *Rocky Mountain News,* "How could I have been so dumb? He (Bob) was sleeping in a bedroom right next to my wife and me, and we had four kids in the house. It's probably one of the least intelligent things I've done. Our thinking at the time was that Spangler wasn't a criminal. He was a victim. He'd just lost his wife and two children."

The one Arapahoe County sheriff's investigator who wasn't feeling sheepish now was Investigator Paul Goodman. All his years of hard work on the case had paid off and he told a reporter, "It was a good feeling to accomplish what we did. I never thought I wouldn't get there. But sometimes it takes a long time. When you finally get there, it's a great feeling."

Jose de Jesus Rivera, the head United States attorney for the District of Arizona, was pleased with Goodman and the whole team as well. He told reporters, "This arrest is a result of the cooperation and dedication of several law enforcement agencies that were determined to solve this reprehensible crime and arrest the person responsible."

Someone not feeling so good in the aftermath of Bob Spangler's confession and arrest was his new wife, Judy Spangler. According to Randy Hampton, Grand Junction KNZZ radio news director, he got a call from a friend who was also a close friend of Judy's. The mutual friend told him that she was being besieged by reporters at her home and asked if Hampton could help. It was getting so bad that Judy couldn't even go out into her yard.

Hampton knew about such things and he telephoned Judy Spangler and told her that the media wouldn't leave until she made some kind of statement. He said it would be best to get it over with all at once. Judy agreed with his assessment and promised to come into the radio station for an interview by him. The agreement spelled out that she would only give this one interview and the radio station was to hand it out to any media sources that wanted it.

Randy Hampton's overall impression of Judy Spangler was "She was very intelligent, concerned about feelings and somewhat New Age in her beliefs. She was well-spoken and interested in the local arts and theater. Bob Spangler had been her kind of man, with similar kinds of interests."

When Judy Spangler showed up at the radio station, she was very jittery and emotional, but she did do the best she could under the circumstances. She told Hampton, "I've never been afraid of Bob. He never showed this side to me. I'm still in love with him."

Wanting to know what he had told her about what had happened to his previous wives, Judy answered that Bob said they had died tragically. Judy recounted, "Bob had encountered tragedy in previous marriages. I never knew or suspected that he had a hand in it." She hadn't pressed him on the subject of his former wives. She and Bob had been living in the present, not the past.

When Bob was first approached by the authorities and made his first interview on September 14, 2000, she had no idea what was coming. She had no inkling until Bev Perry clued her in about all the accusations—it was like a lightning bolt out of a clear blue sky.

That night after she and Bob went home, they talked about how Nancy and Donna had died. Still, he did not tell her about his role in their deaths. He gave her the same lies he had told others over the years and proclaimed his innocence of any wrongdoing.

It was the next day, September 15, while she sat through the interview with him that the whole truth came out. It shocked her, but she knew he was a dying man. She said, "He's not like that now. I had no indication that he was capable of this sort of thing. He always seemed a very gentle person. Always has been with me. He's great with me."

The interview was very hard for her. Several times she seemed almost incapable of going on. Hampton would ask her a pointed question and she would answer, "I'm not ready to answer that."

Randy Hampton was caught between a rock and a hard place. He wanted to conduct a good and thorough interview, but he was also doing this because a friend had asked him to do it. He said later that it was hard to tell where the interview ended and the favor to a friend began. "I would have pushed harder under different circumstances," he said. "But it was hard to tell the line between journalism and friendship."

In the end the interview accomplished what it had set out to do. The news media got what they wanted and quit besieging Judy Spangler. And the overall impression of her was a woman who stuck by her man, no matter what. Many people wondered how she could, knowing what she did now. But the simple fact of the matter lay in her one-sentence answer, "I love him."

Even with Bob Spangler behind bars and the seizure of items from his various homes, the FBI was still collecting data from various friends and associates who had known Bob. The FBI was aware that every bit of evidence against him was just one more weapon in Camille Bibles's arsenal when they went to trial in Arizona. Bob Spangler had been arrested all right, but he was far from convicted.

Comments about Bob Spangler from people who knew him came in from every point of the compass. One was from a friend of Donna's in Durango who said, "She (Donna) wouldn't even get up on an eight-foot beam to water her plants. She was afraid of heights. There's no way she would have stood next to the edge at the Grand Canyon."

Another was someone who had received a telephone call from Donna right before her fatal Easter week hike of 1993. Donna told her that she had just called all her children to say that she loved them. "She had some sort of premonition that something bad would happen."

Another person in Durango commented about

Bob Spangler's memory of Donna after she was dead: "He mocked her for having those fears about the Canyon. And he also mocked the eating disorder that she'd gone through." This person thought it was very inappropriate behavior for someone who had lost his wife so tragically in an accident. It certainly didn't seem like the actions of a grieving husband.

Even more inappropriate was a comment Bob made in Durango to someone who had problems with their kids at the time. He told the person, "Wait until they become teenagers." He said it with such malice that the person wondered how he could utter such a thing, since Bob had recounted how he'd lost his teenage children (with one more of his lies on the subject). The person had the impression that Bob hadn't liked his kids very much and was glad they were out of his life.

But one of Bob's most egregious acts had occurred at the memorial service for Donna after her death. One woman told the FBI, "Everyone, including me, was upset. But not Bob. He seemed like he'd already gotten past the fact that Donna died at the Grand Canyon. It gave me an eerie feeling. And I thought to myself, 'He did it.'"

One of the most intriguing FBI reports was dated November 3, 2000. It concerned the death of Bob Spangler's father in Iowa. The report stated, "Merlin Spangler died under suspicious circumstances when Robert Spangler had been visiting in Ames, Iowa. The Ames Police Department is waiting for disposition of the existing charges against Spangler and is interested in FBI assistance in interviewing him about the death of his father." The FBI further noted, "We were concerned over inconsistencies between Robert telling (name deleted) that his father had a hard time dying and his statement to police that he was not present when his father died."

As fall deepened, another thing on the minds of the FBI, and Spangler himself, was just how long he had to live. One thing was for certain, it wasn't long, and to that end Bob wrote an amendment to his last will and testament. It read: "I hereby direct that my remains be cremated; that my ashes be strewn into the Grand Canyon well away from the peopled rims, specifically along the Boucher Trail below Yuma Point overlooking Hermit Creek Canyon as described in a separate document. There is to be no headstone or marker or funeral; and that all related expenses be kept to a minimum. A gathering to celebrate my life may be held if my family and friends desire."

This may have been Bob Spangler's final wishes, but it remained to be seen if AUSA Camille Bibles would allow this to happen. She loved the Grand Canyon and didn't want his ashes desecrating a place where he had murdered one of his wives. In the past Bob Spangler had called the shots when dealing with women. However, he did not call the shots with Camille Bibles.

Chapter 15

Justice

With the removal of Bob Spangler to Arizona, his travails switched from the squad room to the courtroom. As early as October 17, 2000, documents from Colorado were pouring into the new federal courthouse in Phoenix, Arizona. This initial wave concerned minute entries, docket sheet, financial affidavit and order of appointment of counsel.

It was interesting what Bob Spangler wrote on his financial affidavit for the court. To the question, "Are you employed?" He wrote, "No."

"How much does your spouse make per month?" it queried. "No idea," he answered.

"Have you received within the past twelve months any income from a business, profession or other form of self employment?" Bob wrote, "$944 per month, social security, and $173 per month pension."

"Do you own any real estate, stocks, bonds, notes, automobiles or other valuable property?" He wrote, "No."

This seemed to be an outright lie to the prosecutor. With bonds, mutual funds and real estate, it was estimated that Bob Spangler was worth in the neighborhood of $1 million.

Back on September 15, 2000, Bob had contacted a financial institution that was handling some of his money. He wrote, "Gentlemen, I have an urgent need for instant cash." He had asked them to close certain accounts, which included a municipal bank fund, a prime money market account and some stocks. All of his stocks and bonds and accounts added up to around $545,000. His home on Applewood Street was appraised at $150,000 and was free and clear of mortgage, as was the fixer-upper on Hill Avenue. Bob Spangler was far from being the pauper that he claimed to be. Bev Perry thought that he was trying to hide his assets so that Donna Spangler's children could not touch them after he was dead.

Spangler's original court-appointed counselor for federal court was Bram Jacobson. And for whatever reason, Jacobson put in a withdrawal request so that he wouldn't have to be Spangler's lawyer. This request was denied by the magistrate judge Lawrence Anderson. But this all became academic on October 26 when Bob Spangler dismissed Jacobson and hired his own lawyer, Michael Gordon.

Gordon was a defense lawyer for the highly regarded Phoenix law firm of Quarles and Brady. Bob Spangler's retention of Gordon as his attorney was a clear sign to Camille Bibles that he was going to fight it out in federal court. Attorneys Edward Novak and Darrow Soll would also be helping Gordon in Bob Spangler's defense.

On November 6, 2000, with counsel present, Spangler entered a plea of not guilty before the magistrate judge Virginia Mathis. He was held in detention afterward, though, having been deemed by the judge to be a flight risk and a danger to others. But the court left open the door for attorney Michael Gordon on the detention issue.

Spangler and his lawyers sought and obtained a continuation of trial during November, stating that they had a mountain of material provided by the prosecution to wade through. They asked for a continuation of sixty days and Gordon stated, "This case is complex and the defendant has filed the appropriate notice. The government's allegations arise from and rest largely on a 'confession' of a man dying from lung cancer. The alleged confession is replete with language that gives rise to numerous issues, including invocation of counsel and reliability. Moreover, as the government is well aware, the pretrial services report reflected that Mr. Spangler's cancer had spread to his brain, causing lesions. In filing this case, the government has alleged wrongdoing that occurred many years ago. They charge allegations of first-degree murder that are seven years old and will apparently allege it to be part of a pattern that began over twenty-two years ago, five hundred miles away, in Colorado. While the government wishes to move quickly to trial, with the hope of obtaining a conviction before Mr. Spangler dies, this case demands a deliberative approach that takes into account the uniquely complex facts."

As Camille Bibles had foreseen, Spangler was going to try and say that his brain cancer had made him give a faulty "confession." She explained that the videotapes had been made to show his demeanor during the whole process on September 14 and 15, 2000.

In addition to the plea for a delay of trial, Gordon also brought up the issue of Bob Spangler receiving contact visits with his wife. Judge Paul Rosenblatt, who now presided over the Spangler case, granted Judy the right to visit Bob in jail. He also granted the extension of time before trial.

December brought an unexpected move on Bob Spangler's part—one that Camille Bibles had hoped for. Bob and his counselor advised her that they might be willing to make a deal. In very complex negotiations that involved many jurisdictions, Bibles and Gordon hammered out the framework of a deal. By December 27, 2000, it was in place and everyone met before Judge Rosenblatt to sign off on it. What was evident to Camille Bibles was that even with the high-powered defense team of Gordon, Novak and Soll, Bob Spangler had seen the writing on the wall. If he wanted certain concessions, he was going to have to give something in return. And what he gave was a big one—an admission to the murder of Donna Sundling Spangler at the Grand Canyon. Bibles knew that it was the good work by Lenny Johns, Bev Perry and Paul Goodman that had convinced Spangler to make this move. He had looked in all directions, and every way he turned, there was evidence collected by this team that boxed him in.

Camille Bibles wanted to make sure that the box stayed closed. Bruce Sundling remembered, "My sisters Bernee, Brenda, Bill Burnett and I showed up for the sentencing hearing and at the last minute Camille pulled me aside and wanted me to make sure and say something about supporting the plea agreement. I had to keep my statement under five minutes. I scratched out a bunch of stuff I was initially going to say. Mostly what I scratched out was name-calling and basic anger. I simply referred to Bob as the defendant.

"When it was time, I said, 'I want to thank the court and other law agencies from the absolute bottom of my heart. The law has removed the cancer (Bob) from this family and I am forever grateful we are able to brings [*sic*] some semblance of closure to this nightmare. Our family will continue to succeed. In fact, in the months after my mother's death, when I couldn't simply pick up a phone and call her or visit her, I realized I owned treasured lessons she spent her life teaching. Be a good person. Be honest and truthful. Play fair. Love, and, most of all, enjoy the gift of life.

"'How has the murder affected me? I was devastated. My mom was without a doubt the single most influential aspect [in] my life. When that was stripped away, it has affected every single aspect of my life since then. Mom was my spiritual mentor. Not so much that she was religious or even attended church regularly. Mom loved life. She knew love. Unconditional love.

"'I know we (the children) were all devastated. But I've heard the single hardest thing to do in anyone's life is bury your own child, yet alone, your only child. Grandma stopped living that week. No doubt Mom and Grams had plans, many plans. The defendant not only murdered my mother, he destroyed an absolute sweet, innocent grandmother in the process.

"'What is the best thing for society when they identify a defendant the likes of this one? One of these animals? Well, if you see a cancer, you cut it out. You remove it. If you have a rabid dog, you kill it. I mean it is absolutely incomprehensible to me that a human being can kill and not be absolutely rendered useless as a result of the guilt, shame and pain. Thank God I'm a human being with a conscience. I don't know if a monster, psychopath, coward, murderer best describes the defendant, but he's certainly not human. He's absolutely not a normal human.

"'If I had only one request that this court would entertain, it would be this one. I plead with the court that this defendant or any affiliated parties not be allowed a permit for his ashes to be strewn at the Grand Canyon. He effectively squelched my mother's last dying wish to have a champagne brunch. I also ask the court to deny the defendant's last dying wish. Let him live in eternity the same way he lived his life. A big lie!

"'I suppose ultimately God's in control of all of this. The defendant's cancer is rotting him from the inside out. I guess that's only appropriate in that his heart died years ago. Like an animal, I doubt he ever had a conscience to begin with. I suppose ultimately God will give him his final sentence.'"

With all parties present on December 27, 2000, nearly twenty-two years of lying and deceit were about to come to an end as Bob Spangler sat down and put his name to the plea agreement. It began:

Plaintiff, United States of America and defendant, Robert Merlin Spangler, hereby agree to the following disposition of this matter. Defendant will plead guilty to Count 1 of the Indictment—First Degree Murder a Class A Felony. Defendant understands that the guilty plea is conditioned upon the following terms, stipulations and requirements.

Agreements Regarding Sentencing.

1. The defendant will be sentenced to life imprisonment in this case.

2. The defendant's sentence will not include fines or restitution.
3. This plea is made in conjunction with an agreement with Coconino County Attorney that the state will not file charges in conjunction with the death of Donna Sundling Spangler.
4. This plea is in conjunction with an agreement from Arapahoe County District Attorney's Office in Colorado. The agreement is that one year after the conviction and sentence are final, the three First Degree Murder charges pending in Arapahoe County resulting from the 12/30/78 deaths of Nancy, David and Susan Spangler, will be dismissed with prejudice.
5. This plea is also in conjunction with an agreement from Story County Attorney in Iowa that they will not prosecute the defendant for any offenses which may have occurred in their jurisdiction.

Criminal History Option: This plea agreement is especially conditioned upon the accuracy of the defendant's criminal history as known by the government at the time of the plea. The discovery of any criminal history in addition to that known shall entitle the government to withdraw from this agreement.

Elements And Factual Basis:

1. The defendant killed Donna Sundling Spangler.
2. The defendant killed Donna Sundling Spangler with malice and forethought.
3. The killing was premeditated.

As a part of the agreement Judge Rosenblatt went over every word of the factual basis and made Bob Spangler agree to each. Camille Bibles noticed that Bob Spangler hated doing this, but he complied nonetheless. He also complied in a written statement compiled by Bibles about the actual murder. One statement by Bibles really stuck in Spangler's craw. It was that he had decided to murder Donna on Easter morning.

Bob sneered to the judge, "Well, Ms. Bibles may think that's significant, but I don't." But in fact he had said on National Public Radio in 1993, "We were only a couple of hundred yards up that trail when on one of those switchbacks came this beautiful sunrise. Easter sunrise as a matter of fact." Despite his protestations, he agreed to the wording of the document, just to move the process along.

Bev Perry, who was watching all this, noted that Bob Spangler did not like Camille Bibles. He seemed to blame her for his present situation. He made several other disparaging remarks that pertained to her and often glared at Bibles. Here was one woman he couldn't control.

Right after the plea agreement was finalized, Bob's attorney Michael Gordon went back to his desk. Then, according to Camille Bibles, she was talking to Lenny Johns when Bob Spangler suddenly moved in her direction and came very close to her. He snarled, "I'm sorry I can't give you another death penalty!"

She shot back, "So am I!"

The federal marshals grabbed Bob immediately and hustled him out of the courtroom.

Very soon thereafter that same day, a press release was sent out to the media from U.S. attorney Jose de Jesus Rivera. Underneath the title was the bold statement, **Spangler Pleads Guilty to Killing Wife in the Grand Canyon.** It retold the story and added, "Spangler is a vicious killer who has been brought to justice. It is difficult to comprehend how he could kill his wives and children in such a cold-blooded manner. The tenacity of those who were determined to bring the killer to justice is to be commended."

News stories ran in Colorado, Arizona and Iowa with headlines such as SPANGLER SENTENCED IN MURDER; SPANGLER GETS LIFE SENTENCE FOR MURDER; KILLER OF 4 GETS LIFE IN CANYON MURDER; and FORMER AMES MAN SENTENCED TO LIFE IN PRISON.

There were a few more loose ends to tie up in the following months. In January the Arapahoe County prosecutor made it official that they would not go forward on a trial in their county against Bob Spangler for the deaths of Nancy, Susan and David. The prosecutor talked to the relatives of Nancy Spangler and determined that they didn't feel the time, effort and money would be worth it. Prosecutor Michael Knight said, "It just didn't seem like a prudent expenditure."

Nancy's stepbrother, David Fitch, agreed. He told the *Rocky Mountain News,* "We have to be practical. If the man truly has terminal cancer, it's very unlikely he'd survive until the end of the trial."

But Fitch was glad that Spangler had to agree that he had murdered Nancy and the children during his federal plea agreement. "It's part of the official record," he said.

In February 2001 Bob's attorney was writing another brief to Judge Rosenblatt about contact visits between Bob and Judy. Bob hadn't received any visits from her in months, his health was failing and he was now incarcerated in a cell operated by the Corrections Corporation of America (CCA). In the brief Gordon wrote: "I have contacted CCA who has advised that the United States Marshals contract provides for no contact visits. However, CCA further advised that the other inmates at CCA are permitted contact visits and that no additional security will be required. The request is made because 1. Mrs. Hilty [*sic*] is traveling approximately 600 miles to visit her husband, 2. Mr. Spangler has not been able to see his wife for an extended period of time, 3. Mr. Spangler will not be able to see his wife for even longer periods and 4. The pretrial services report reflects a terminal illness."

Judge Rosenblatt granted a motion for Judy to visit Bob in prison on February 17, 18 and 19, and March 10, 11 and 13. But March 12 was a special day for Bob Spangler. It was when the final sentencing took place and not only put the final touches on the plea agreement, but it determined whether Judge Rosenblatt would allow Bob's ashes to be scattered in the Grand Canyon after he was dead.

The sentencing went pretty much as expected. Judge Rosenblatt stated, "It is the judgment of this court that the defendant is hereby committed to the custody of the Bureau of Prisons for a term of life on Count One, First Degree Murder."

Then he added, "It is further ordered that any applications to the Grand Canyon Park to have defendant's ashes to be spread into the Grand Canyon be denied." Neither Bibles nor the judge wanted any of his ashes there. They considered it a form of desecration to one of the premier national parks in the nation.

As Camille Bibles had said, "Bob Spangler used

the Grand Canyon, a place that is one of America's cathedrals, as a murder weapon."

And her superior, Jose de Jesus Rivera, weighed in as well. "He has devastated many lives over a long period of time. Hopefully, this will bring some closure to those families."

Even Judge Rosenblatt made a short statement after sentencing: "His (Spangler's) lack of remorse for the killings proves him to be devoid of the common decencies of humanity."

One of Donna Sundling's sons held an impromptu memorial for his mother after the sentencing. But Bob Spangler had no comment to anyone as he was led away by United States marshals to his final home at a federal prison in Missouri. It was ironic that the place he was going to end his days was not far from the place where Sharon Cooper had been born. It is not known whether this thought crossed his mind—if he had never met Sharon in 1976, perhaps he never would have been a killer. Or perhaps it was beyond his knowing. Not even those who had tracked his career in crime knew for sure if he had become a killer out of opportunity or because it was in his makeup all the time. Bob Spangler may have always been a killer just waiting for the right opportunity to happen. His life was filled with mysteries, from the classmate he hated who died at a sewage treatment plant in 1944 to Donna Spangler tumbling off a cliff at the Grand Canyon. Even his adoptive father, who had taken care of him and given him every opportunity in life, died suddenly and mysteriously when Bob Spangler arrived at his door in 1986.

Chapter 16

Aftermath

With the successful conviction and incarceration of Bob Spangler, well-deserved praise was showered on the team of investigators. The Phoenix Headquarters of the FBI wrote in a memo: "Special Agent Lenny Johns is to be commended for the outstanding work he did on this investigation. He developed an excellent rapport with Spangler which ultimately led to Spangler's confession and conviction."

Camille Bibles said of Special Agent Johns, "He has an amazing track record when it comes to talking to violent offenders about their deeds. He is, hands down, the finest interviewer I have ever seen." Of the Spangler case in particular, she said, "Lenny was the key to the case in many ways."

Special Agent Lenny Johns said later, "This case was a great learning experience. It shows how important the pattern of relationships are. How Bob Spangler treated all his wives with a particular style. A certain control. He always looked for common characteristics in his women, and he knew how to exploit these. He got them to trust him when they should have been wary. The teamwork in this case was just phenomenal. If there had been only one missing link, it wouldn't have happened. Paul and Bev and Camille were all essential parts of the whole. They performed their assigned tasks brilliantly and with dedication. We all had a common goal. This was probably the biggest case I will ever work on."

Bev Perry received praise from her superior, Paul Berkowitz, head of the National Park Police Section at the Grand Canyon. He said that her work on the Spangler case was "absolutely sterling." Not long after the conclusion of the case, Perry left the Grand Canyon to become a teacher at the Federal Police Officer Training School in Georgia. She is still a special agent and an instructor in the Behavioral Science Division. She also teaches interviewing techniques to new park rangers as they attend their initial academy for certification as federal law enforcement officers.

A great deal of what Bev Perry learned on the Spangler case she passes on to others. One of the chief messages she gives is "Never give up on a case, no matter how old it is. This just shows you what can be done. It also shows that law enforcement agencies don't have to squabble over territory."

Paul Goodman was in for his share of praise as well. The Colorado Homicide Investigators Association honored him with its highest award. At the Denver ceremony he gave advice to the gathered guests: "Don't give up. Read and examine the evidence." And just like Lenny Johns, he added, "This is one case I'll never forget."

Camille Bibles's career after Bob Spangler went on to even greater heights. She joined the International Criminal Tribunal for the former Yugoslavia at The Hague, Netherlands. She became part of a team investigating war crimes perpetrated during the war in Bosnia. She initially prosecuted defendants in connection with the Keraterm Detention Camp. The place had essentially been a concentration camp, where torture and murder were commonplace.

In a twist of fate, Camille Bibles arrived at The Hague on September 11, 2001, just as the World Trade Center was being attacked. She recalled, "It was difficult to sit overseas and watch. But I was comforted by the sympathy of the people of the Netherlands. All flags were at half-mast. Even down at the beach cafés they lowered the Pepsi flag to half-mast."

Her most memorable day at The Hague was when she donned the black robe that prosecutors wore and walked into court. "Suddenly I had a strong sense as to the importance of the work here," she said.

Before long, she had an even greater task. She joined the team prosecuting Slobodan Milosevic, the former president of Yugoslavia. Despite the seriousness and importance of her new role, she never forgot Bob Spangler or his victims. She said, "That case taught me, more than any other, the horrible price that innocent people pay for the acts of a monster when the crimes are not discerned. I can't imagine what it was like for Nancy's family to spend years having to believe that their sweet, wonderful Nancy murdered her own children. I believe her mother died under this misconception. The horror of what Spangler did to his wife and own children may be outweighed by the torment that the family and friends had to endure in trying to reconcile the awful lie that he left them with for years. I guess I believe in the power of the truth and wonder what other lies about death might be in his past. Somewhere in my current office I've seen a quote, something to the effect [that] 'to the living we owe respect, to the dead we owe the truth.' Spangler's case brought that concept home to me."

And Donna Spangler's own children wanted more than just criminal justice. They wanted financial justice as well. Despite Bob Spangler's protestations otherwise, he had always profited by the deaths of all his wives. Especially that of Donna Sundling Spangler. He may have been covered in the criminal plea agreement, as far as not having to pay restitution, but that did not cover him in civil court. And it was there that Donna's children took him and Judy to try and regain some of the assets lost when Bob murdered Donna.

In the spring of 2001 the civil suit against Bob Spangler contended that in a will made out by Donna in 1991, she left her interest in the Durango home and everything she owned—except some jewelry, furniture and clothing—to Bob. After her murder Bob used the profits from the Durango home to buy the house on Applewood Street in Grand Junction, the home that Linda Wallace had called "palatial." He eventually signed this house over to Judy. Donna's children brought suit against Bob and Judy Spangler on this property, and as in federal court this was settled without a trial. The lawyer for Donna's children said in a press release, "I can't give any details, but I can say at least my clients are very happy with it."

That summer, Judy Spangler won something as well. The court ordered that she receive all the items that had been taken during the search and seizures performed after Bob's arrest on October 3, 2000. Among all the items she got back were the computers, Grand Canyon journals and videos, and Bob's last will and testament.

The only person left with nothing at all, except for a small prison cell, was Bob Spangler. And soon he didn't even have that. His condition became worse and he was transferred to the U.S. Medical Center for Federal Prisoners.

At 3:15 A.M. on August 5, 2001, Bob Spangler died of lung and brain cancer. He was sixty-eight years old. Instead of his ashes being scattered over the Grand Canyon, his remains were cremated at the Ozark Wilbert Cemetery in Springfield, Missouri.

About three hundred miles up the road in Ames, Iowa, there is a cluster of graves on a small knoll in the Municipal Cemetery. One large headstone there is dedicated to the memory of Merlin and Ione Spangler. Surrounding it are the graves of Nancy, Susan and David. None of their graves bear the last name Spangler, as if they wished to expunge Bob from their lives and deaths. And in even a more profound way, the only person not present on that knoll is Bob Spangler. He had turned his back on them in life, but in death it was they who shunned him.

Turn the page for a preview excerpt from
Kill or Be Killed,
the next exciting Robert Scott true crime
coming soon from Pinnacle.

Chapter 1

The Package

Cottonwood, California, April 28, 1998, Midnight

Darkness covered the hills over the sleeping northern California town of two thousand souls as the clock struck midnight. Winding Cottonwood Creek ran silently through the dense trees as a pair of headlights swept along Gas Point Road and swung into a driveway near a mobile home. It was mainly a rural area with long distances between houses, and the locale was deserted at this hour. The driver dimmed the lights of his SUV, cut the engine and stepped into a yard. He carried a large orange-colored 11" x 14" manila envelope in his hand as he walked toward the mobile home on the wooded property. Underneath his jacket, protected from the cool air and prying eyes, his right arm displayed an Irish Republican Army (IRA) tatoo. The tattoo portrayed an American flag and an Irish flag, with the words "One But Not the Same" written beneath the banners. The tattooed man who stepped out of the shadows and into a pool of light in front of the mobile home was twenty-seven-year-old Todd Jesse Garton.

Slowly another man stepped into the circle of light and faced him. Even though the man's face was boyish-looking for a twenty-eight-year-old, his jaw was now set with grim determination, reflecting the seriousness of the moment. The boyish- looking man was Norman Daniels III and occupant of the mobile home.

The two men were not strangers. In fact, they had been on an assassination mission together. It had taken them across state lines up into Oregon with a vehicle filled with weapons, a huge cache of ammunition, disguises and silencers. As Garton handed the package to Daniels, Daniels looked down at the lettering on its cover. Two strips of clear plastic tape revealed letters spelled out in block form. The letters read: NEWBIE RECRUIT, PATRIOT RECRUITER. Daniels knew that he was the "newbie recruit" and that Garton's code name was Patriot. It was a name given to him by a shadowy organization of hired killers. The organization seemed to be filled with ex-CIA operatives, former military Black Ops specialists and just plain soldiers of fortune. Daniels had gathered all this information by listening to Garton's stories about his dangerous exploits on behalf of the organization.

Daniels turned the package over and noticed a wax seal that appeared to bear the head of a ram. But his eyes deceived him. In fact, it was an impression from Garton's U.S. Navy SEAL ring. The wax displayed the headpiece of a diving bubble, the insignia of the SEALs. It was an emblem steeped in stealth, covert operations and quick death.

Just as Daniels began to place his thumb under

the seal, Garton spoke up and said, "Hold on. Wait a second! I warn you, before you open that, if you open it, you are going to have to do what it tells you in that package. Or you will end up dead."

Daniels responded, "Well, I already opened the seal, so it looks like I'm going to have to go through with this."

Garton grunted and said, "Okay."

As Daniels looked at the contents of the package, he immediately noticed a small pager. It had instructions and an 800 number to call on how to make the pager operational. There were also instructions made of labeling tape, the same kind of labeling tape used on the front of the package. These instructions advised Daniels that he must give his recruiter the pager number. In other words, Todd Garton.

Also in the package were several news articles related to the turmoil in Northern Ireland. They spoke of the Irish Republican Army and Sinn Féin, their political affiliate. One of the articles dealt with an IRA leader who had died recently and showed a picture of people mourning at his funeral. Another photo was of a crowded Belfast street in Northern Ireland. One of the articles discussed an anonymous female who dealt with IRA "political prisoners." Another was about an unknown female who planted a bomb at a British bookstore. Daniels vaguely wondered if the women in the articles might be Todd's wife, Carole Garton. Todd had told him previously that Carole had been an IRA operative in Ireland when she was a teenager. He'd indicated that she'd helped plant bombs and even gun down British soldiers. He said she was a crack marksman.

The most potent material in the package were three photographs. The first photograph portrayed Carole Garton, a woman that Nor4man Daniels knew well, wearing a completely black outfit and dark sunglasses. She was looking back over her shoulder at the photographer. It was hard to read the expression on her face.

The second photo was of Carole Garton at a waterfall near a bridge and rocky cliff area along a stream. There were dense woods in the photo. Strangely enough, the scene looked like an area east of Cottonwood where Norman Daniels and Todd Garton had gone rappelling in years past. As a matter of fact, the photo itself looked familiar. Daniels was sure he'd seen it in Garton's home. Maybe in a photo album. He asked Garton about this, but Garton replied, "I've never seen this photograph before."

The third photograph was the most graphic of all. It portrayed Carole Garton, Todd Garton and an anonymous male on a stage. There was sound equipment in the background and a large audio speaker. Todd was sitting on the stage up against a wall. The unknown male was standing with his arms crossed. Carole was front and center. She wore a hat and sunglasses, and she held one arm aloft with her head tilted to the side. She seemed to be posing for the camera. The most unusual thing about the photo was that both Todd and the unknown male's heads were x-ed out with a marking pen. Carole's head, though, had a large circle drawn around it in yellowish green ink. Daniels knew from previous instructions that his target to kill was whoever had their head circled in a photograph. He was not to do it with a rifle from ambush. He was to kill them up close and personal with a pistol.

On the back of this photograph, in clear tape with black lettering, was information and instructions. The information gave Carole Garton's birth date, Social Security number and the license plate number of her Jeep Wrangler. The instructions read: "Carole Garton—TO." "TO" meant *target of opportunity.*

The instructions also stated: "WO—12:01 on the 28th of April until May of the 20th." "WO" meant *window of opportunity,* in other words the amount of time Daniels had to carry out his mission.

The very last thing on the instructions was the admonition "If you don't complete this mission, you will be terminated." Daniels understood this to mean that he would be killed.

Even though Daniels had been on the assassination mission to Oregon, this one startled him. He knew and admired Carole Garton. He turned directly toward Todd and said, "No way!"

Todd took the photo of Carole from Daniels, looked at his wife's face and sighed heavily.

"I can't do this!" Daniels exclaimed. "I'll get caught. You've got to call someone and change this."

Garton reluctantly took Daniels's cell phone and began to dial some numbers. Then suddenly he pressed the power button and hung up. He ran his hand over his head as Daniels kept repeating, "I can't do this. I'm going to get caught. I'm a dead man."

"You've got to do it," Garton finally replied. "There's no way out."

Then Garton sat down heavily on a chair near the porch of the mobile home, saying that they both ought to get drunk. He looked as forlorn as Daniels felt.

Finally after staring at his wife's circled face in the photo once again, Todd Garton sighed and said, "Well, at least it isn't me."

Norman Daniels first met Todd Garton at Shasta College on the north side of Redding, California, in the spring of 1993. With its buildings tucked in a beautiful rolling wooded area, the campus looked more like a park than a college. To the northeast, fourteen-thousand-foot snowcapped Mount Shasta rose majestically over the countryside. Surrounded by myths and legends, ethereal Mount Shasta at times seemed to float above the terrain as if it were not really connected to the earth. There were stories of underground passages beneath the mountain and lost kingdoms. New Age devotees flocked there seeking enlightenment. More sportsmenlike devotees flocked there for good hunting and fishing. The area lived up to its chamber of commerce title, "the Shasta Cascade Wonderland."

Norm Daniels bumped into Todd Garton in the college's Mac lab—a room filled with Macintosh computers for students to do homework and assignments. Garton happened to be doing homework on a Mac when Daniels noticed him wearing a military shirt. Since Daniels had been an army paratrooper, he asked if Garton had been in the military as well. Garton said that he was still in the military. They struck up a conversation and Todd said that he was a lieutenant in the marines and had injured both of his legs in a mission. He was currently in the process of being rehabilitated and not on active duty at the present time. During his period of convalescence he was taking classes at Shasta College to further his education. As a matter of fact, that was the reason why he was in the Mac lab. He was doing an assignment for his geography class.

Daniels sat down beside Garton and they continued to talk about the military and the world in general. As they talked, Daniels noticed that Garton was having trouble with his computer program, and it was obvious that he was a novice in this regard. The same could not be said of Norman Daniels.

Daniels in 1993 was a computer science major with experience in programming in Basic and C++ 3.1. He knew DOS, Disk Management Plus Systems operation for Linux machines and had Internet experience. He was also a computer program designer.

As Daniels watched Garton fumble around with his program on world geography, he offered to help. Soon they were both looking at maps of the world. Todd Garton pointed at Central America and said, "I've been there." The conversation that followed led Norman Daniels into a world he had never dreamed of. It was filled with romance, danger and excitement.

Garton explained that he was a field grade officer; in other words, he had not gone to officer's school but had enlisted as a private and risen in the ranks to lieutenant because of his abilities in the field. He pointed at Guatemala and El Salvador and said that he had done anti-drug-cartel work there with the marines. Of course it had all been very hush-hush and covert in nature.

Daniels vaguely knew about these secret operations. He'd heard of the Iran-Contra Affair and U.S. Marine Corps colonel Oliver North's involvement in it. And he'd heard of other operations concerning the CIA that were mostly kept hidden from the public eye. These tales generally concerned covert operations and sometimes assassination missions. Every once in a while stories would filter into the newspapers about some drug operation destroyed or some drug lord killed.

Garton said he'd been so good at his job that the marines had loaned him out to the Drug Enforcement Agency (DEA). If the marine missions had been secretive, the DEA missions were doubly so. He'd done scouting and reconnaissance work. On his recon missions he would spy out the enemy positions and ascertain how many people were there and what kind of weapons and vehicles they had.

Garton also said, "I did missions where I had to destroy drug labs and the like. I was sometimes a sniper and had to take out people."

Daniels knew that "take out" meant *kill*.

Garton wove an intricate picture of a shadowy world where the ethical lines between the "good guys" and the "bad guys" blurred into a haze. Todd said that he had been on these missions until recently. He'd been rappelling from a helicopter when suddenly the copter was fired upon. Knocked off balance, he lost his grip and had fallen from the rappel line and broke both of his legs when he hit the ground. That was the reason he was being rehabilitated back in the States.

Norman Daniels was fascinated by these stories. But they were only a prelude to Garton's next words.

Todd Garton related that before he was a marine—in fact, when he was only sixteen years old—he had stolen a credit card and gone to Northern Ireland to help fight with the IRA. To

prove it, Garton undid his shirt and showed Daniels
an IRA tattoo on one of his shoulders. It displayed
a Celtic cross. He said that he had always been sympathetic to the IRA cause and that he was of Irish
ancestry himself.

When he landed in Belfast, he had hooked up
with a cell of IRA sympathizers. Before long, he was
showing them how to maintain their weapons. As
a boy Todd Garton had grown up with guns. He
knew how to shoot well and how to maintain his
weapons. By the time he was seventeen, his services
to the IRA went far beyond just cleaning weapons.
He was sent out to snipe at British soldiers who patrolled the streets of Belfast.

One particular incident stood out in his memory
and he conveyed it to Daniels with the art of a master storyteller. He and an IRA friend were lying in
wait in an alley for a squad of British soldiers to pass
by. They were hidden behind obstructions and
both carried weapons with thirty-round "banana
clips." The banana clips were so named because of
their distinctive semicircular shape that somewhat
resembled a banana. Unfortunately, Todd's friend
was not as familiar with weapons as he was. This
friend had put two clips together upside down and
taped them. Unlike Garton, he didn't know that
this was a bad idea. When he jumped into a prone
firing position and opened fire on the British soldiers, he bent one of the clips on the ground. This
caused it to jam. While he was trying to fix his gun,
he was shot and killed.

Garton had made no similar mistake. From his
ambush position he opened up on the soldiers.
Even though they were wearing helmets and flak
jackets, he managed to shoot several of them in the

face, killing them instantly. Todd's marksmanship as a boy paid off. He held the British survivors at bay and didn't take off for safety until he'd emptied most of his clip. He escaped down the alley and disappeared from the scene of carnage.

These stories of Northern Ireland really filled Norman Daniels with a thirst for adventure. By comparison to Garton, his stint in the paratroopers had been dull and prosaic. Before long, he and Garton were meeting over drinks at the American Legion Hall in Anderson and shooting the bull. Garton kept up his stream of war stories and Daniels drank it all in, imagining scenes in the steaming jungles of Central America or of the windswept rainy streets of Belfast. Daniels knew he had what it took, the same as Garton. But he had never been presented with the opportunity.

Once Garton's legs were better, he and Daniels went rappelling off an eighty-foot cliff face near a bridge and waterfall near Shingletown. It was the same area that would look so familiar to Daniels in the photo of Carole Garton near a waterfall. To show how good he was at rappelling, Garton even did it off the bridge, which was a straight shot to the ground below. He may have been inept at computers, but he was good with guns and certain outdoor activities.

As they went on these forays, Todd Garton regaled Daniels with more and more stories. Norman Daniels believed all of them. After all, Garton used certain military terms that weren't common knowledge. And as Daniels said later, "I'm a trusting person. It's a fault, I guess. If someone told me they had a million dollars in the bank, I wouldn't ask to see their bankbook."

But in Todd Garton's case, Daniels should have looked at his "bankbook." In fact, Todd Garton had never been in Central America, never helped on a DEA mission, never been a Navy SEAL and had only been a corporal in the marines, not a lieutenant. He'd hurt his leg in a training exercise and had been given an honorable discharge from the marines. He'd never been on a rappelling mission from a helicopter that took enemy fire. And most of all, he'd certainly never been to Northern Ireland as a teenager nor anywhere near the Irish Republican Army.

Todd Garton was the biggest con man since P.T. Barnum, and he had Daniels falling for his stories hook, line and sinker. These stories were vivid, exciting and filled with adventure. There was just one flaw—they weren't true.

Yet Garton was so consistent with his lies, so exact in his embellishments, that he had a lot more people than just Norman Daniels fooled. All of this might have added up to no more than good storytelling at the American Legion Hall except for one thing—Garton's cons weren't ultimately harmless like P.T. Barnum's. Todd Garton's deceptions were about to lead down a road to conspiracy and murder.

MORE MUST-READ TRUE CRIME
FROM PINNACLE